C000176571

Dubai

WHAT'S NEW | WHAT'S ON | WHAT'S BEST

www.timeout.com/dubai

Contents

Dubai by Area

Essentials

Published by Time Out Guides Ltd
Universal House
251 Tottenham Court Road
London W1T 7AB
Tel: + 44 (0)20 7813 3000
Fax: + 44 (0)20 7813 6001
Email: guides@timeout.com
www.timeout.com

Managing Director Peter Fiennes
Editorial Director Ruth Jarvis
Business Manager Dan Allen
Editorial Manager Holly Pick
Assistant Management Accountant Ija Krasnikova

Time Out Guides is a wholly owned subsidiary of Time Out Group Ltd.

© **Time Out Group Ltd**
Chairman Tony Elliott
Group General Manager/Director Nichola Coulthard
Time Out Communications Ltd MD David Pepper
Time Out International Ltd MD Cathy Runciman
Production Director Mark Lamond
Group IT Director Simon Chappell
Head of Marketing Catherine Demajo

Time Out GCC
Publisher Zoë Cooper-Clark
Group Editor James Alexander

Time Out and the Time Out logo are trademarks of Time Out Group Ltd.

This edition first published in Great Britain in 2009 by Ebury Publishing
A Random House Group Company
Company information can be found on www.randomhouse.co.uk
Random House UK Limited Reg. No. 954009
10 9 8 7 6 5 4 3 2 1

Distributed in the US by Publishers Group West
Distributed in Canada by Publishers Group Canada

For further distribution details, see www.timeout.com

ISBN: 978-1-84670-077-4

A CIP catalogue record for this book is available from the British Library.

Printed and bound in Germany by Appl.

The Random House Group Limited supports The Forest Stewardship Council (FSC), the
leading international forest certification organisation. All our titles that are printed on
Greenpeace approved FSC certified paper carry the FSC logo. Our paper procurement
policy can be found at www.rbooks.co.uk/environment.

Time Out carbon-offsets all its flights with Trees for Cities (www.treesforcities.org).

Dubai Shortlist

The **Time Out Dubai Shortlist** is one of a new series of guides that draws on Time Out's background as a magazine publisher to keep you current with everything that's going on in town. As well as Dubai's key sights and the best of its eating, drinking and leisure options, the guide picks out the most exciting venues to have recently opened and gives a full calendar of annual events. It also includes features on the important news, trends and openings, all compiled by locally based editors and writers. Whether you're visiting for the first time in your life or for the first time this year, you'll find the *Time Out Dubai Shortlist* contains all you need to know, in a portable and easy-to-use format.

The guide divides central Dubai into five areas, each containing listings for Sights & Museums, Eating & Drinkiing, Shopping, Nightlife and Arts & Leisure, and maps pinpointing their locations. At the front of the book are chapters rounding up these scenes city-wide, and giving a shortlist of our overall picks. We also include itineraries for days out, plus essentials such as transport information and hotels.

Our listings give phone numbers as dialled within Dubai. From abroad, use your country's exit code followed by 9714 (the first three digits designate the country of the UAE, while the remaining '4' indicates the emirate of Dubai) and then the number given, dropping the initial '0'.

We have noted price categories by using one to four dollar signs ($-$$$$), representing budget, moderate, expensive and luxury. Major credit cards are accepted unless otherwise stated. We also indicate when a venue is NEW.

All our listings are double-checked, but places do occasionally close or change their hours or prices, so it's a good idea to call a venue before visiting. While every effort has been made to ensure accuracy, the publishers cannot accept responsibility for any errors that this guide may contain.

Venues are marked on the maps using symbols numbered according to their order within the chapter and colour-coded as follows:

❶ Sights & Museums
❶ Eating & Drinking
❶ Shopping
❶ Nightlife
❶ Arts & Leisure

Map key	
Major sight or landmark	
Hospital or college	
Railway station	
Park	
Water	
Motorway	
Major road	
Main road tunnel	
Airport	✈
Area name	DEIRA

Time Out Dubai Shortlist

EDITORIAL
Managing Editor Chris Anderson
Editor Matt Farquharson
Assistant Editor Ananda Shakespeare
Proofreader Simon Cropper

DESIGN
Art Director Scott Moore
Art Editor Pinelope Kourmouzoglou
Senior Designer Henry Elphick
Graphic Designers Gemma Doyle,
    Kei Ishimaru
Advertising Designer Jodi Sher
Picture Editor Jael Marschner
Deputy Picture Editor Lynn Chambers
Picture Researcher Gemma Walters
Picture Desk Assistant Marzena Zoladz
Picture Librarian Christina Theisen
Picture Editor (Dubai) Celia Topping
Picture Research (Dubai) Celia Topping,
    Holly White

ADVERTISING
Commercial Director Mark Phillips
International Advertising Manager
    Kasimir Berger

International Sales Executive
    Charlie Sokol

ADVERTISING DUBAI
Commercial Director Walid Zok
Group Advertising Manager
    Gareth Lloyd-Jones
Senior Advertising Manager
    Kamel Heikal
Advertising Manager Michael Smith
Advertising Manager Milena Kovijanic
Senior Sales Executive Charlotte Hurst

MARKETING
Marketing Manager Yvonne Poon
Sales & Marketing Director,
    North America Lisa Levinson
Senior Publishing Brand Manager Luthfa
    Begum
Marketing Designers Anthony Huggins,
    Nicola Wilson

PRODUCTION
Production Manager Brendan McKeown
Production Controller Damian Bennett
Production Co-ordinator Julie Pallot

CONTRIBUTORS
The editor would like to thank the writers of previous editions of Time Out Dubai and
Time Out Abu Dhabi magazines, and the Time Out Dubai, Abu Dhabi and the UAE Guide,
whose work forms the basis for this book. Additional original material by Matt
Farquharson and Ananda Shakespeare.

PHOTOGRAPHY
All photography ITP, except page 42 Getty Images
Cover photography Burj Al Arab, Dubai by Chris Caldicott/Axiom

MAPS
Maps by JS Graphics Ltd (john@jsgraphics.co.uk). All maps are based on material
supplied by Netmaps except the overview map which is based on material supplied
by Lovell Johns Ltd.

About Time Out

Founded in 1968, Time Out has expanded from humble London beginnings into the
leading resource for those wanting to know what's happening in the world's greatest
cities. As well as our influential what's-on weeklies in London, New York and Chicago,
we publish more than a dozen other listings magazines in cities as varied as Beijing
and Mumbai. The magazines established Time Out's trademark style: sharp writing,
informed reviewing and bang up-to-date inside knowledge of every scene.

Time Out made the natural leap into travel guides in the 1980s with the City Guide
series, which now extends to over 50 destinations around the world. Written and
researched by expert local writers and generously illustrated with original photography,
the full-size guides cover a larger area than our Shortlist guides and include many
more venue reviews, along with additional background features and a full set of maps.

Throughout this rapid growth, the company has remained proudly independent,
still owned by Tony Elliott four decades after he started Time Out London as a single
fold-out sheet of A5 paper. This independence extends to the editorial content of all
our publications, this Shortlist included. No establishment has been featured because
it has advertised, and no payment has influenced any of our reviews. And, for our critics,
there's definitely no such thing as a free lunch: all restaurants and bars are visited
and reviewed anonymously, and Time Out always picks up the bill.

For more about the company, see www.timeout.com.

Don't Miss

Souks in Deira p58

WHAT'S BEST
Sights & Museums

Sightseers in other cities might roam through castles, nose around historical forts or stroll through museums, but Dubai is a little different. There is a smattering of historical buildings by the Creek (p58), but most visitors focus on beaches, malls, five-star hotels and swanky restaurants. Visitors searching for a spectacular meal can pick from scores of fancy hotels, but those keen on Dubai's past face more of a challenge. However, with a little planning and perseverance, some hidden treasures can be found.

'Old' and 'New'

With tongue firmly in cheek, residents speak of 'old' and 'new' Dubai, the former being anything that has been around for more than five years. 'New' Dubai typically refers to the Marina and the residential areas inland from it.

But the original town grew up either side of the creek, and in the shadow of uncompromising hotels and offices, heaving souks and forlorn shipyards still offer the briefest glimpse of this fishing village swallowed up by a big city. Although it may be tempting to cling to the beachy splendour of Jumeirah (p101), a trip down town to the Creek is not to be missed. It has abras (water taxis), souks, Iranian dhows loaded with cargo and character not found elsewhere in the city. It also has Dubai Museum (p82), which reveals how the city came to be.

S H O R T L I S T

Mosque-sees
- Bidiya Mosque (p152)
- Grand Mosque (p82)
- Jumeirah Mosque (p101)

Souks you, sir
- Fruit & vegetable souk (p65)
- Gold souk (p66)
- Spice souk (p69)
- Textile souk (p89)

Best for Creek crawling
- Abra crossing point (p79)
- Bastakia (p82)
- Dhow Wharfage (p59)

Best for wildlife
- Al Khor Wildlife Sanctuary (p92)
- Sir Bani Yas (p155)

Old Dubai
- Al Ahmadiya School (p59)
- Majlis Ghorfat Um Al Sheef (p101)
- Sheikh Saeed Al Maktoum House (p83)

Best for history
- Dubai Museum (p82)
- Heritage Village (p82)

Best for new history
- Afternoon tea at the Burj Al Arab (p125)
- Driving through the Palm (p142)

Best for a day trip
- Bait al Naboodah (p151)
- Hatta (p152)
- Museum of Islamic Civilization (p151)

Best for desert scenery
- Liwa (p154)

Best for east coast exploring
- Fujairah Museum & Fort (p152)
- Khor Kalba (p153)

This part of town developed a little haphazardly, and housed the first Asian immigrants to Dubai. The buzzing, claustrophobic streets inland either side of the Creek give a flavour more akin to Mumbai, Jalalabad or Manila than the Arabian peninsula. Heading away from the Creek on the Bur Dubai side leads to Dubai's first signal that it had big, brash ideas: the World Trade Centre and Sheikh Zayed Road. Compared to the shiny glass and steel monoliths that now line this drag like a giant game of dominos, the 30-year-old trade centre looks quaintly reserved and old fashioned.

Roughly parallel to Sheikh Zayed Road, Jumeirah Beach Road has a few public beaches and a smattering of smaller malls and restaurants; although pleasant, it'slargely residential. The Jumeirah Mosque (p101) at the road's northern end is perhaps the most significant sight. It's the only

THE BIG BUS COMPANY DUBAI

- Magnificent views from an open top, double-decker bus
- One ticket covers two exciting routes
- Ticket valid for 24 hours
- Hop on and Hop off at all major sights in Dubai
- Guided English commentary or choice of 8 digitally recorded languages
- Buses operate 7 days a week from Wafi and City Center main entrance from 9 am to 5 pm
- No Advance booking necessary
- Free daily Arabian Dhow Cruise
- Free Walking tour daily from Oct -April
- Free entry to Dubai Museum and Sheikh Saeed Al Maktoum's House
- Free Wafi Welcome Card (Up to 20% discount at selected outlets)

10 % discount on Big Bus Sightseeing Tours
Promotion offered upon presentation of the voucher and valid for one person
"Time Out Shortlist"

www.bigbustours.com
infodubai@bigbustours.com

+971 4 340 7709

Al Mamzar Beach p70

mosque in the emirate that allows non-Muslims to enter, and has guided tours three times a week. Most of the action of interest to tourists begins at the other end of the road, with Madinat Jumeirah, the Burj Al Arab, Wild Wadi water park, the Marina and a clutch of resort hotels with private beaches.

Sight-hopping

The city is not very well served by public transport, but the first parts of the Dubai Metro are expected to open in September 2009. In keeping with Dubai's taste for braggadocio, it will be the longest fully automated metro system in the world. Until then, there's only the city's unreliable bus network.

The best way to get around is by car, and as a result, traffic problems are increasing. The road network is mostly new and generally easy to navigate, but unannounced construction work can cause congestion.

Taxis are the easiest way to get around, but they can be hard to find. Major hotels are usually a good bet, as are big malls (though these can have hour-long taxi queues at peak times). Bookings can be made by calling 04 208 0808. Drivers are generally courteous and knowledgeable, and all cars have meters; more and more accept credit cards. Unlicensed drivers occasionally pull up next to hot and bothered tourists to tout for trade. They are generally not insured beyond third party claims (a big negative on Dubai's roads), and never have meters.

All aboard

Since 2002, Dubai has had its own double-deckers imported from London. These operate every day of the year and offer fine views of the city from the open upper decks.

The Big Bus Company (04 324 4187, www.bigbus.co.uk) offers entertaining, open-top sightseeing tours. As with the firm's tours in other countries, there is a hop on/hop off option at all 20 stops, which allows you to explore at your own pace, then catch a water bus to continue your journey. You'll have live commentary in English on every bus, and the firm has just introduced a two-hour beach tour at no extra cost. The distinctive vehicles leave from outside Biella restaurant at Wafi City every 20 minutes from 9am to 5pm, but you can join the tour at any of its stops. Ticket prices (Dhs175; Dhs100 reductions; Dhs450 families) include entry to Dubai Museum (although this is only Dhs3 anyway) and Sheikh Saeed Al Maktoum House (p83), plus a cruise on an Arabian dhow.

Whereas London sent over double decker buses, New York sent over the amphibious Wonder Bus to the city (04 359 5656, www.wonderbusdubai.net). This more unconventional look at the city offers a road trip around Dubai's landmarks before splashing headlong into the Creek to take in the city's sights from the water. The 90-minute trip (Dhs125; Dhs85 reductions; Dhs390 families), complete with onboard TV, leaves from the BurJuman Centre and takes in Wafi, the Grand Hyatt hotel and Creekside Park before hitting the Creek by Garhoud Bridge. Gimmicky, yes, but lots of fun. Tours are conducted in English.

Out of town

Some of Dubai's grandest sights are beyond the city, out in the farther reaches of the emirate. The desert can be spectacular, and beyond the city are wadis, waterholes and isolated beaches. Although dune bashing requires a masterful hand, plenty of tour operators offer 4x4 safaris that often include a barbecue and camel rides. See Worth the Trip, p150.

Shisha smoking

Rhodes Mezzanine p147

Eating & Drinking

Hungry? You've come to the right place. Most parts of this gluttonous city have restaurants, and the range of nationalities here ensures that there is plenty of choice. You can find food from just about any country on earth, from Ethiopia and France to Mexico or Sri Lanka. And more often than can be considered healthy, hotels serve up coronary-inducing all-you-can-eat deals that might have limitless champagne thrown in and cost Dhs400, or be as cheap as Dhs30 for a feast of Filipino boiled fish.

But most people don't come to sit on the floor of an authentic Yemeni restaurant; they usually visit for a taste of the good life, and that means fancy gourmet food in five-star settings. In Dubai, glitz and glamour are very affordable: you don't need a second mortgage to eat at the best restaurants, and visitors who want to woo their taste buds have many options. There are more than 40 five-star hotels in the emirate, and each has a few dining areas. The celebrity chef culture has also reached this corner of the Middle East, and Gordon Ramsay (Verre, p63), Gary Rhodes (Rhodes Mezzanine, p147) and Indian TV chef Sanjeev Kapoor (Khazana, p95) all have venues here.

Many visitors don't eat outside the city's top-end resorts, but this can mean missing some culinary diamonds in the rough. There are plenty of out-of-the-way spots where you can eat, without fear of food poisoning, for under

Dhs50 a head. The drawback for drinkers is that these cheap, independent places are not usually allowed to sell alcohol. But they're still worth bursting that bubble of luxury for.

World tour

Certain parts of Dubai have become synonymous with particular types of cuisine. Karama has a cluster of places serving south Indian food; just head to the area around the park opposite the LuLu shopping centre. Most of these restaurants offer authentic grub cooked by chefs from Kerala and Tamil Nadu; for a spicy mix 'n' match experience, try thali in any one of them. For between Dhs7 and Dhs10, you'll get a selection of six or seven different curries in little metal dishes, and a stack of chapattis and rice to mop it all up.

Al Diyafah Street in Satwa is a strip of garishly lit Arabic and south-east Asian spots. Head here for shawarmas and hummus or cheap Chinese, Thai or Filipino food. Around the corner on Satwa road, there's more of an Indian flavour, with Ravi Restaurant (p107) the best known. Its cheap and simple dishes are classic Punjabi, and the streetside diners are as likely to be British bankers as Pakistani taxi drivers.

At the southern end of Jumeirah, Souk Madinat and Jumeirah Beach Hotel have international restaurants in slightly fancier surroundings. The former is popular with tourists and also has a few lively bars. New international venues are also beginning to open in the Marina, as the residential towers and hotels are completed.

Sheikh Zayed Road was the original home of Dubai's urban glam, and the hotels at either end of the main drag, like Dusit Thani

SHORTLIST

Best in the city
- The Noble House (p96)
- Verre (see p63)

Best Arabic
- Mezza House (p116)
- Al Nafoorah (p116)

Best al fresco
- The Irish Village (p75)
- The Terrace (see p62)

Best waterside meal
- The Boardwalk (p75)
- Majlis Al Bahar (p128)
- Pierchic (p131)

Most romantic
- Beach Bar & Grill (p144)
- Eau Zone (p145)
- Pai Thai (p131)
- The Roof Top (p147)

Best shisha cafés
- Aroma Garden Caffe (p93)
- Ego (p75)
- Zyara (p121)

Best for late night munchies
- Al Mallah (p105)
- Ravi Restaurant (p107)
- Zaatar W Zeit (p121)

Best by the beach
- Barasti Bar (p137)
- Saluna (p132)

Best sports bar
- Nezesaussi (p119)

Best for tasting
- Belgian Beer Café (p71)
- Oeno (p146)

Best for posh curry
- Iz (p95)

Most outrageous interior
- Al Mahara (p129)

renew your perspective

The Westin Dubai Mina Seyahi Beach Resort & Marina. Book your next stay with us and experience fresh thinking

For bookings and more information visit
westin.com/dubaiminaseyahi
or call 971 4 399 41 41

This is how it should feel.™

THE WESTIN
DUBAI
MINA SEYAHI
BEACH RESORT & MARINA

(p164) or Crowne Plaza (p164), remain popular. Another stalwart for the hungry and thirsty is the Wafi complex in Oud Metha (p98).

Brunching out

The Friday brunch is a staple of the city's social scene, and many residents indulge in these gorgefests as a regular treat. The tone can vary from the Torremolinos-styled anglo-buffoonery of Waxy O'Connners (a fry-up, five pints and a roast for Dhs70; p86), to more sophisticated affairs, like at Al Qasr hotel (p176), which has oyster stations, top quality cuisines from around the world and a far more sedate feel. Most of Dubai's large hotels will have at least one venue that offers such a deal, and depending on your taste, they can be a cost-effective way to try lots of different cuisine types prepared by talented chefs, or a shameless food orgy on the cheap.

Table manners

All restaurants have air-conditioning, and in most fine dining places dress codes are less stringent than in many Western countries. Although you won't be welcome at top-end spots in shorts and a T-shirt, only the Burj Al Arab insists on jackets and bans denim at dinner. Reservations are essential when eating in hotels, because popular restaurants get oversubscribed and have an annoying habit of regularly changing their opening hours.

During the holy month of Ramadan (falling on 1 September in 2008 and 21 August in 2009), most restaurants don't open for lunch, and many change their opening times in the evenings. You will, however, be able to enjoy iftar tents, where expats and UAE nationals congregate at sunset to break their day-long fast with mezze, dates, coffee and shisha over

Verre p63

Unearthly Japanese.

Ascend to a new level of Japanese cuisine

a game or two of backgammon. During Ramadan, eating in public during daylight hours is illegal and can incur fines.

When dining out, be mindful that water is routinely served prior to a meal and often without your consent. You will be charged for it unless you make a point of sending it back. If you want the cheapest water available, ask for local water – a brand such as Jeema, Masafi or Aquafina. Otherwise you might end up with the expensive imported water that restaurant staff are told to subtly force upon you.

Wherever and whenever you eat in Dubai, don't forget to tip when you find good service: ten to 15 per cent is standard, although most hotel restaurants simply add a charge of ten per cent to the bill.

Pubs & bars

Strictly speaking, only venues attached to hotels can serve alcohol, and they can only serve it to non-Muslims. But most hotels have the necessary licence and a decent range of beers, wines and spirits, and five-star hotels normally have a few rare vintages and premium brands. The high import duty makes prices expensive.

By confining its watering holes to hotel premises (and some big sports clubs), Dubai may have robbed itself of charming 'locals' or low-key beach shacks, but in their place are sumptuous terraces, sleek designer bars and, rather less impressively, facsimile copies of the West's worst chains.

Larger hotels tend to have several pubs and bars, whereas the grand resorts, such as Madinat Jumeirah, house enough drinking dens to challenge the most hardened booze hound. In Bur Dubai and Deira, there are plenty of one- and two-star hotels that

seem to exist purely to serve alcohol – some have almost as many bars as they have guestrooms. These dens tend to be shabbier, tackier and utterly free of pretension. They can be a giggle, but may not satisfy sophisticates.

There are themed English, Irish and Australian venues to cater for the large population of Western expatriates, and the city's hectic work culture ensures that bars aren't short of customers in the evenings. Don't expect the pubs here to be brimming with character. Instead, you'll find – with a few notable exceptions listed here – cliche-ridden boozers incongruously tacked on to hotel lobbies.

Pubs open at around noon and generally don't close until around 1am during the week, or 2am on the weekends. The bars, meanwhile, tend to open their doors at around 4pm and close between 1am and 3am. The distribution of alcohol in the UAE is handled by just two companies, a+e and MMI. This, combined with the difficulty and expense of importing stock means that the big brands rule, so your favourite real ale, wheat beer or organic cider probably won't make it to Arabian shores. The Belgian Beer Café (p71) in Festival City and the new Left Bank (p129) in Souk Al Barsha are perhaps the only two exceptions. Don't make plans to sample the local tipple – it is illegal to produce alcoholic beverages in the UAE.

Smoking

A smoking ban came into force in January 2008. All Dubai restaurants are non-smoking indoors, but terraces are often supplied for those in need of a gasper. Indoor smoking is allowed if the restaurant has a designated room, but most venues do not.

S*uce p112

WHAT'S BEST
Shopping

Tourists flock to the sandy city to see if the rumours are true: are there really more than 100 shopping malls? Well, yes and no. The sizzling heat of summer means that the environment isn't right for strings of stores in the open air. To pull in the punters, top shops amalgamate in the air-conditioned safety of malls. But don't expect every shopping centre to be a hotbed of great labels and well-known brands; there are only around a dozen malls worth jumping in a taxi for; the others serve day-to-day needs and have only basic shops.

The Dubai Mall, with its Olympic-sized ice rink, huge aquarium and gold souk, opened in 2008 to steal the crown of 'biggest mall in the Middle East' away from the Mall of the Emirates (p134). MOTE is large enough to have its own ski slope, and both malls are large enough to make a simple shopping trip a feat of Olympian endurance. But more is to come, the even larger Mall of Arabia is due to open in 2010 and will have almost a square kilometre of retailers.

The shops within these mega malls are tax free, but if you're expecting rock-bottom prices, you might be disappointed. Although certain brands are considerably cheaper, on the whole you'll pay similar prices to those in other major cities. The main exception is during the Dubai Shopping Festival (p40), which takes place from January to February, a much-hyped extravaganza that shopaholics might want their trips to coincide with. Away from the malls, there is the notorious Karama area in Bur Dubai (p79), a treasure trove of small shops brimming with knock-offs from bags to watches and games.

The shopping experience doesn't have the colour and variety that might be found in London or New York, but Dubai is upping the ante every year, with bigger malls and independently owned boutiques. The souks aren't quite the bustling thoroughfares found in Egypt or Syria – most are covered markets – but you can still haggle to your heart's content and walk away with gold, silks and spices. Typical shop opening hours are from 10am until midnight, with stores opening later on Fridays, usually at around 2pm.

Bargaining

Haggling is a tradition in Dubai's souks, and it really is rare to pay the first price quoted. Even the 'best price' isn't necessarily as low as you can go. Take your time, be polite and decide what you are willing to pay. A common starting point is to offer half the quoted price and bounce numbers back and forth. If you can't get the price down, simply walk away; many shop assistants will follow to secure a purchase. A handshake is considered binding. Bargaining isn't common practice in malls, although it doesn't hurt to ask for a discount, especially if you're paying in cash.

Refunds

Visitors used to generous return, exchange and refund policies should be aware that consumers don't have as many rights in Dubai. Many stores, even global franchises, will not offer cash returns, and in some cases exchanges aren't available either. When exchanges are possible, rather than having weeks to take your purchase back, the norm here is between three and seven days, with some places conceding just 24 hours. Check before you buy.

DON'T MISS

S H O R T L I S T

Best newcomers
- Kurt Geiger (p66)

Best local designs
- Ayesha Depala (p107)
- S*uce (p112)

Best independent
- Boom & Mellow (p133)
- Five Green (p97)
- Rage (p135)

Best malls
- Boulevard at Emirates Towers (p121)
- BurJuman (p87)
- Mall of the Emirates (p134)

Best for words
- Magrudy's (p111)

Best gems
- Cartier (p122)
- Tiffany & Co (p69)

Best for labels
- Ginger & Lace (p97)
- Harvey Nichols (p134)
- Saks Fifth Avenue (p89)

Best for kids
- Favourite Things for Mother & Child (p112)

Best bargains
- Priceless (p68)
- Sell Consignment Shop (p98)

Best chocolate
- Chocoa (p133)
- Jeff de Bruges (p134)
- Patchi (p135)

Best for fancy scents
- Ajmal Perfumes (p63)

Best funky tees
- Twisted (p136)

Best entertainment centre
- Magic Planet at Mall of the Emirates (p134)
- Smart Discovery at Palm Strip (p112)

under a dream sky — and all that Light
shining — like animal eyes — and the Wind
Holding us there in long whisper arms —
All our Friends — and those who would becom

REPLAY

Books

Until recently, it was difficult to find contemporary fiction beyond the bestseller list, but new Jashanmal and Magrudy's bookstores, the expansion of Virgin's stores and the arrival of Borders means that the range is broader than ever. However, censorship laws mean that all books coming into the country are checked; off-limits subjects include Israel and Judaism, gay and lesbian interest, alcohol, drugs and sex, and nudity and anything controversial to do with Islam is also likely to be blacklisted. International magazines are painstakingly leafed through, and anything deemed indecent is blacked out using a marker pen. Although books are sold at roughly the UK/US price, imported magazines can double in price by the time they've reached Dubai's shelves.

Rugs

Dubai offers a vast range of rugs, from contemporary to traditional, antique to new, and cheap to expensive. They come from a number of countries, including Iran, Turkey, Pakistan and central Asia. If you're planning to buy an antique rug, you should examine its reverse side. The more knots there are on the underside, the better the rug's quality and the longer it's likely to last.

The gold rush

The malls may be home to the likes of Tiffany & Co, Cartier and Damas, but to find real bargains you can't beat a trip to the gold markets. Investing in gold may be a centuries-old practice, but it's still a major factor in the UAE economy. It's valued according to its carat – the amount of gold in the mixture – which falls into four categories: 22, 18, 14 and nine.

Gold prices are based on a standard rate per gram that changes daily, according to world markets. Typical rates in Dubai are around Dhs60 per gram of 18 carat gold, Dhs75 for 22 carats, and 24 carats at around Dhs80. What makes the difference is the work that has gone into the piece, and most stores charge a workmanship fee of approximately ten to 20 per cent. The gold market in Dubai has stringent laws to ensure that all gold is valued and labelled correctly, and government officials regularly check these markings.

Duty calls

It's not uncommon for tourists to arrive extra early at Dubai airport for their flight home, such is the appeal of Dubai Duty Free. There is a vast array of cosmetics, perfumes, electronics, music, tobacco and alcohol, although the range of clothes is more limited. Arriving in Dubai, each passenger is permitted to buy up to four items of alcohol (be it bottled spirits, wine or a case of beer) and two cartons of cigarettes.

Shipping

To send goods home, contact a cargo or shipping agency among those listed at www.yellowpages. ae. Crown Worldwide (04 289 5152), DHL (04 299 5333), UPS (04 339 1939) and Federal Express (04 299 5484) are all represented in the city. A good agency will give you a quote for shipping bulk items home, and most operate globally. The cost of export depends on the item (electronic goods can be more expensive) and quantity. In the end, visitors may find it isn't worth shipping items home, as export tax makes the process very expensive.

The Roof Top p147

Nightlife

Dubai's nightlife is easily
the best in the Gulf, and is
developing all the time. It's a scene
focused on house and R&B, with
occasional outbreaks of live music.
The main comedy supply comes
from www.thelaughterfactory.com,
which visits for a few nights each
month, with a decent calibre of
Western comedians.

Clubbing

Most clubs are open until 3am, but
patrons are always fashionably
late, meaning places don't get going
until 1am. Dubai's clubbers are a
notoriously fickle crowd, and one
month's 'in' place is passé almost
before the paint is dry. The result
is a cynical, and cyclical, hedonistic
and invariably expensive club
scene: a night at one of the city's
top clubs can easily cost over

Dhs700 when entrance fees,
extortionately priced drinks and
taxis are factored in. It's this high-
end market that dominates Dubai's
scene, and for a place that prides
itself on being the biggest and best,
it's no surprise to see superstar
DJs on a regular basis.

The rise of the city's nightlife has
resulted in some out-of-this-world
venues. First among them has to
be 360° at Jumeirah Beach Hotel
(p136). Set on a stone pier 200
metres out to sea, and with a
stunning location next to the Burj
Al Arab, it offers panoramic views
of Dubai's ever-expanding skyline.
Factor in some excellent resident
DJs and the long-running Friday
events that showcase the finest in
underground electronica, and you
have the best bar Ibiza never built.

Unsurprisingly, weekends see
the biggest events, with Thursdays

dominated by the gargantuan outdoor venue at Chi Club (p98), where you can expect a soundtrack of house, hip hop and R&B. On Fridays the four different areas at Chi regularly pull in more than 2,000 punters, with indie, R&B, house and commercial '80s classics played in separate rooms. The one significant drawback here is the door policy. Guestlists (discounted and free) can close without warning if promoters don't think they've taken enough money on the door.

You can also amuse yourself during the working week. Tuesday night, for example, is a citywide ladies' night, which means free drinks for the fairer sex at a number of bars. The concept may seem quaintly, patronisingly retro, but although some places can feel like a meat market, it can mean a jolly night of free drinking.

The schedule of touring DJs also sees big-league beat merchants playing midweek, with Zinc Bar & Club (Crowne Plaza Sheikh Zayed Road, 04 331 1111) being one of the most popular hangouts.

Live nation

Until recently, the lack of live music meant the UAE was seen as a dirham-spinning stop-off for bands that the rest of the world thought had given up. But in the last few years, Muse, Robbie Williams, Elton John and Shakira have all pitched up, and Bon Jovi went as far as to claim that 'the lost highway leads to Abu Dhabi'.

There has also been a marked upturn in the number of local bands making an impact. Rockers Juliana Down, soul-funk four-piece Abri and Bahraini group Manakin (formerly Brothermandude) have all made inroads in the international market, having cut their teeth on Dubai's burgeoning scene. Local

SHORTLIST

Best new clubs
- Alpha (p77)
- Elegante (p91)

Best for cheesiness
- Chi (p98)
- Submarine (p91)

Best ladies' nights
- Boudoir (p113)

Best for cocktails
- Ginseng (p99)
- Vu (p120)

Best for superstar DJs
- 360° (p136)
- Chi (p98)

Best for house
- Mix (p99)

Best for grunginess
- Jimmy Dix (p95)
- Rock Bottom Café (p86)
- Touch (p91)

Best for comedy
- Zinc (p25)

Best for showoffs
- The 400 Club (p123)
- Cin Cin (p116)
- Lotus One (p123)

Best for beautiful people
- Sho Cho (p113)

Best for alternative nights
- Step on at Chi (p98)
- Submarine (p91)

Best for clubbing outdoors
- 360° (p136)
- Sho Cho (p113)

Best live music
- Desert Rhythm (p37)
- The Original Music Festival (p44)
- Desert Rock Festival (p43)

The first lifestyle club
in the world.

cavalli club

event organisers have spotted this trend too, with the Dubai Original Music Festival showcasing around 20 local, original acts.

Held at the start of every March, the Desert Rock Festival is now a true Dubai institution, with thousands of metalheads emerging for the two-day rock-a-thon. If you prefer your listening a little easier, the annual Dubai International Jazz Festival might be your taste.

Covers bands are rife in the city's cheaper pubs, and the standard varies wildly. Occasionally these acts give pitch-perfect renditions of guitar-based classics. More often than not though it will be an Anglo-Filipino-Uzbek conglomerate mercilessly warbling an old Bangles number at a volume to make your ears bleed.

If you're not on the list

Although the majority of bars and clubs are based in hotels, some venues have a separate entrance to keep well-oiled patrons away from hotel guests. Entry to most bars and pubs is free, but be prepared to pay anywhere from Dhs50-Dhs200 for an evening at one of the city's larger clubs. Finally, although there is a plethora of venues in Dubai, there is a clear-cut 'birds of a feather' mentality, in other words clubbing is quite segregated in the city, with few hedonists venturing outside, their cultural clique.

At its best, this can mean the opportunity to gad about at an authentic(ish) replica of a night out in Beirut or Manila. At its worst, this 'stick to your own' policy can translate as pure racism disguised by members-only policies. Certain bars, predominantly old-school pubs patronised by Western expatriates, will block the admittance of anyone they feel is 'unsuitable', with 'suitability' measured in skin tone

and English proficiency. Although many bars' licences do depend on operating such a system, if you're white you are likely to breeze through unhampered. Maddeningly, there is little that can be done short of boycotting such establishments, and arguing with the bouncer is liable to yield nothing more than laryngitis. One or two venues have been shamed in the local press, but the situation doesn't appear to have changed much.

The rest of the scene in Dubai, however, is constantly evolving. Many new bars and clubs open after the quiet period caused by long, hot summers and the month of abstinence that is Ramadan. The Muslim holy month sees the city's clubs fall silent, and begins on 1 September in 2008 and 21 August in 2009 (these dates rely on sightings of the new moon and so may change). The best thing you can do is pick up a copy of *Time Out Dubai* magazine or visit www.timeout. com/dubai to keep up to date.

Lotus One p123

Art Dubai

WHAT'S BEST
Arts & Leisure

Dubai has always done leisure well. The city is full of spas and beach clubs, all with a service culture so indulgent that dedicated loungers may find themselves unable to function in Western society ever again. From cold face towels at the pool side, to rose-infused waters for reflexology massages, it can be overwhelmingly lordly.

What the city has long lacked is arts. This has not been a place to visit for a cultural break, but that is beginning to change. Where there was once industry, arts are now developing, and the unlikely setting of the Al Quoz industrial zone is the focus of a blossoming of galleries and studios. It's not quite Berlin or Beijing (or even Beirut), but during

the last year a cultural scene has begun to develop that promises to offer art-lovers a little more reason to visit.

The art scene

This is a city of shopping malls, high-rise apartments and lurid materialistic dreams. It might seem that you've come to the wrong place for art.

But that is changing, because Dubai, along with neighbouring Sharjah and big brother Abu Dhabi, has designs on becoming a regional arts hub. The past few years have seen dozens of commercial galleries opening in Dubai, displaying contemporary and traditional work from the Middle East and beyond. There are now two informal art 'quarters' in the city, one in Al Quoz and the other in Bastakia. Every March, Art Dubai (p43) showcases works from across the world.

The billion-dollar Culture Village is Dubai's bid to become the artistic capital of the Arab world – though in true Dubai style, it will be mixed with luxury apartments. The city has also been hosting record-breaking auctions, courtesy of Christie's, and Abu Dhabi is set to become home to outposts of the Guggenheim and the Louvre franchises. What's more, on the doorstep is the cerebral Sharjah Biennial (p151), which is packed with works by international artists every two years.

Most of Dubai's residents are foreigners, and the nature of the work seen across the city is diverse. People seeking genuine Emirati art can now visit the new Flying House gallery (p138), as well as occasional local student shows.

Indian art is extremely popular, and well served by establishments such as 1x1 Art Space (p114) and Bagash Gallery (p91), which put on eclectic shows of contemporary work from across the subcontinent. The Red Gallery (p140), meanwhile, revives a long-standing Dubai love affair with Far Eastern work, with a focus on Vietnamese art.

Younger art-lovers tend to head towards the contemporary galleries in the Al Quoz area. Here you'll find professionally curated shows, with art of a high standard from the Middle East and North Africa. For contemporary painting, photography and installations, it doesn't get much better than B21 (p137) and the Third Line (p141) galleries. Located within minutes of each other, they offer a rich palette of work, and are the places most likely to exhibit anything challenging or ground-

SHORTLIST

Best for local art
- The Flying House (p138)

Most cutting-edge art gallery
- The Third Line (p141)

Art in old-style venues
- Majlis Gallery (p92)
- XVA (p92)

Best community venue
- DUCTAC (p137)

Best for Arabic-language theatre
- Al Ahli Club Experimental Theatre (p78)

Best cinema
- CineStar at Mall of the Emirates (p137)

Best spas
- Amara (p69)
- Cleopatra's (p99)
- Talise (p141)

Best for beach bums
- Club Mina (p137)
- Hiltonia Beach & Pool (p138)

Best for free paddling
- Al Mamzar Public Beach (p70)

Best for sailing away
- Bluesail (p91)
- Ocean Explorer Fishing Charters (p140)

Best for swingers
- Dubai Creek Golf & Yacht Club (p78)
- Four Seasons Golf Club (p74)

Best for chilling out
- Ski Dubai (p141)

Best at organising it all for you
- Blue Banana (p149)

Capture the Spirit

FIFTH AVENUE · KNIGHTSBRIDGE · FAUBOURG SAINT HONORE
VIA MONTENAPOLEONE.
NOW THE WORLD'S FINEST STORES ARE ONE AT JUMEIRAH ROAD.

ENJOY OUR HOSPITALITY ON YOUR PREVIEW VISIT
ANY DAY BETWEEN 10AM TO 8PM AND CAPTURE THE SPIRIT.

SAGA
WORLD

P.O. BOX: 111398; 356-948 JUMEIRAH BEACH ROAD, UMM SUQUEIM 1, DUBAI - U.A.E.
TELEPHONE: 971 4 3959071-73, FAX: 971 4 3959074 EMAIL: SAGADUBAI@CIEWORLD.COM

breaking. Nearby, you'll also find the Courtyard (p137), run by Iranian expatriate Dariush Zandi, who regularly shows some of the best in modern Persian work. Further away from the main drag is the Meem Gallery (www.meem.ae), which exhibits the cream of contemporary Arabian art in exciting and hugely instructive exhibitions dedicated to Islamic and pre-Islamic pieces.

Down by the Creek lies the historic Bastakia district, home to the Dubai Museum (p82) and the few relatively old buildings left standing. Here, among the wind towers and coral and stone buildings, the XVA (p92) and the Majlis Gallery (p92) hold frequent shows by contemporary and more traditional artists respectively.

The silver screen

Cinemas are extremely popular in Dubai. Despite the difference in the cultural backgrounds of audiences here, Western films remain the most watched, with Hollywood blockbusters filling auditoriums for weeks on end. There is no arthouse scene to speak of, apart from a few dedicated individuals who hold free screenings in galleries. Yet as the population expands, so does the breadth of material. The Dubai International Film Festival (p39) has achieved much during its short lifespan, bringing some impressive and eclectic films to the city for a week every December. A regional forum, the Emirates Film Competition, aims to give Emiratis an amateur film community, and the newly developed Dubai Studio City hopes to attract world-class production talent.

Although Western titles are frequently shown completely out of kilter with other major territories, Bollywood releases play to large and appreciative audiences pretty much

Flying House p29

Time Out
Travel Guides

Worldwide

All our guides are
written by a team of
local experts with a
unique and stylish
insider perspective.
We offer essential tips,
trusted advice and
honest reviews for
everything you need
to know in the city.

Over 50 destinations
available at all good
bookshops and at
timeout.com/shop

Time Out
Guides

in step with Indian release dates, and often a few days in advance.

There is an IMAX cinema at Grand Cinema's Megaplex at Ibn Battuta Mall. It is especially popular on weekends, so it's advisable to call ahead to make a reservation. Another welcome innovation is the Gold Class cinema at CineStar Mall of the Emirates (p137), where, for a Dhs100 ticket, you can stretch out in a luxury recliner, enjoy table service and view a film in far more convivial surroundings than the usual bear pits. Call ahead to book.

Time Out Dubai magazine lists and reviews the week's screenings, but distributors and cinemas can change the programme with little warning, so it's always best to phone and check the line-up in advance. Although the UAE uses a similar certificate system to the USA and UK, it sometimes gives the film a different category or age bracket.

Censorship

Until recently, all films released for public screening were censored at a central office in Abu Dhabi. Now each emirate has been granted autonomy to cut and filter releases as they see fit. Broadly speaking, the Dubai Department of Censorship will cut any nudity and overt sexual references as well as any homosexual scenes. Scenes of drug taking are also forbidden. Political comments relating to Arab governments or anything deemed defamatory towards Islam is also cut, as is anything that comes close to recognising Israel. These cuts can be heavy-handed, with films lurching awkwardly past the offending scene. Films that are deemed to be too contentious for exhibition will simply be banned altogether.

Local talent

Dubai's Emirati minority, who have watched their once tiny city boom and grow over the past few decades, have stories of their own to tell, and more and more UAE nationals are turning to film to chronicle their lives. Although

DON'T MISS

Meem Gallery p31

BLACK
vs. COLOUR

Ayyam Gallery - Dubai

Featuring

Youssef **ABDELKE**   Ammar **AL-BEIK**
Safwan **DAHOUL**   Asaad **ARABI**
Nassouh **ZAGHLOULEH**   Khaled **TAKRETI**

ayyam
gallery
damascus | dubai

Dubai Showroom, 3rd Interchange, Al Quoz 1, P.O.Box 283174 Dubai, UAE
t. +971 4 323 6242, f. +971 4 323 6243, e. dubai@ayyamgallery.com, w. www.ayyamgallery.c

the UAE's feature films can still be counted on the fingers of one hand (the first such example is *Al Hilm,* from 2005), the grassroots amateur film industry is thriving under the aegis of the Emirates Film Competition. The competition is held each March, and the standard of films – with steadily improving production and scripts – is growing.

Theatre

There are a couple of full-sized auditoriums in the city – the Madinat Theatre (p140) and the Dubai Community Theatre and Arts Centre (DUCTAC; p137) – and a few smaller enterprises, but on the whole, quality drama is hard to find.

There is a growing market for international productions, and *Chicago, Simply Ballroom* and *Mamma Mia!* have all packed out Dubai theatres recently.

Theatre schedules at the Madinat Theatre tend towards a crowd-pleasing blend of cabaret-style acts and mainstream dramas. In the purpose-built theatre at DUCTAC, a more multicultural programme is in place: giant Iranian puppet shows and traditional folk dancing have been shown. DUCTAC has also hosted productions by the Al Ahli Theatre Club, a small but dedicated troupe of performers who seek to promote Arabic-language theatre.

One of the largest companies to visit Dubai in recent times was Cirque du Soleil, which held a month-long residency in a purpose built tent in 2007. The run was so successful that Cirque has announced plans to have a permanent venue and show at the Palm Jumeirah by 2010.

Other performing arts

Public performances of Emirati poetry, song and dance are mainly limited to ceremonial occasions and traditional displays at the Heritage & Diving Village (p82).

During religious and national holidays, you're also likely to see ayyalah performances, which re-enact battles and hunting expeditions with groups of men beating sticks, and hurling swords high into the air. Dressed in the bright abayas (cloaks) of the desert, groups of women engage in separate na'ashat dances, swinging their long hair and swaying to music. As for international dance, there are some ballet schools and there's a lively salsa scene, but performances of Western classical dance are rare.

The sporting life

Once completed, Dubai Sports City will be part of the mind-boggling Dhs18 billion Dubailand development. The largest stadium will be a 60,000-seat multi-purpose arena for football, rugby and athletics. There will be a 5,000-seat hockey stadium, a 30,000-seat cricket stadium, and an indoor arena for events such as trade shows and concerts. It is hoped that in the near future the city can lure events such as the ICC Cricket World Cup, the Twenty 20 Cricket Series and the Hockey World Cup.

For now, the main spectator sports are big annual set pieces known as much for their social element as sporting endeavour. The Desert Classic golf tournament (p41) attracts the world's best players, and the Dubai World Cup (p44) is the world's richest horse race, with a purse of around US$6 million each year. The IRB rugby sevens (p37) gets the Test-playing sides and their supporters out in force for three days each November.

DON'T MISS

Calendar

Desert Rhythm

What follows is a list of the best events in Dubai in 2009, from those that had been announced as we went to press. For up-to-the-minute event details, pick up a copy of *Time Out Dubai* magazine or consult www.timeoutdubai.com. Most of these events take place annually but dates for future years were unavailable at press time, so check the website given for details.

January 2009

To Mar **Camel racing**
Lisaili, Al Ain Road, 35km
from Dubai
04 338 8170
The camel racing season runs from October to March. Races usually take place on Thursdays and Fridays at around 7am; you can watch training

sessions most mornings at around 10am and from 2-5pm. See box p42.

To Mar **Horse racing**
Nad Al Sheba Racecourse, off the
Dubai-Al Ain Road
04 327 0077/www.dubairacingclub.com
The country's principal venue for horse racing is in Dubai at Nad Al Sheba, where local and international steeds and their jockeys compete through a winter season that starts in November and culminates with the Dubai World Cup in March.

Early Jan **Spinneys Cup**
Desert Palm Polo Club
www.spinneys.com
The event includes horse trials, dressage, show jumping and cross-country. All the proceeds go to Riding for the Disabled.

8-10 **Toyo Tires 24 Hours
of Dubai**

Dubai Autodrome
www.dubaiautodrome.com
Over 90 cars battle it out in a 24-hour
endurance race.

**15 Jan-15 Feb Dubai Shopping
Festival**
Various venues
www.mydsf.com
A month of bargain hunting.

18 Dubai Marathon
www.dubaimarathon.org
The 2008 race saw Ethiopian legend
Haile Gebrselassie win the men's race,
following a route that went up and
down Jumeirah Beach Road. Beyond
the start and finish lines, spectators are
pretty thinly spread, so you are guaranteed a good view if you want to cheer
the runners on.

23-24 Gulf Gaelic Games
www.dubaicelts.com
The games have been going since 2007,
and there's been a growing interest in
them. A curious crowd heads down to
find out exactly what hurling and
carnogie are.

23-24 24 Hours of Dubai
Dubai Autrodrome
www.dubaiautrodome.com

The inaugural round of the 2009 event,
which brings racing drivers together
from all over the globe.

**26 Jan-1 Feb Dubai Desert
Golf Classic**
Emirates Golf Club, off Interchange
5, Sheikh Zayed Road
*04 380 1777/www.dubai
desertclassic.com*
Every winter the Emirates Golf Club
welcomes some of the finest swingers
in the world (Tiger Woods was the
victor in 2008) to compete on pristine
greens for an impressive purse of
US$2.4 million.

February 2009

Ongoing Camel racing
(see January), Horse racing
(see January), Dubai Shopping
Festival (see January)

**13 RAK International
Half Marathon**
Ras Al Khaimah
www.rakmarathon.org
'The richest half marathon in the
world', apparently. There's also a team
relay challenge.

13-20 Maktoum Sailing Trophy

UAE Desert Challenge

the
400
A Clubbing Legacy

Dubai Marine Club, Le Méridien
Mina Seyahi Beach Resort & Marina
*04 399 4111/www.maktoumsailing
trophy.com*
Inshore and offshore races, which are
popular with local sailing enthusiasts.

16-28 Barclays Dubai Tennis Championship
Dubai Tennis Stadium, the Aviation
Club, Garhoud Road
*04 282 9166/www.dubaitennis
championships.com*
The Dubai Open sees the world's top
players grunting it out at the Aviation
Club. Federer, Nadal, Henin and
Davenport have all won in the past.

19-28 Dubai International Jazz Festival
Dubai Media City
*04 391 1196/www.chillout
productions.com*
In 2008, acts included the Puppini Sisters
(a trio that sings a mixture of '50s and
modern hits in a '50s style), Courtney
Pine and, strangely, Robin Gibb.

27 Feb-7 Mar 24-Hour Cycling Race
www.wbs.ae
Cycling enthusiasts jump on the sad-
dle and pedal for six, 12 or 24 hours.
Run by favourite independent retailer
Wolfi's Bike Shop.

28 Feb-1 Mar Emirates Airline International Festival of Literature
Dubai Festival City
www.eaifl.com
Promised participants include Kate
Adie and Paulo Coelho.

March 2009

Ongoing Camel racing (see
January), Horse racing (see
January), 24-Hour Cycling Race
(see February)

3-7 Dubai International Boat Show
Dubai International Marine Club
www.boatshowdubai.com
Even if you're not planning to splash
out yourself, drop by to see some beautiful boats and Dubai's elite snapping
up yachts left, right and centre.

Culture clubs

Dubai has been maligned in the
past (often fairly) as a bit of a
cultural vacuum. The argument
is that local traditions have
been paved over in the race to
develop, and the only Western
cultural imports have been the
worst kind of bland: malls and
action flicks, rather than
Monets and arthouse, and
sculpted golf courses rather
than any sort of sculpture. But
this is gradually beginning to
change, with the introduction
of a few arty events.

The **Dubai International
Film Festival** (www.dubaifilm
fest.com) always gets the
black-rimmed-spectacles
brigade justifiably excited,
as it gives obscure shorts,
documentaries and features
their Gulf premiere, and in many
cases, their only Gulf showing.
Many films don't get a general
release, and those that are
shown do not fall foul of the
censor's scissors.

The **Creek Art Fair** (p43;
www.creekartfair.com) will be
on its third year in 2009, and
is suitably housed in Bastakia,
Dubai's most atmospheric area.
Artists from the Middle East and
further afield show their work,
and a special effort is made to
give local, Emirati artists a
platform. **Art Dubai** (p41)
(www.artdubai.ae) does much
the same, but in line with its
claims to be the biggest art fair
in the Middle East, does it on
a grander scale. Corporate
sponsors ensure plenty of
coverage and lots to see.

Dubai Rugby Sevens

6-7 **Dubai Desert Rock Festival**
Various venues
*04 333 1155/www.desertrock
festival.com*
The 2007 incarnation of this growing
event featured Iron Maiden, Incubus
and the Prodigy, and for the fifth
anniversary in 2008, 28,000 fans turned
up to see Marky Ramone, Velvet
Revolver and Muse.

11-14 **Taste of Dubai**
Dubai Media City
04 366 8888/www.tasteofdubai09.com
A week-long excuse to eat extravagantly, as chefs from around the world
descend on Media City to host gala din-
ners, talks and classes. Names are likely to be of the calibre of Anthony
Worrall Thomson and Sanjeev Kapoor,
2008's guest hosts. Local restaurants
also showcase dishes.

17-22 **Art Dubai**
Madinat Arena, Madinat Jumeirah,
Jumeirah Beach Road
*04 366 8888/www.madinat
jumeirah.com*
Big names in the art world come to
show off some impressive pieces, such
as the Andy Warhol *Dollar Sign*.

19-21 **MEFIT**
The Aviation Club
04 321 4646/www.mefit.net
Health and fitness is big business in the
UAE. MEFIT (which stands for Middle
East Health & Fitness Summit) is
geared towards both professionals and
the general public looking to learn how
to achieve a healthy lifestyle. Tickets
cost Dhs150-850.

19-21 **Dubai International
Horse Fair**
Dubai International Convention
& Exhibition Centre
www.dihf.ae
Horses are a national obsession, and all
the equipment, services and care products you could think of (and more) will
be on sale here.

20 **Mina Mile Open Water
Swimming Race**
Le Méridien Mina Seyahi
www.supersportsdubai.com
Actually a 1,600-metre and 800-metre
event with a 200-metre relay. The event
has been going since 2005.

Mar **Chill Out Festival**
04 397 3728/www.ohmrecords.com

Richard Dorfmeister, Andy Smith of Portishead and the fantastic regional band Furat Qadduori have all taken part in the Chill Out Festival. The organisers are promising some excellent DJs for 2009.

Mid Mar **Creek Art Fair**
Bastakia, Bur Dubai
www.creekartfair.com
A satellite fair to Art Dubai. You'll come across the odd Andy Warhol displayed alongside the works of up-and-coming artists and pieces by Emirati artists and students.

Late March **Red Bull Air Race**
Abu Dhabi corniche
www.redbullairrace.com
Abu Dhabi has been the first port of call for the Red Bull Air Race since 2005. A trip down to the Corniche with your camera is a must for this event. The planes are afine sight.

28 **Dubai World Cup**
Nad Al Sheba stadium, off the Dubai-Al Ain Road

04 327 0077/www.dubaiworldcup.com
The Dubai World Cup is the richest horse race in the world, but it's as much about dressing up as giddy-up.

April 2009

10-11 **Grand Racing Weekend**
Dubai Autodrome
www.dubaiautodrome.com
International and local racers push their V8 engines to the limit.

Apr **Urban Desert Festival**
04 339 0550/
www.urbandesertfestival.com
The first Urban Desert Festival ran in 2008, themed around hip hop, rap, funk and R&B. The line up included Akon, American rapper Fat Joe, hip hop DJ Cutmaster Swift and DJ Ready D.

May 2009

1-2 **24 Hours of Dubai at the Kartdrome**
Dubai Autodrome
www.dubaiautodrome.com

Ernie Els, Dubai Desert Golf Classic

Camel racing

With their lolloping gait and heaving humps, camels are not the most graceful creatures. But the iconic Arabian quadrupeds can reach speeds of 40kph (25mph), and watching 20 of them hurtle around a track is a rare and peculiar sight that is unlikely to be matched elsewhere. Races are followed by trainers who keep up with their steers by driving alongside in 4x4s. Until recently the jockeys were typically boys from Afghanistan and Pakistan (some aged as young as eight) who were strapped to a hump and ordered to whip for all they were worth. International pressure to curtail this exercise (some jockeys were smuggled against their will) threatened to put an end to the sport, but in keeping with Dubai's reputation for unusual ideas, a solution was found: robots. Mechanical jockeys are now strapped on to the camels, with the whipping and rein pulling remotely controlled by a trainer. The robo-riders have their own silks, so the spectators can see who is winning.

Races begin at 7am, and are usually held on Thursdays and Fridays between October and March – as there is no fixed timetable, catching the camels in action can prove tricky. The Dubai Racing Club (www.dubai racingclub.com) can sometimes provide details; call the day before you intend to go.

The track is near the Nad Al Sheba horse racetrack, on the road to Al Ain. Visitors with their own 4x4 can get trackside, but it is not something that should be tried by drivers with limited off-road experience. The terrain has some hard lumps and bumps, and if you get in the way of a trainer he is likely to get pretty irate. Most taxi drivers will know the spot, and although they are unlikely to go trackside, they should take you to the main stand, where you can park up and watch the show. It is a predominantly male event, so women should dress modestly.

Racing drivers from all over the world roll into town for this endurance event.

May **Sir Bu Na'air Traditional Sailing Race**
www.dimc-uae.com
A spectacular event: dozens of traditional dhow sailing boats battle it out in the Arabian Gulf waters.

Mid May **Jumeirah Beach Hotel Tennis Open**
Jumeirah Beach Hotel
04 348 000/www.jumeirah beachhotel.com
Tennis players from the region thrash it out on court.

June 2009

June **The Original Music Festival**
Local music talents take to the stage at various venues. See Time Out Dubai for gig details.

19 June-22 Aug **Dubai Summer Surprises**
Various venues
www.mydsf.com

A shopping festival featuring the odd bargain and an endless stream of free children's entertainment.

August 2009

Ongoing **Dubai Summer Surprises** (see June)

Mid Aug **Hopfest**
The Irish Village
www.irishvillage.ae
Normally held over three days, this event introduces the public to over 100 beers that aren't usually found in Dubai.

22 Aug-21 Sept **Ramadan**
The Muslim holy month is marked by the practice of fasting from sunrise to sunset. Non-Muslims must do the same in public settings. The exact dates depend on the lunar calendar.

September 2009

21-23 **Eid Al Fitr**
After Ramadan, Muslims wait for the new moon to show that it's time for Eid Al Fitr – 'Feast of Breaking the Fast'. The date depends on the lunar calendar.

October 2009

Oct-Mar Camel racing (see January)

Oct **UAE Desert Challenge**
Various locations
www.uaedesertchallenge.com
The second largest motor sport event in the Middle East, the Desert Challenge pits the world's finest endurance bike riders and cross-country drivers against each other.

Oct **Desert Rhythm**
Dubai Festival City
04 339 0550/www.desertrhythm festival.com
Desert Rhythm, a two-day festival of world music, is Dubai's answer to WOMAD. Joss Stone, Kanye West, Madness, Mika and Ziggy Marley have all headlined.

November 2009

Ongoing Camel racing (see January), Horse racing (see November)

Early Nov **Red Bull Flugtag**
www.redbullflugtag.ae
Teams attempt to build flying machines and launch them over the Creek. 'Flugtag' means 'flying day in German. Though some craft descend straight into the water...

16-20 **Middle East International Motor Show**
Dubai International Convention & Exhibition Centre
www.dubaimotorshow.com
A lavish display of luxury and custom-built cars, bikes, trikes and quads in 11 exhibition halls.

Nov **Dubai Rugby Sevens**
Al Ain Road
04 321 0008/www.dubairugby7s.com
The IRB World Sevens Series features 16 international teams (usually including all the Test nations) and plenty of local and regional teams competing for a variety of trophies over three days.

Late Nov **Dubai Shamaal**
Nr the Palm
www.dubaishamaal.com
An annual surf ski event – a load of people competing in kayak-type boats with a pedal operated rudder to you and me. It's fun to watch.

28 **Eid El Adha**
Festival of sacrifice.

December 2009

Ongoing Camel racing (see January), Horse racing (see January)

2 **National Day Festival**
Various venues
The anniversary of the formation of the United Arab Emirates in 1971 sees all major monuments and tourist attractions open to the public, and in the evening there are fireworks displays and concerts.

18 **Eid Al-Hijira**
Islamic New Year.

Dec **Dubai International Rally**
Various venues
04 228 4019/www.aaauae.com
After the Desert Challenge cup comes the International Rally championship, which is the final leg of the FIA's Middle East events.

Dec **World Offshore Powerboat Championship**
Dubai Marine Club, Le Méridien Mina Seyahi Beach Resort & Marina, Al Sufouh Road, Jumeirah
399 4111/www.class-1.com
The UIM Class 1 World Offshore Powerboat Championship takes place over two days.

Dec **Dubai International Film Festival**
Various venues
www.dubaifilmfest.com
Although Dubai cinemas rarely stray from a popular mix of Hollywood blockbusters and corny action flicks, the increasingly popular Dubai International Film Festival showcases cinema that is otherwise impossible to see in the UAE. As its slogan has it: Bridging cultures, meeting minds.

Itineraries

Burj al Arab p125

The Right Altitude

Dubai is as flat as a pancake, but still manages to offer some spectacular man-made views. So it's not a bad idea to spend an afternoon and evening taking in some vertiginous vistas. Start at 2pm and don't make any other plans for later in the day.

By the end of 2009, the best view in town will (if the developers stick to their word) be from **Burj Dubai** (p118). As this book went to press, the main structure and spike were finished, but the opening had been delayed until September 2009. In May 2008 it became the world's tallest man-made structure, reaching 636 metres and topping the KVLY TV mast in North Dakota, USA. When finished, it will reach above 800 metres, and look like a big game of pick-up-sticks before the drop. The world's fastest lifts, reaching 40mph, will whizz visitors to an observation deck near the top. The tower will

also house the Armani Hotel, with design and finishing touches overseen by Giorgio himself.

Until then, there are plenty of other ways to get acquainted with the clouds. Deira's tallest building is the National Bank of Dubai tower, its big, gold, curved shield of glass a landmark that's often seen in photos of the Creek. But unless you're a banking bigwig, you're unlikely to get asked to the top; so start at the other end of town, at the Jebel Ali Golf resort and Spa. This is about 25 minutes along Sheikh Zayed road (heading south to Abu Dhabi) from the Creek. This part of town is pretty flat. But bobbing up and down on the water by the hotel's private beach is a seaplane. **Seawings** (www.seawings.com) will take you for a 30-minute scenic flight over the **World**, two **Palm** developments and the **Marina** (p142) for Dhs895 per person.

The Palm

Once you're back on dry land, head 20 minutes down the road to **Burj Al Arab** (p125). The UAE's most photographed building is likely to be the first thing that the people back home ask you about, apart, possibly, from the heat and the camels. This building has been the aesthetic battering ram used to get people to take notice of Dubai, and golfer Tiger Woods and tennis players Roger Federer and Andre Agassi have all (rather gingerly) demonstrated their skills on the hotel's precariously perched helipad about 200 metres up. Just below this, forming a long, sea-facing horizontal cross against the sail-shaped hotel's main 'mast', is the **Skyview** bar (p132) and **Al Muntaha** restaurant (p130). The blurb for the former speaks of stylish sophistication, but giddy psychedelia is more accurate. It's a violent collision of colour, and some of the decor would be more fitting in an Iberian airport than a self-appointed 'seven-star hotel'. But aesthetic quibbles aside, the views out to sea and along the

coast are great, and best enjoyed during daylight. With an advanced booking (and a minimum spend of Dhs250 per person), Skyview does high tea between 2pm and 5pm. The bar, like the hotel itself, is a stunning victory of wealth over taste, style and practicality. It really must be seen. Staff are serious when they say no jeans or trainers, and gents must wear a collar.

Having sipped what may be one of the priciest cuppas you'll ever have, take a golf cart and driver (they are lined up in front of the hotel entrance) and trundle next door to the waved-shaped **Jumeirah Beach Hotel** (p176). This other icon of the city has similar sea views, but from lower, less kitschy surroundings. Head to Uptown Bar on the 24th floor to sip an aperitif while the sun goes down (around 6pm in winter). Appetite sufficiently whetted, you can take dinner at **La Parrilla** (p131). The quality of its modern Latin American cuisine (and views from the window seats) outweighs the drawback of a slightly overbearing tango show. The steaks are spectacular, and the ceviche is sumptuous.

Next, hop in a taxi (the JBH has some nice private motors that charge more than regular taxis but feel a touch more sophisticated) to the **Dusit Dubai** (p164). Its distinctive inverted Y shape is a well known landmark next to Defence roundabout. It's designed to look like two hands pressed together in the prayer shape of a traditional Thai greeting. Others have suggested that it looks more like an upside-down tuning fork. Either way, head up to the **Splash** pool bar on the 36th floor to enjoy a cocktail and take in the views up Sheikh Zayed Road.

Cocktail number two should be had in the **Jumeirah Emirates Towers** hotel (p167), just a little way down the city's main artery (though you'll need to take a taxi). Dubai's twin towers are a prominent landmark, and the hotel lobby is as impressive inside as

the 50-plus storey building is from outside. Ask your cabbie to take you to the main hotel entrance, rather than the shopping strip one level below. Unfortunately, the fancy lifts are reserved for hotel guests, mere visitors have to make do with the regular lifts just behind. Ears tend to pop somewhere around floor 37, and up on 51 the doors open directly into **Vu's** bar (p120) in the angled glass roof of the building. The dinky seats in front of the window fill pretty quickly, but the bar space is comfortable and allows you to take in the wonderful view of Satwa and Jumeirah with a superb cocktail.

Finish the sky tour at **Raffles Dubai** (p174) in Oud Metha. The pyramid design has a glass apex over the last three floors, with two rather swanky spots to visit. Noble House (p96) was crowned Restaurant of the Year in 2008 by *Time Out Dubai* for its contemporary Chinese fodder. But, as this is a cloud-hopping tour, ascend one more level to the China Moon Champagne Bar; just make sure you call ahead to book a table. There are views from all four sides (including a glass wall behind the wash basin in the toilets), and the bar, with its black stone floor and sparkling city skyline feels luxurious. It also serves tasty cocktails.

And if the thought of pottering around the city by taxi seems drearily land-based, there are some more adventurous options available. A number of firms offer helicopter flights, with whirlybird tours that can cover Sheikh Zayed Road, the World and Marina, the Creek and Ras Al Khor wildlife reserve. **Aerogulf** (04 220 0331, www.aerogulfservices.com) does a 30-minute tour for Dhs3,200 for up to four people.

Burj Dubai p46

Textile Souk

Creekside Stride

The casual observer would be forgiven for thinking that it is impossible to walk anywhere in Dubai. From airport to beachside hotel, it looks like a series of giant, unforgiving flumes of concrete. And it's true that this is not a city that is kind to pedestrians; most of its roads are big highways more suited to Hummers and cargo trucks than inquisitive walkers. But the **Creek** as the heart of what Dubai was before the oil, is a plodder's paradise. It has shaded alleys and curious crannies, and takes just a couple of hours to explore. Start at 2pm and you'll be finishing around sunset.

The best place to begin is the **Dubai Museum** (p82). It's small and can be a little cramped, but it's the only place that offers a historical view of the city. The introductory video near the entrance runs like an excitable promotional blurb for the

city, but does have a few interesting old images. The large boards around this room show the growth of Dubai through the 20th century. Other rooms have exhibits on pearl diving, dhow building, nomadic life and local flora and fauna. Although some of the displays are a little twee, the simple explanations of life before Dubai's hyperdevelopment (particularly the harshness of a pearl diver's existence) can be fascinating.

The museum is on a roundabout just outside the **Bastakia** area (p82). As you exit, turn left and head along Al Fahidi Street. Before you reach the next roundabout, turn left into one of the alleys next to the Sheikh Mohammed Centre for Cultural Understanding. You are now in Bastikia. Iranian traders settled in this district more than a century ago, and built homes out of coral, topped with wind towers that served as natural air conditioning units. Today, the wind towers are merely decorative, but in the past Dubai's citizens occasionally hung wet cloths in them when the summer was especially cruel. These would cool the air before it entered the home, giving inhabitants some much needed respite from the heat. Aside from the wind towers, this neighbourhood is home to some of the city's best art galleries and a few quaint outdoor cafés.

Start at the **Majlis Gallery** (p92), just off Al Fahidi Street. It houses a wonderful collection of local art, including paintings, illustrations, sculpture, silverwork and Arabian trinkets. You can browse the entire collection in half an hour, and leave anything you buy with the owners to collect later. Step out of Majlis, turn right, and a few metres down you'll see the **Basta Art Café** (p85), a beautiful courtyard eaterie. After looking at their limited range of local crafts, get a table in the shade of the central tree and order some super-healthy Arabian wraps or salads, washed down with mint and lime juice.

Once you're refreshed, continue the heritage walk by turning right down the narrow alleyway that separates the Majlis Gallery and Basta Art Café. At the end of the alley you'll see the back of **XVA Gallery** (p92) an idyllic slice of old Arabia hung with white fabric and home to regular exhibitions. It also has a hotel upstairs, with some cute, atmospheric rooms. Climb up to the roof and you'll get a view over the area's wind towers, minarets and cobbled streets. Take in the art and the local jewellery, clothing and magazines in the store before stopping for lunch in the courtyard.

Leaving XVA, head out of the wind tower quarter and down towards the Creek. You'll emerge next to the Bastakia Mosque, near a clutch of abras for hire. Walk past

Basta Art Café

these as far as you can and turn left into the **Textile Souk** (p89). The wares on offer are firmly aimed at tourists, and anyone after a genuine material bargain would do better to head to Satwa. Weave through this network of cloth-pushing salesmen and you'll rejoin the Creek. You may find abra skippers approach and offer tours for anything up to Dhs100. Politely decline and head for the **Bur Dubai Abra Station** (p79), directly in front of you. You'll see turnstiles that lead down a walkway to the public abras. You'll be hustled on with everyone else, and pay just Dhs1 for the five-minute journey over to Deira. These water taxis chug back and forth, ferrying a quarter of a million people a month across the Creek, and are a vital means of transport for the city's low-paid workers.

As your abra barges its way into the **Sabkha Abra Station** on the other side, you'll notice the battered old dhows to your left. These come from Iran and across the gulf, packed high with spices, toys,

TVs and household goods, which are then stacked by the side of the road for collection. The dhows also serve as accommodation for the crews, and a stroll along the wharf gives the opportunity to sneak a peak at the sailor's life. Opposite the abra station, a narrow road runs into the **Old Souk**. As you enter, the first few stalls to the left sell fairly generic tourist trinkets – wooden camels, glowing Burj Al Arabs and the like – but just past these to the right is the more scenic **Spice Souk** (p69). The name sounds grander than the reality, but this run of eight or nine shops down one cramped street is quite atmospheric and smells wonderful.

Push on up the main drag and you'll pass more souvenir stalls and touts selling 'copy watches' and fake Louis Vuitton, and reach the cornea-troubling sparkler that is the **Gold Souk** (p66). Prices here are fixed according to the day's gold price per gram, with an extra charge for workmanship. The more intricate the piece, the more you

have to pay – and if you are buying, haggle heartily. If you're just there for a look, 20 minutes of strolling through the alleys is usually enough. Then, retrace your steps and take an abra back to Bur Dubai. As you disembark, turn right, and walk around the Creek.

It's a ten-minute saunter to Al Shindagha, the other remaining pocket of the old town, where you can take a trip around Sheikh Saeed's childhood home. The **Heritage Village** and **Diving Village** (p82) are also here, but displays can be uninspired. Sometimes Bedouins set up camp in the former, complete with camels and open fires. At other times it's just a desolate bit of scrubland with a few shops selling tourist tat. If they're around, the Emirati women selling fried dough balls covered in date syrup are worth a visit. And once the strolling is all done, head to the terrace of one of the Arabian restaurants nearby for a shisha and lashings of mint tea, and watch the sun set over the Creek.

Dubai's markets

Image Conscious

Dubai's image makers present a pristine city of white beaches and gleaming towers. But, for the avid hobby snapper, the city has a photogenic underbelly. So charge up your camera for a full day of snapping, from dawn to dusk.

Your day will begin before sunrise. Assuming this is during the cooler months (October to March; spending a day outdoors during summer is not a good idea), this will mean a 6am start. Get a taxi to take you to the **Deira** (p58) side of the Shindaga tunnel. At this time of day (and a weekday will work best, so go between Sunday and Thursday), allow 15 minutes from Bur Dubai, 20 from Jumeirah 2 or half an hour from Umm Suqeim.

Hop out at the **corniche**, near the Deira market, and point the camera (with a tripod) back over the cranes and monolithic cargo ships of Port Rashid. These are

lit up through the night, and you should be able to get some artily industrial shots while it's still dark. As dawn breaks, the light will be behind you, and cast a fiery orange glow that glints off the Gulf waters and the clanking metal monsters at the dock. This might also be a good time to turn around and shoot into the sun as it rises over Deira and Sharjah.

Next, walk to the **fish** (p65), **meat** (p68) and **veg markets** (p65) just behind you. They are a chaotic affair, full of colour contrasts and vibrant human life. The stacks of blue, yellow, green and red plastic crates are particularly impressive, and stacked high can look like a vast, dysfunctional Rubik's cube.

Inside, the long, low buildings have some dim corners, so a flash will be necessary. Stalls are piled high with veg, meat and fish from India, Pakistan, Iran, the Gulf,

and Africa, with traders involved in a manic effort to set out their stalls and holler their prices to potential buyers. This is the spot for close-ups and abstracts of the food on show, and, if you ask very nicely, the characterful faces of people at work. Cheerier souls may even be willing to strike a pose with their stock for the benefit of inquisitive tourists.

Your next stop is the **bus station** (p179). It's an unromantic sight, but can be quite revealing about life in Dubai for so many residents. The city's laughable attempt at public transport is relied upon by the thousands of service industry staff and less wealthy workers who keep Dubai functioning. The long queues of commuters hoping for a spot on the overcrowded and under funded buses offer a much truer snapshot of the city's population than strolling through a mall.

Head back out on to Baniyas Road and turn left, following the loop around the Creek. Here you will be able to get some shots of the

Bur Dubai Abra station (p79) across the water, but there will be a better opportunity to photograph this later. The Ahmadiya school, just behind you by the St George Hotel, is worth no more than a quick snap. Carry on along the side of the **Creek** and you'll come to some tatty old dhows at the waterfront, with their load stacked haphazardly by the side of the road.

The boats come from other emirates and Iran, and act as accommodation for the sailors. Some may even allow you to hop on board to take some close-ups, but even from the water's edge they make for some decent shots. However, there is a much larger **dhow wharfage** (p49) further up, which you should reach at around lunchtime, when the decks of boats become dining areas for sailors to cook curries, dals, rotis and rice.

Directly behind you is the **Old Souk**. Head straight in, and to your right is the **Spice Souk** (p69). This is an opportunity to snap some vast bags of cardamom, dried lemons, saffron and other regional whiffs and flavours. Venture further up the main street and you'll come to the gaudy spectacle that is the **Gold Souk** (p66). But for more atmospheric shots, like light seeping through old wooden roofs onto cobbled streets, or traders sleeping on their trolleys, head across the road from the spice souk and amble around. Once you're finished, retrace your steps back to the Creek, where you entered the souks.

The nearby **Abra Station** is an obvious spot for a touristy snap, but still visually interesting. Spend Dhs1 on the five-minute chug across to the Bur Dubai station. Here, get out, turn left and walk through the **Textile Souk** (p89) to the next abra station. Cross the Creek again and you'll be deposited a few hundred yards up from where you left. The round trip is a great chance for some shots of the city from the water.

Hop off your tug and turn right, walking along the Creek and around the Sheraton Dubai to the dhow wharfage. The scale and number of these boats is more impressive than those mentioned earlier. Amble around the wharves and shoot away to your heart's content. It should be early afternoon by now, and you'll find some of the sailors huddled around curry tins and cooking up a storm.

Next, step back on to Baniyas Road and hail a taxi. Ask your driver to take you to **Chili's** (Saleh Building) in Garhoud, a ten-minute (and Dhs15) ride up the road. This isn't an uninspired suggestion for lunch, but the closest well-known landmark for your next shots. Step out and walk up the alley to the right of the restaurant. Cross the road at the back and turn left. After about ten minutes you will come across what is developing into an unofficial wrecker's yard. Around

20 vehicles have been dumped here, after horrific prangs as a result of the demented driving on Dubai's roads. They're a sinister reminder of how easily the Dubai dream can go wrong.

Suitably chilled, it's time to hail another taxi (fasten your seatbelt) and head for **Lulu Centre Karama**. This shouldn't take more than 15 minutes to reach (though traffic here can be heavy), and leads to lunch, a reward for your long morning's snapping. Directly opposite Lulu is a park surrounded by Indian restaurants. Across the park is a vegetarian spot called **Saravana Bhavan**. This should get you upstairs and order yourself a thali (Dhs7 for seven pots of curry, a stack of chapattis, rice and a banana for desert, all served in metal dishes resting on a banana leaf in a metal tray). Eat heartily to replenish your strength, but not before you've photographed the tray as it arrives. Step back out into the park and you'll find office workers having a postprandial nap, and families making use of the kiddies' playground.

Then it's back in a taxi, though finding one around the park can be tricky. Instead, take one of the alleys near Saravana Bhavan that lead through to the three-lane highway behind. This is Za'abeel Road. Stand at the entrance to the slip road and you should flag down a cab soon enough. Your destination is **Dubai Drydocks** for a uniquely Dubaian human migration. Get your driver to go straight down Sheikh Rashid road towards the port. He'll go through three major crossroads, the last of which is Al Mina Road. After this you'll reach a small crossroads. Bear left here as though heading to Jumeirah Beach Road. Before you get to that strip, stop outside the workers' accommodation to your left. Each day between 4pm and 5pm, hundreds of dock workers in light blue boiler suits ride bicycles from the dock to their digs. They flow across like a tide of colour, a strong visual reminder of the labour that goes into the city's economic miracle.

By now it will be nearing dusk (generally between 5.30pm and 6.30pm during the winter), and time to set up for a sunset shot on the beach. Hail a taxi (or hop back in the one that you've kept waiting) and head down the beach road to the **Dubai Marine Beach Resort** (p174). Next to this is the city's most popular public beach (colloquially known as Russian Beach). There is usually a good cross section of Dubai's population here, from blubbery westerners to fully clothed Muslim women paddling in the sea. There are palm trees, sun loungers and other beach paraphernalia, and on a clear day the sunsets can be very impressive.

Another option, if you have time, might be to head further along the coast to **Umm Suqeim public beach**. Here you can get a shot of sunset with the Burj Al Arab in the background. It's a little beyond your 'underbelly of Dubai' photo brief, but could be your one concession to touristic papping. Wherever you chose for your sunset shot, catching a taxi from the beach road should be straightforward. Your final stop is **Satwa** (p100), for its nightlife. This area is prime real estate, so the colourful, eclectic scene won't survive for long.

Take a cab to **Al Maya Lal's** supermarket on Plant Street. Grab a shawarma (and a few snaps) from the stall next door and have a wander. You'll find Fillipinos chatting on the supermarket steps, Emirati men smoking shisha outside ramshackle cafés, groups of Indian and Pakistani men crowded around TVs showing cricket, and the chance to take a few final pictures of a Dubai that will soon disappear.

The photogenic Creek

Cuisine that's simply Exquisite

LA VILLA

CITY CENTRE HOTEL | + 971 4 603 8080 | bqt@citycentrehotel.ae | WWW. SOFITEL.COM

Information correct at time of print. Subject to change with or without prior notice at management's discretion.

Dubai by Area

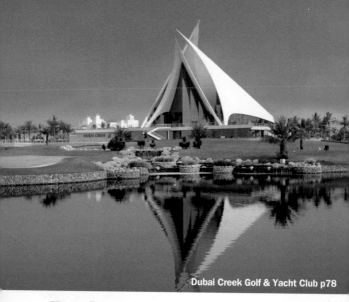
Dubai Creek Golf & Yacht Club p78

Deira

Broadly speaking, the term Deira is used to describe everything north of the Creek, but in reality, it is an amalgam of districts. Garhoud has the airport, with a few vibrant nightspots and restaurants clustered at the **Méridien** hotel and around the tennis stadium. Nearby **Festival City** is a shopping, dining and drinking hub that remains quiet for the moment, but is growing in popularity (box p72). The most exciting part for the visitor, though, is the original Deira alongside the **Creek** – the heart and soul of old Dubai. It is a bustling, chaotic, dusty commercial hub where plate-glass office blocks tower over old souks.

Walk along the Creek, and you'll see old meet new with full force. Five-star hotels such as the Sheraton Dubai Creek and Radisson SAS are just yards away

from wharfs that haven't changed in 60 years. On the roads, limousines and 4x4s jostle for space with rickety, multicoloured pick-up trucks, while sharp-suited business folk wait at zebra crossings alongside sarong-clad workers pushing handcarts, and fishermen in work-stained *khanduras*. Traditional **dhows** still line the **wharf**, and day and night goods are unloaded, destined for the many tiny shops that make up Dubai's oldest trading area.

What Deira lacks in refinement it makes up for in atmosphere and character. And to experience it first hand, all you have to do is walk along the corniche. But bear in mind that Deira is by no means pristine; despite the Dubai municipality's efforts, litter abounds, and spitting in the street is commonplace.

Sights & museums

Al Ahmadiya School & Heritage House

Nr Gold House building, Al Khor Street, Al Ras (04 226 0286/ www.dubaitourism.co.ae). **Open** 8am-7.30pm Mon-Thur, Sat, Sun; 3-7.30pm Fri. **Admission** free. **Map** p60 B1 ❶

Established in 1912, Al Ahmadiya was the first school in Dubai, and it was renovated as a museum in 1995. Next door lies the Heritage House, a traditional home with interiors dating back to 1890. When you visit, guides and touch screens will take you through the tour of these two small – and ever so slightly dull – museums.

Dhow Wharfage

Beside the Creek. **Map** p60 B3 ❷

Set along the Creek where the towering National Bank of Dubai building curves elegantly over the water, the Dhow Wharfage is a reminder of the city's past. The many dhows that dock alongside each other on the Creek, bringing in spices, textiles, and other goods from neighbouring countries, are more than just vessels. In many cases, the seafarers who brave the Gulf and the Indian Ocean also live in these colourful wooden beauties. A stroll along the Creek will yield plenty of opportunities for great holiday snaps.

Eating & drinking

Ashiana

Sheraton Dubai Creek (04 228 1111). **Open** 1-3pm, 7.30pm-12.30am daily. **$$. Indian. Map** p60 B2 ❹

Ashiana is a gem amid the sparkling array of Indian restaurants in Dubai. As cross-legged musicians bounce mysterious vibes off the dark wood and soft fabric finishes, tuck into the gosht boti kebab, monolithic boulders of tender, spice-infused lamb. The murgh Ashiana consists of chicken strips, engulfed in a thick sauce of pepper and spice, packing an almighty, moreish kick. The food is heavenly, the atmosphere is fantastic, and service is top notch.

The Bombay

Marco Polo Hotel (04 272 0000). **Open** 12.30-3pm, 7.30pm-2am daily. **$$. Indian. Map** p60 B2 ❺

The Marco Polo Hotel is no Burj Al Arab, but the Bombay's location proves that sometimes you have to dig a little deeper to find the most valuable treasures. When going for an Indian meal in Dubai, it's easy to plump for cheap and cheerful or go to the other extreme and opt for luxury and high prices. Somewhere in between the two, the Bombay is a mid-range discovery that will cater for hungry city explorers.

The China Club

Radisson SAS Hotel (04 205 7333). **Open** 12.30-3.30pm, 7-11.30pm daily. **$$$. Chinese. Map** p60 B2 ❻

This is one club that can be joined with no membership fee and no initiation ceremony. It's open to everyone who appreciates fine Chinese food and great service in a relaxed atmosphere. When you open a steaming basket of siew mai dim sum underneath the fading 70s-style lampshades encircling the ceiling, you might start considering full-time membership.

Focaccia

Hyatt Regency (04 209 1100). **Open** 12.30-3.30pm, 7-11.30pm daily. **$$. Italian. Map** p60 B1 ❼

When Italian decor is attempted anywhere other than Italy, the result can be wonderfully cosy or horrendously tacky. Focaccia manages the first, with only the odd touch of the second. The menu is an eclectic mix of Italian staples such as gnocchi with four cheeses, with some experimental dishes such as the beetroot risotto with hammour.

Handi

Taj Palace Hotel Dubai (04 223 2222). **Open** noon-3.30pm, 7-11.30pm daily. **$$. Indian. Map** p60 B3 ❽

We've always been impressed by the Taj Palace Hotel's Indian restaurant. The dahl Handi with black lentils and the fresh okra masalam are great as an accompaniment or for vegetarians. The meatier dishes are also excellent, but

Deira

Al Hamriya Port

Al Manzar

Cairo Street

Al Wuheida Rd

Al Rasheed Rd

Hor Alanz East

Al Khaleej Rd

Abu Hail Rd

Al Muheida

Al Rasheed Rd

Hor Alanz

Corniche Deira

Dubai Hospital

Al Baraha

Abu Hail

Al Muteena

Al Baker Al Siddique

Al Khabaisi

Al Rasheed Rd

Salahuddin Rd

Al Murar

Al Maktoum Hospital Rd

Al Nahe

Al Khaleej Rd

Hyatt

Al Regency

Al Maktoum Hospital

Al Muraqqabat

Al Buteen

Fish, Meat & Veg Market

Al Buteen

Al Rigga

Sheraton

Hilton Dubai Creek

Riggat Al Buteen

Clocktower Roundabout

Old Souk

Baniyas Road

Radisson SAS Dubai Creek

Sheraton

Dhow Wharfage

Maktoum Br

Al Shindagha Tunnel

Al Ras

Al Daghaya

Dhow Stations

Al Seef Road

Al Waleed Road

Hamriya

Umm Hurair

Trade Centre Road

Tariq Bin Zeyad

1 km
1000 yds

© Copyright Time Out Group 2009

BAGHDAD RD (D 95 RD)

AL NAHDA

AMMAN ROAD

AL NAHDA RD

AL QUSAIS

DAMASCUS STREET

82

AL TWAR

ABU HALI RD (D 91 RD) (107TH RD)

AL RASHIDIYA RD (D 90 RD)

RD)

Dubai
International
Airport

AL KHAWANEEJ RD (D 89 RD)

Le Meridien

73
67 68 81
76 80

Millenium
Airport Hotel

Aviation
Club
84 83 72
79 75

MARRAKECH STREET

AL GARHOUD

AL RAMOOL

77 69
70

UMM RAMOOL RD (D 83 RD)

Park Hyatt
15
14
45 13

Dubai Creek 78
Golf & Yacht
Club 66
74

AL GARHOUD RD

Dubai Creek Park

Dubai Creek

Crowne
Plaza

Dubai
Festival City

33 56 57 58 59
60 61 62 63 64

BUSINESS
BAY BRIDGE

AL GARHOUD BR

InterContinental

55 58
52

65
54

DUBAI
FESTIVAL
CITY

UMM
SURAIR

ADDAF

86

Sights & museums
Eating & drinking
Shopping
Nightlife
Arts & leisure

Shabestan

The fireplace here is fake – video screens only generate limited heat – but the dancing flames in the kitchen are reassuringly real. The view into the kitchen, and of chefs using huge quantities of butter and cream in many of the dishes, will tell you you're in for a calorie-heavy feast. The Australian filet mignon steak is particularly magnificent. On most nights of the week a talented jazz pianist performs, making this a fine spot for a romantic, if rather pricey, dinner.

Shabestan
Radisson SAS Hotel, Deira Creek (04 222 7171). **Open** 12.15-3.15pm, 7.15-11.15pm daily. **$$. Middle Eastern.** Map p60 B2 ⑪
Shabestan is a beautiful, spacious Persian restaurant that offers great views of the Creek during the day, and is a moody, romantic affair with live entertainment from accomplished musicians at night. The mirza ghasemi is a tomato and aubergine starter that makes a rich and hearty beginning, and the main courses are huge portions of meat and rice. The plate of peanut brittle, heart-shaped shortbread and macaroons that comes with the bill is an extra treat.

Sumibiya
Radisson SAS (04 205 7333). **Open** 1-3pm, 7-11pm daily. **$$$. Japanese.** Map p60 B2 ⑫
At Sumibiya, grills at every table let you cook meat, fish, crustaceans and chicken to your own specifications. The produce here is impeccable, and if you are prepared to splash the cash, it pays to follow your starters with pieces of wagyu tenderloin, a cut prized the world over for its intense flavour.

The Terrace
Park Hyatt (04 317 2222/ www.dubai. park.hyatt.com). **Open** noon-2am daily. **Bar.** Map p61 B4 ⑬
Blessed with year-round sunshine and endless blue skies, Dubai demands an alfresco drink or two, and the sumptuous Terrace bar is one of the best places at which to see the light of day.

it's a shame the hotel is not licensed to sell alcohol. If you're looking for good Indian food in an atmospheric and beautifully finished restaurant, you should pay Handi a visit.

Miyako
Hyatt Regency Dubai (04 209 1100). **Open** 12.30-3pm, 7.30pm-12.30am daily. **$$. Japanese.** Map p60 B1 ⑨
Miyako is a cosy, tidy and tranquil dining spot, which is decorated in light oranges and browns that allow for quiet contemplation of life over a bento box. Miyako's location, a stone's throw away from the fish market, ensures that the sashimi slices and sushi appetisers are as fresh as any in the city. It's such a mellow, welcoming restaurant that dealing with the endless traffic outside the Regency's doors seems like a minor inconvenience.

Palm Grill
Radisson SAS Hotel (04 205 7333). **Open** 7.30pm-midnight daily. **$$$$. Steakhouse.** Map p60 B2 ⑩

The cocktail list is almost as impressive as the panoramic views, which take in the Creek-side marina – replete with envy-inducing schooners – and Dubai's haphazard skyline.

Thai Kitchen

Park Hyatt (04 602 1234). **Open** 7pm-midnight Mon-Thur, Sat, Sun; noon-4pm, 7pm-midnight Fri. **$$**. **Thai**. **Map** p61 B4 ⑭

Elegant arches, candlelit walkways, the gentle lapping of the Creek in the background and the restaurant's sleek decor all point to great things at the Thai Kitchen. The food on the menu is slightly hit-and-miss, but standout dishes include the spicy pomelo salad, which zings with fresh citrus and kicks with peppers. The shrimp toast with sesame is fried to crispy perfection, and the roast duck curry comes saturated in a moreish spicy sauce, which is thick with coconut milk.

Traiteur

Park Hyatt Dubai (04 602 1234). **Open** noon-3.30pm, 7pm-midnight daily. **$$$**. **French**. **Map** p61 B4 ⑮

Traiteur's high ceilings and marble floors make it ideal for power lunches. If the menu could recapture the majesty it once displayed, this would be a great restaurant. But for now there's room for improvement, as the food doesn't always live up to the classy setting.

Verre

Hilton Dubai Creek (04 227 1111). **Open** 7-11pm daily. **$$$$**. **French**. **Map** p60 B3 ⑯

Consistent excellence has defined Verre since its explosion onto Dubai's scene in 2001, and Gordon Ramsay's Creek-side restaurant is dependably superb. The Menu Prestige showcases everything Verre does brilliantly. The vine tomato minestrone with basil pesto is fresh and zingy, and the tender roasted sea scallops with caramelised pork belly are tempered by the coolness of the pan-fried watermelon and ginger. The restaurant has a chic, understated elegance that complements the fabulous food. Book well in advance.

Vivaldi

Sheraton Dubai Creek (04 228 1111). **Open** 6.30am-1.30am Mon-Thur, Sat, Sun; 6.30am-4pm, 7pm-1.30am Fri. **$$**. **Italian**. **Map** p60 B2 ⑰

Maybe it's the Deira location, or perhaps it's the tacky mock-Venetian paintings, but Vivaldi rarely gets the plaudits when the city's best Italian restaurants are mentioned. It deserves better. The carpaccio di manzo starter is faultless, with circles of melt-in-the-mouth beef drizzled in lemon oil and served with light and fresh rocket. The foie gras is good, and the meat is wonderfully tender. Nab a seat on the terrace, and you can enjoy fine Italian with the Creek in the background.

Shopping

Ajmal Perfumes

Deira City Centre (04 295 3580/www.ajmalperfume.com). **Open** 10am-10pm Mon-Wed, Sat, Sun; 10am-midnight Thur; 3pm-midnight Fri; 10am-midnight Sat. **Map** p60 B3 ⑱

Miyako

A unique dining destination
on par with
a spectacular golf course

FOUR SEASONS
GOLF CLUB
Dubai Festival City

Whether an avid golfer or diner you're destined to succumb to the dining choices
on offer at Four Seasons Golf Club.
Savour in the authentic Italian Cuisine and the dramatic interiors at the chic Milanese-influenced Quattro
Enjoy a multi-cultural dining experience at the contemporary Blades
Unwind at the casual Spikes and pamper your taste-buds with an eclectic mix of international delights
or grab a quick satisfying bite at The Tee Lounge, located under the Club's striking spiral glass atrium.
Your discerning dining choice will be enhanced by Four Seasons' signature service, par excellence.

Phone: 04 6010101 Email: restaurants.dub@fourseasons.com Visit: www.fourseasons.com/dubaigolf

Ajmal is a swanky Arabian perfume shop at which you can pick up scents from the region. However, a word of warning to the uninitiated: Arabian scents are much headier and spicier than Western perfumes.

Calvin Klein
Deira City Centre (04 295 0627).
Open 10am-10pm Mon-Wed, Sun; 10am-midnight Thur-Sat.
Map p60 B3 ⑲
A whole shop dedicated to Calvin Klein underwear – all classic, with lots of cotton and simple black and white designs. Wonderful if you're on the slim side, but otherwise you may want to give this shop a miss.

Club Monaco
Deira City Centre (04 295 5832/www.clubmonaco.com).
Open 10am-10pm Mon-Wed, Sun; 10am-midnight Thur-Sat.
Map p60 B3 ⑳
Two decades after its launch, Club Monaco has finally reached the Middle East. This store is home to chic essentials, which are aimed at urban men and women. With plenty of A-list fans, Club Monaco is a great alternative if you can't afford high fashion labels. Colours tend to be subdued.

Damas
Deira City Centre (04 295 3848/www.damasjewel.com). **Open** 10am-10pm Mon-Wed, Sun; 10am-midnight Thur-Sat. **Map** p60 B3 ㉑
The most advertised and popular jewellery chain in the Middle East prides itself on its quality gold creations – and there's not a knuckle-duster in sight. With Lebanese singing sensation Nancy Ajram as the face of the brand, Damas caters for women of all ages.

Deira City Centre Mall
Deira/Garhoud area (04 295 1010/www.deiracitycentre.com). **Open** 10am-10pm Mon-Thur, Sat, Sun; 2-10pm Fri. **Map** p60 B3 ㉒
Once the jewel in Dubai's shopping crown, Deira City Centre has had to work hard to fight off stiff competition from the likes of Mall of the Emirates and Ibn Battuta Mall. It's putting up a good fight, having introduced a flood of new titles including Club Monaco, H&M and New Look. There's also a massive branch of French hypermarket Carrefour, the amusement centre Magic Planet, and a multiplex cinema. Taxi queues to get out, though, can be heartbreakingly long.

Fish market
Opposite Hyatt Regency Dubai & Galleria. **Open** 9am-1pm, 4-10pm Mon-Thur, Sat, Sun; 4-10pm Fri.
Map p60 B1 ㉓
A huge hall contains stall upon stall of fresh fish, as an army of men in blue uniforms rush around boxing, weighing and carving up the day's catch. While splashing your path past the stalls – this is not a place for flip-flops – expect to see black hammour, koffer, kingfish, safi, shark and plenty of brawny king prawns.

For Love 21
Deira City Centre (04 294 3038).
Open 10am-11pm Mon-Wed, Sun; 10am-midnight Thur-Sat.
Map p60 B3 ㉔
Aside from hundreds of gold heart pendants and other pieces of glitz, there are also ethnic-inspired wooden beads and bangles, oversized sunglasses, cute underwear, print canvas handbags and patent pumps. It's cheap to shop here, which means you'll probably leave armed with enough accessories to last you the entire season.

Fruit & vegetable souk
Opposite Hyatt Regency Dubai & Galleria. **Open** 9am-1pm, 4-10pm Mon-Thur, Sat, Sun; 4-10pm Fri.
Map p60 B1 ㉕
If you enter here from the adjoining meat market, it's like dying and being reborn. Bright, colourful and fragrant, with an upbeat aura, it's a fun place to look around even if you have no intention on stocking up on fresh goods. Pick up some ice-cold coconut water to keep you refreshed as you ogle everything from bog-standard bananas to

DUBAI BY AREA

more intriguing buys, including bitter gourds, custard apples, dragon fruits and mangosteens.

Al Ghurair City Mall

Al Rigga Road (04 222 5222/ www.alghuraircity.com). **Open** 10am-10pm Mon-Thur, Sat, Sun; 4-10pm Fri. **Map** p60 B2 26

This veteran mall (the oldest mall in Dubai) combines Arabian decor with modern design. Popular outlets include Nine West and Paris Gallery. It's quite a maze, spread over two floors with corridors branching out at all angles, but it's worth persevering; tucked in the alleyways are excellent speciality stores selling everything from Arabian jewellery and rugs to South African beauty products.

Gold Souk

Nr Baladiya Street. **Open** 7am-noon, 5-7pm Mon-Thur, Sat, Sun; 5-7pm Fri. **Map** p60 B1 27

The old gold souk is an open market down a wide alley, framed by a wooden monster of an entrance with the text 'Dubai City of Gold'. The souk is formed of a crazy collection of walkways, lined with window displays of exotic, mind-boggling pieces. If you get bored with all the glitter, there are a few hidden spots where you can find clothing for sale, and towards the eastern end is the perfume souk, in which you can blend your own scents or purchase copies of designer brand names.

Jacky's

Deira City Centre (04 294 9480/ www.jackys.com). **Open** 10am-10pm Mon-Wed, Sun; 10am-midnight Thur-Sat. **Map** p60 B3 28

One of the giants of the electric scene in Dubai, Jacky's has come a long way since opening its first store in 1988. Now with seven outlets, the City Centre branch goes head-to-head with fellow superpower Jumbo Electronics next door. A vast selection of fridges, freezers, washers and dryers is complemented by an assortment of culinary essentials such as blenders, toasters, kettles and irons.

Jumbo Electronics

Deira City Centre (04 295 3915/ www.jumbocorp.com). **Open** 10am-10pm Mon-Wed, Sun; 10am-midnight Thur-Sat. **Map** p61 B4 29

This popular shop is one of the largest Sony distributors in the world, and has 16 outlets scattered around the city. Jumbo Electronics boasts an enviable supporting cast of leading international brands. The store layout aims to be interactive, so that you can road test potential buys such as the PSP or the PlayStation 3.

Kanz Jewels

Gold Souk (04 226 5639). **Open** 8am-11pm Mon-Thur, Sat, Sun; 8am-noon, 4-11pm Fri. **Map** p60 B1 30

Kanz is another big name in the business, with more than one outlet in the old souk. The pieces that stand out here are the traditional Gulf necklaces – delicate gold chokers with inlaid gems from all over the region. The store also boasts a collection of UAE-made chokers that tie with a traditional red cord and cost around Dhs11,000 each.

Kurt Geiger

Deira City Centre (04 294 3395). **Open** 9.30am-10pm Mon-Wed, Sun; 9.30pm-midnight Thur-Sat. **Map** p60 B3 31

This recently opened shop is taking Dubai's shopaholics by storm, as shoe shops have always been tastelessly stocked here. This is the first Kurt Geiger branch to open in the city, and it stocks Kurt Geiger, KG, Carvela and French Connection.

MAC

Deira City Centre (04 295 7704/www.maccosmetics.com). **Open** 10am-10pm Mon-Wed, Sun; 10am-midnight Thur-Sat. **Map** p60 B3 32

MAC is used by professional makeup artists around the globe, and it's no wonder, with their plethora of foundations, glosses and beauty tools, and show-stopping, bright and glittery eye shadows. The staff are helpful and on hand to give you a makeover and tips.

Abracadabra

What's the best way to cross the Creek?

Creekside

Dubai's Creek forms a significant psychological barrier for many people who live in the city. Like Londoners who refuse to go south of the water, or New Yorkers who won't countenance leaving Manhattan Island, many Dubaians are put off heading to 'Deira side'. It's perceived as being a bit low rent compared to the sparkly towers of Sheikh Zayed Road, the yachty opulence of the Marina, or even the bustle of Bur Dubai. Even for those who realise how worthwhile a trip can be, simply getting there can be off-putting. Traffic across the bridges can add an hour to the journey, particularly coming from Deira in the morning and going back in the evening. The quickest way to get across is on the water. Abras pootle back and forth for a dirham a time, and a trip on the ramshackle old tugs is an atmospheric way to get across. They go from each side of the Bur Dubai textile souk to Sabkha station (next to the spice souk) or Baniyas (further up the Creek).

The new waterbus provides an air-conditioned alternative for the same routes, and costs Dhs4 each way. The Road Transport Authority bills these as 'amazingly spacious high tech boats'. To the uninitiated, they may appear like barges with a greenhouse on top, but they're dry, cool and as quick as the old abras. Berths are next to abra stations.

Another step up the ladder of nautical grandeur is the water taxi. Like road taxis, these can be called to come and collect you from the same stations as waterbuses and abras. As this book went to press, fees and routes hadn't been fixed, but the boats can carry up to 11 on a private cruise across the Creek.

The cheapest option, though, is to go under the water. Down next to Shindagha tunnel, near the mouth of the Creek, is a seldom used pedestrian tunnel. It runs from just past the Diving Village on the Bur Dubai side to near the bus station on Baniyas Road on the Deira side. It won't cost you a fil and offers views out to the Gulf.

DUBAI BY AREA

Massimo Dutti

Marc by Marc Jacobs

Dubai Festival City (04 232 6118/ www.marcjacobs.com). **Open** 10am-10pm Mon-Wed, Sun; 10am-midnight Thur-Sat. **Map** p61 A6 ③③

Marc Jacobs' '50s-inspired designs can make anyone look classy. A dress will cost around Dhs1,200, a bag Dhs2,500, and a watch Dhs1,100, which is still a lot cheaper than usual. Our advice? Head to the back, which is a little less crowded, to check out the bags. You'll also find baby tops for a pricey Dhs500.

Massimo Dutti

Deira City Centre (04 295 4788/ www.massimodutti.com). **Open** 10am-10pm Mon-Wed, Sun; 10am-midnight Thur-Sat. **Map** p60 B3 ③④

Stacks of sophisticated suits, crisp cotton shirts, rugged leather jackets, ultra-glam eveningwear, well-finished accessories and catwalk-savvy pairs of shoes make Massimo Dutti one of the city's most popular shops. The clothes effortlessly exude class and don't have sky-high price tags.

Meat market

Opposite Hyatt Regency Dubai & Galleria. **Open** 9am-1pm, 4-10pm Mon-Thur, Sat, Sun; 4-10pm Fri. **Map** p60 B1 ③⑤

It's unlikely you'll want to invest in half a lamb carcass while on holiday, but for anyone with an interest in food, the meat market will be fascinatingly repulsive. Duck behind the huge carcasses that swing from intimidating meat hooks while butchers busy themselves by hacking away at cow heads – watch out for flying jawbones as fragments are thrown in various buckets. If that hasn't put you off, meat eaters can find plenty of bargains here.

Nine West

Deira City Centre (04 295 6887/ www.ninewest.com). **Open** 10am-10pm Mon-Thur, Sat, Sun; 2-10pm Fri. **Map** p60 B3 ③⑥

Nine West can be a bit hit and miss when it comes to catwalk looks, but for everyday basics it consistently delivers the goods. It's also one of the few shoe shops in Dubai to stock large sizes, and prices are very reasonable.

Paris Gallery

Deira City Centre (04 295 5550/www.uae-parisgallery.com). **Open** 10am-11pm Mon-Wed, Sun; 10am-midnight Thur-Sat. **Map** p60 B3 ③⑦

This stalwart of the UAE's beauty industry has the ambience of a boudoir. Staff can be over eager, but most international brands are stocked, with goods tantalisingly displayed on carousels. There's also a spa on the upper level.

Priceless

Al Maktoum Street (04 221 5444). **Open** 10am-10pm Mon-Thur, Sat, Sun; 2-10pm Fri. **Map** p60 B2 ③⑧

You'll love Priceless. All the big names, such as Gucci, Yves Saint Laurent, Jimmy Choo, Giorgio Armani and Akris, are here. The only difference is the price tag: there's a whopping 85 per cent off (think Gucci shoes for Dhs250). They can hold pieces for around five hours – but no longer.

Rituals

Deira City Centre (04 294 1432/ www.rituals.com). **Open** 10am-10pm Mon-Wed, Sun; 10am-midnight Thur-Sat. **Map** p60 B3 **❸❾**

The face, body and hair ranges at Rituals, a Dutch lifestyle brand that embraces Eastern philosophies, are a little more expensive than regular toiletries, but they're worth the investment: the quality is superb.

Ruby Damas

Gold souk (04 226 3648). **Open** 9.30am-10pm Mon-Thur, Sat, Sun; 9.30am-11.30am, 4.30-10pm Fri. **Map** p60 B1 **❹⓿**

This UAE-based company has stores in countries all over the world, including a few in the old gold souk. This particular branch is the only one that bears the name of Ruby Jewellers, an Indian jeweller that was purchased by Damas. Take a look at the tempting diamonds (which are mainly from Italy) and the wide selection of fashionably modern gold accessories. The Arabian pieces include a simple strand of Bahraini pearls for Dhs27,000.

Sona Jewellers

Gold souk (04 226 6012). **Open** 9.30am-2pm, 4-9pm Mon-Thur, Sat, Sun; 9am-11.30am, 4-10pm Fri. **Map** p60 B1 **❹❶**

Sona Jewellers is the only spot in the souk with an interesting collection of gold statuettes. The elaborate mini models, which are hollow and made in Asia from mould casts, are based on mythical figures and Hindu gods. Glistening Ganeshas start at around Dhs150 per gram.

Spice Souk

Between Al Nasr Square & the Creek, nr Gold souk, Deira. **Open** (most stalls) 8am-1pm, 4-9pm Mon-Thur, Sat, Sun; 4-9pm Fri. **Map** p60 B1 **❹❷**

Postcard-pretty sacks of aromatic ingredients line the small shop fronts at this colourful spice souk. Expect to find frankincense, nutmeg, cardamom, star anise, vanilla pods and saffron imported from Iran. Despite the fact that it only occupies a few streets, this is one of the most atmospheric souks in town, and gives you a glimpse into old Dubai. Just don't expect to have a leisurely stroll: getting through the area without being lured into several shops is hard work.

Stradivarius

Deira City Centre (04 294 1221). **Open** 10am-10pm Mon-Wed, Sun; 10am-midnight Thur-Sat. **Map** p60 B3 **❹❸**

Most of the clothing in this store is aimed at fashionable teenagers. Big on brilliant colours, Lycra, short skirts and funky accessories, it's certainly eye-catching. The shoe and bag selection is impressive too.

Tiffany & Co

Deira City Centre (04 295 3884/ www.tiffany.com). **Open** 10am-10pm Mon-Wed, Sun; 10am-midnight Thur-Sat. **Map** p60 B3 **❹❹**

The aura of Audrey Hepburn glamour will always linger around the iconic Tiffany. This outlet may be small in size, but it still squeezes in a flabbergasting selection of classy jewellery, chic accessories and gift items. Check out the highly coveted engagement rings and signature heart chains. It's worth asking for a discount if you're buying something expensive.

Arts & leisure

Amara

Park Hyatt Dubai (04 602 1660/ www.dubai.park.hyatt.com). **Open** 9am-10pm daily. **Admission** Dhs420 1hr massage. **Map** p61 B4 **❹❺**

Amara is probably the trendiest spa in the city. If the surroundings matter to you as much as your treatment, book yourself in here and it's unlikely you'll be disappointed. Each of the treatment rooms comes with a private courtyard and an outdoor rain shower. After your session, you'll be treated to herbal tea and dried fruits in the courtyard, and given some relaxation time. You can also use the swiming pool and gym facilities for the day.

Amara p69

CineStar

Deira City Centre mall, Garhoud (04 294 9000). **Admission** Dhs30. **Map** Map p60 B3 46

Screens current Hollywood fare.

Club Olympus

Hyatt Regency Hotel, Deira Corniche (04 209 6802/www.dubai.regency. hyatt.com). **Open** 6am-11pm daily (incl swimming pool). **Admission** (non-members) Dhs150. **Map** p60 B1 47

Friendly, professional staff attract a varied clientele to this city centre club. Classes range from aerobics to yoga, and there's also a gym and a running track, which encircles the two floodlit tennis courts. A pair of squash courts, an outdoor swimming pool, a sauna, a steam room, a jacuzzi and a splash pool complete the line-up of extensive facilities at the club. The outside deck is particularly popular during the cooler winter months.

Grand CineCity

Above Spinneys supermarket in Al Ghurair City mall, Al Rigga Road (04 228 9898). **Admission** Dhs30. **Map** p60 B2 48

An eight-screen cinema that typically shows an even split of Hindi films and safe Hollywood fare.

Lifestyle Health Club

Sofitel City Centre, Port Saeed (04 603 8825/www.accorhotels.com). **Open** 6.30am-11pm Mon-Thur, Sat, Sun; 8am-8pm Fri. **Admission** Dhs50. **Map** p60 B3 49

This hotel-based club stretches over three floors: the reception, the two squash courts, sauna and steam room are on one level; the gym and aerobics studio on the next; and an outdoor swimming pool and floodlit tennis court are on the roof. The gym is packed with resistance and cardiovascular machines; different aerobic classes (Dhs30) are held each day in the studio.

Al Mamzar Beach

Al Mamzar Creek, by the Sharjah border (04 296 6201). **Open** 9am-6pm daily. **Admission** Dhs5. No credit cards. **Map** p60 E2 50

If you don't fancy the crowds at Jumeirah Beach Park, head for Al Mamzar. It doesn't have a café, but shower facilities and kiosks are dotted along the coast. There are sun loungers, but these tend to be in the main areas, so if you want a quieter spot, take a beach mat and camp down for the afternoon. As with everywhere in Dubai, it's busy on Friday, but if you venture out to Al Mamzar during the week (Beach 5 is the best), you should enjoy some peace and quiet.

Radisson Health Club

Radisson SAS (04 222 7171/www. deiracreek.dubai.radissonsas.com). **Open** 24 hours daily. **Admission** Dhs55 Mon-Thur, Sun; Dhs85 Fri, Sat. **Map** p60 B2 ⑤

What makes this gym stand out is that it is one of only two 24-hour gyms in the city, which means that you've got absolutely no excuse for neglecting to fit a session into your busy schedule. Facilities include an outdoor swimming pool, a tennis court, a squash court, a steam room and a sauna. There are no group sessions.

Taj Spa

Taj Palace Hotel, Al Maktoum Street (04 211 3101/www.tajhotels.com). **Open** 7am-8pm daily. **Admission** Dhs275 1hr massage. **Map** p60 B2 ⑤

Three different styles of massage are available at the atmospheric and relaxing Taj Spa; a one-hour basic Balinese, Ayurvedic or Swedish massage costs Dhs320. Friendly staff will happily recommend appropriate treatments according to the desired effect, and facials are available. As well as separate saunas and steam rooms, the Taj Spa also features a pool and a jacuzzi.

Festival City

Eating & drinking

Belgian Beer Café

InterContinental hotel, Dubai Festival City. (04 701 1111). **Open** 5.30pm-2am Mon-Wed, Sun; 4pm-2am Thur; noon-2am Fri, Sat. **Café. Map** p61 A6 ⑤

All the food and the competitively priced beers are strictly Belgian (including Stella for the less adventurous), right down to the correct glasses for the different brews. Indeed, the management has even introduced Belgian drinking traditions, such as 'the shoe stealer.' No, we didn't have a clue what it was until we asked a

Belgian friend. Apparently, when you order a certain beer, it comes in a huge, expensive glass. So when barmen serve it they ask the customer to take off a shoe, which is kept in a same-sized glass until they finish their drink.

Quattro

Four Seasons Golf Club, Dubai Festival City (04 601 0101). **Open** 6.30am-1am daily. **$$. Italian. Map** p61 A6 ⑤

Expect tantalising amuse-bouches to come over first, such as soft goose liver with fruity red onion marmalade. For starters, try the excellent beef carpaccio. On the mains front, the black squid ink maltagliati pasta is a delight. Market-fresh mixed seafood stew is cooked cartoccio style, with its paunchy prawns, plump scallops, juicy mussels and flaky fish fillets swamped in a rich red sauce. With its atmospheric setting and first-rate Italian food, Quattro is a restaurant worth savouring.

Reflets par Pierre Gagnaire

InterContinental hotel, Dubai Festival City (04 701 1111). **Open** 5.30pm-2am Mon-Wed, Sun; 4pm-2am Thur; noon-2am Fri, Sat. **$$$$. French. Map** p61 A6 ⑤

A new high point for Dubai's dining scene and for six-time Michelin-starred chef Pierre Gagnaire. The jewel-box interior and ceremonial presentation is entirely appropriate for somewhere that serves such divine, inspired creations of molecular gastronomy. This is absolutely somewhere worth blowing the budget on.

Shopping

Converse

Dubai Festival City (04 232 5906/ www.converse.com). **Open** 10am-10pm Mon-Thur, Sat, Sun; 11am-11pm Fri. **Map** p61 A6 ⑤

There are cool and brightly coloured Converse trainers displayed on all the walls of this hip store, but the service leaves room for improvement. For the kids, a pair of kicks will cost around Dhs90, whereas grown-ups will get a

DUBAI BY AREA

Festival of food

Dubai's newest area in which to eat, drink and be merry.

Reflets par Pierre Gagnaire p71

One of Dubai's many ironies is that a city with so much vision has so little imagination when it comes to names. A collection of training centres becomes Knowledge Village, which is next to Internet City and Media City. The place where boxes get lost is called Cargo Village; the vast theme park on the city's outskirts is to be Dubailand; and there are also Heritage Village, Diving Village, Jumeirah Village (which isn't, confusingly, actually in Jumeirah but is about 10km from the coast), Jebel Ali Village and plain old the Village.

Add to that list Dubai Festival City, which has at least held a festival or two. For many in town, this is the only reason to cross the Creek other than getting to the airport. It's a vast shopping mall, but hosts concerts outside (including 2008's Desert Rock Festival, with Muse and Velvet Revolver), and has plenty of bars and restaurants with outdoor seating around the Creek and man-made canals. There are over 60 spots to eat, with 20 along the Canal Walk, where you can watch abras chug back and forth on a route that is more expensive and much less fun than the real thing further down the Creek.

A couple of big hotels add to the entertainment options. There's the Belgian Beer Café (p71) at Crowne Plaza, a favourite of ale-lovers and one of the few places to sell beers that don't sponsor the European Champions League. Over at the InterContinental, you'll find Reflets par Pierre Gagnaire (p71), a swanky spot from multi-Michelin-starred chef Gagnaire. A Four Seasons, due to open in 2010, promises more top-end chow.

This part of town remains fairly undiscovered. Most residents have a psychological block about crossing the Creek because of the heavy commuter traffic going to Deira every evening. But time your trip on a weekend, and this can be a pleasant spot for waterside eating and drinking.

pair for Dhs155. Although the actual shopping experience leaves a lot to be desired, at least you'll walk out with some pretty good trainers.

Dubai Festival City Mall
Garhoud (04 375 0505/232 5444/ www.dubaifestivalcity.com). **Open** 10am-10pm daily. **Map** p61 A6 ⑥⑦
These connected centres opened in early 2007 to an avalanche of hype, with a whopping 500 stores and a fantastic location by the water. The spacious corridors are bathed with natural light, and several good restaurants are scattered along the waterfront. Few malls offer such variety: there's Calvin Klein, Kenzo, Lacoste, Mark Jacobs, Marks & Spencer and a gigantic Ikea to boot. The picturesque Festival Square at the heart of the venue offers a regular programme of entertainment.

New Yorker
Dubai Festival City (04 232 9744). **Open** 10am-10pm Mon-Thur, Sun; 10am-midnight Fri, Sat. **Map** p61 B6 ⑤⑧
We're always dubious about shops named after cities, but we're big fans of the cheap and cheerful ethic of New Yorker. On par with H&M, it has a raft of apparel for under Dhs100 that's colourful, wearable and, most importantly, durable. From slogan T-shirts to electric blue jeans, and trilby hats to Converse-esque pumps, you could pick up an ensemble for less than Dhs250.

Paul Frank
Dubai Festival City (04 232 5915/ www.paulfrank.com). **Open** 10am-10pm Mon-Thur, Sun; 10am-midnight Fri, Sat. **Map** p61 A6 ⑤⑨
This store is a colourful, animated space, and although images of Julius the monkey smirk away at you from all sides (there's a vinyl leather Julius-covered couch to sit on), you'll also find trendy items that aren't covered in monkey print. The Small Paul collection is ridiculously cute. Not surprisingly, Romeo Beckham (Posh and Becks' son) has been snapped in some of the range (T-shirts start at Dhs95).

Puma
Dubai Festival City (04 232 5966/ www.puma.com). **Open** 10am-10pm Mon-Wed, Sat, Sun; 10am-midnight Thur-Sat. **Map** p61 A6 ⑥⓪
Here are a few tips before you enter the store. Firstly, pair a sporty piece like track pants with something simple and feminine like a sexy tank top. Also remember that athletic shoes may be high fashion, but they look best when worn as a dress-down ensemble. Finally, there's a way to get sporty without the treadmill.

Sephora
Dubai Festival City (04 232 6023/ www.sephora.com). **Open** 10am-10pm Mon-Wed, Sun; 10am-midnight Thur-Sat. **Map** p61 A6 ⑥①
Anyone who has ever visited Sephora will tell you that it's a beauty junkie's paradise, thanks to the relaxed atmosphere, interesting decor and helpful staff. The French beauty giant has quickly drawn a following of loyal customers around the world. Along with the cool cosmetics and toiletries that are available to buy, the staff are extremely friendly (and look immaculately groomed). So if you're one to fuss over mascara, this store alone is reason enough to come to Dubai Festival City.

Ted Baker
Dubai Festival City (04 232 6053/ www.tedbaker.com). **Open** 10am-10pm Mon-Wed, Sun; 10am-midnight Thur-Sat. **Map** p61 A6 ⑥②
Ted Baker's quirky sense of humour is everywhere in this store – from the 'I love Ted' badges worn by the sales people to the over-the-top, decadent couch. There are also mountains of cool clothes, which all embody the signature Ted Baker style: British heritage meets eccentric contemporary clothing. Hip Londoners have always loved Baker's shirts and trousers with laser-cut pockets; the feminine floral skirts and sexy little black dresses will appeal to women; and the colourful, smart, sleek shirts and ties should tempt most men here.

Tommy Hilfiger

Dubai Festival City (04 232 6187/ www.tommy.com). **Open** 10am-10pm Mon-Wed, Sun; 10am-midnight Thur, Fri. **Map** p61 B6 63

According to Hilfiger, here's what every woman should have in her wardrobe: a tailored white shirt, a pair of great-fitting jeans, a classic navy blazer, a strapless dress and a chic trench. Apparently, girls will also need stilettos and classic pearls to complete the look. As for the boys, they'll need a practical – yet polished – carryall, a couple of smart signature polo tops, a tailored blazer (navy or white) and some casual canvas trousers.

Vintage 55

Dubai Festival City (04 232 6616/ www.vintage55.com). **Open** 10am-10pm Mon-Wed, Sun; 10am-midnight Thur-Sat. **Map** p61 B6 64

This store could almost double as a photography exhibition of famous Hollywood film stars. A large photograph of Audrey Hepburn hangs above the cashier, while Marilyn Monroe and James Dean gaze down moodily from the wall. Empty black wooden boxes are stacked to the ceiling, displaying items of clothing like quirky T-shirts, cute white capri pants embellished with the name 'Jackie O', striped vests featuring the words 'First Lady', well-cut jeans and cool, comfy shorts. There are also kitsch ornaments along with a range of cult books, such as Marlon Brando's biography.

Arts & leisure

Four Seasons Golf Club

Al Rebat Street, Festival City (04 601 0101/www.fourseasons.com/dubaigolf). **Open** 6am-sunset daily. **Admission** Dhs775. **Map** p61 A6 65

Al Badia golf course is the focal point of this Dubai Festival City golfing wonderland. Designed by Robert Trent Jones II, the 18-hole championship course has a desert oasis theme, and boasts a golf academy.

Alpha p77

Garhoud

Eating & drinking

The Boardwalk
Dubai Creek Golf & Yacht Club (04 295 6000). **Open** 8am-midnight daily. **$$**.
European. Map p61 B4 66
When it comes to alfresco dining, few places in Dubai have the same panache as the Boardwalk. Built on a wooden terrace over the Creek, this place lets diners take in a gorgeous marina view while abras – and some more ostentatious sea crafts – chug by. The fish and chips are reasonable, and the burgers are a safe bet, with sizeable patties complemented by a good range of fresh garnishes. The unforgettable vista makes the Boardwalk worth a visit.

Café Chic
Le Méridien Dubai (04 282 4040).
Open 12.30-2.45pm, 8-11.45pm daily.
$$$. **French**. Map p61 B4 67
This place would be fit for Louis XIV himself. There's all manner of jus, consommé and crottin on the menu, along with the requisite amuse-bouches (smoked salmon and cream cheese mini sandwiches, for example) and a bread selection to rival the most fastidious Parisian bakery – the black olive, tomato and cheese bake is nothing short of exquisite. And that's a bread roll we're talking about.

The Dubliner's
Le Méridien Dubai, Airport Road, Garhoud (04 282 4040/www.starwood hotels.com). **Open** noon-1.30am
Mon-Thur, Sun; 11am-1.20am Fri, Sat.
Bar. Map p61 B4 68
A cosy Irish bar serving decent pub food and some of the biggest pies in town, the Dubliner's is a jovial place for a beer. The decor incorporates dark wood, the obligatory Guinness posters and the back end of a truck, alongside acres of Celtic paraphernalia. It's a good bet for televised sports, and its proximity to the airport makes it worth a visit if you've only got a few hours in town and aren't feeling adventurous.

Ego
Garhoud (04 283 2444). **Open** 10am-midnight daily. **Café**. Map p61 B5 69
This trendy café serves lentil soup, which comes liquidised and full of cumin flavour, with the obligatory wedge of lemon on the side and some warm, soft flatbread; an absolute bargain at Dhs9. Try the shish taouk, hunks of charred chicken in a thick white baguette with gherkin, green pepper and mayonnaise. Despite the good-value food, this is primarily a shisha and internet café.

Golestan
Next to Computer College, Garhoud (04 282 8007). **Open** 12.15pm-midnight daily. **$$**. **Middle Eastern**.
Map p61 B5 70
From the carved, dark wood partitions and the beautifully arranged mosaic finishes to the wonderfully evocative music, this low-key Persian restaurant, Golestan, gets everything right. For starters, try the kashk-o-bademjan, a creamy puree of fried aubergine, yoghurt, tomato garlic and crispy onion. Save some dip to accompany the main course of chelo kebab sultani, with skewers of tender and juicy lamb, and steak and basmati rice. Once you've finished, delay the return to the outside world a little longer by ordering a twin-action dessert of falooda and saffron ice cream, and muse contentedly on a fantastic meal.

The Irish Village
The Aviation Club, Garhoud (04 282 4750/www.irishvillage.ae).
Open 11.30am-1am daily. **Bar**.
Map p61 B5 71
The Irish Village is a great option if you're looking for a pint of beer, a snack and a crowd to enjoy them with. The burgers are particularly satisfying if you're feeling hungry. The main draw during the winter months is the fantastic outside terrace that hugs a duck pond, yet the vast assortment of draught beers available – including old favourites Guinness and Kilkenny – keep people flooding in all year round.

JW's Steakhouse

JW Marriott Hotel Dubai (04 262 4444). **Open** 12.30-3.30pm, 7.30-11pm daily. $$$. **Steakhouse**. Map p61 C3 ⓒ

This steakhouse has the feel of an exclusive gentlemen's club, but to join the flesh-chomping fraternity here you don't have to belong to an old boys' network (but you do have to be willing to part with a significant sum of cash). The no-fuss menu lists hearty comfort food: oysters or foie gras, followed by a bewildering variety of steak cuts, from Australian grass-fed fillet to Wagyu sirloin, as well as lamb and seafood dishes. The brass nameplates on each table, which can be earned by visiting JW's a belt-busting 24 times in six months, are testament to its popularity.

Kiku

Le Méridien Dubai (04 282 4040). **Open** 12.30-2.45pm, 7-11pm daily. $$. **Japanese**. Map p61 B4 ⓒ

Kiku is a fantastic Japanese restaurant, and if you don't want to take our word for it, trust the huge throng of Japanese people that visit on a nightly basis. The authentic and well-priced food dished up by friendly staff leaves its mark. There are three bento boxes and four different set menus, which, at around Dhs70, constitute such good value it's tempting to share one between two and then go off piste for the rest of the meal.

Legends

Dubai Creek Golf & Yacht Club (04 295 6000). **Open** noon-2.30pm, 7pm-midnight Mon-Thur, Sun; 11.30am-2.30pm, 7-11.30pm Fri. $$. **Steakhouse**. Map p61 B4 ⓒ

With the lush greens of the golf club in one direction and the Creek in the other, this restaurant consistently serves great meals at mid-range prices. From the tenderness of a perfectly cooked 14oz New Zealand rib eye to the succulent US prime Angus tenderloin, these cuts are stirringly juicy, sliced like butter and melt in the mouth. It's worth investigating their early bird deals, which consist of three-course meals with wine for about Dhs170 per person.

Al Mazaj

Century Village, Garhoud. (04 282 9952). **Open** 12.30pm-1.30am daily. $. **Arabian**. Map p61 B5 ⓒ

If gongs were handed out for undemanding conviviality, Al Mazaj would secure its fair share of nominations. Ambition and innovation are thin on the ground, but the absence of airs and graces makes for a pleasant dining experience. Once ensconced in one of the cosily ergonomic seats, kick back with a shisha pipe and let your stress drift away. The food doesn't quite match up to the atmosphere, but there are several acceptable dishes on offer. There is better Lebanese food elsewhere in Dubai, but decent grub and good vibes is a winning combination that Al Mazaj has down to a fine art.

Al Mijana

Le Méridien Dubai, Garhoud (04 282 4040). **Open** noon-3pm, 8pm-12.30am daily. $$. **Arabian**. Map p61 B4 ⓒ

From the dramatic wooden ceiling to the open kitchen and wine cellar, Al Mijana is reminiscent of the classy restaurants perched on the edge of Lebanon's mountains. Here you can gorge on wonderful fattoush, raw minced lamb and a note-perfect mixed grill. Finish off with an apple shisha and a brew of Turkish coffee, and let the oud player's tear-jerking tunes take you back to Lebanon's glory days.

More

Behind Lifco supermarket, Garhoud (04 283 0224). **Open** 8am-10pm daily. $$. **Café**. Map p61 B5 ⓒ

The eggs Benedict is superb here, and the salads and sandwiches, on the whole, do the trick. The pumpkin, feta and spinach salad is a favourite with vegetarians, and comes dripping with a thick and nicely tart dressing. The fillet steak with peppercorn sauce is always good – pair it with a thick milkshake or smoothie. The sandwiches are enormous, as are the vats of soup that come with thick, crusty bread. Despite the occasional off day this café will have you coming back.

DUBAI BY AREA

QD's

Dubai Creek Golf & Yacht Club (04 295 6000/www.dubaigolf.com). **Open** 6pm-2am daily. **Bar**. Map p61 B4 ⑦

In the cooler months, the setting at QD's is as evocative as anywhere in the city. As wafts of fruit-tinged shisha whisper through the air, lazy dhows chug by against the twinkling backdrop of the Creek at twilight. The food certainly isn't anything to write home about – it offers a menu of passable bar food presented without any real flair, and QD's biggest problem remains the inattentive and unreliable service. However, the pricing is fair and the setting quite wonderful, with some seats right next to the water.

Sarband

Century Village, Garhoud (04 283 3891). **Open** 11am-2am daily. **$$**. **Middle Eastern**. Map p61 B5 ⑦

The contemporary Mediterranean decor and outdoor terrace are more than pleasant, but what keeps people so interested in Sarband is the excellent Persian food. Simply presented (and in vast quantities) the saffron-infused chicken kebabs or the sweet and sour chicken with barberries (rather like a cross between a cranberry and a raspberry) are crammed with sumptuous meat, and so flavoursome they could make a hungry man dizzy. Round things off with falooda, a blend of frozen vermicelli and syrup. Value for money should be guaranteed here.

Sukhothai

Le Méridien Dubai (04 282 4040). **Open** 12.30-2.45pm, 7.30-11.30pm daily. **$$$**. **Thai**. Map p61 B5 ⑧

With a majestic wood panelled interior and unquestionably authentic food, Sukhothai has been one of the leading Thai restaurants in Dubai for many years. Viscous flowers of crabmeat dumplings explode with flavour, and chubby prawns arrive enveloped in tight jackets of dried noodles. You can't go wrong with the red and green curries, either. It's clear why Sukhothai has been winning over Dubai hearts since its inception.

Nightlife

Alpha

Le Méridien, Airport Road (04 282 4040/www.starwoodhotels.com). **Open** 6pm-2am Tue; 6pm-3am Thur; 4pm-3am Fri. Map p61 B4 ㉛

The newest club in town is dishing up an electro-infused indie night on

Aviation Club p78

Tuesdays, with house on Thursdays and Fridays. They're promising a monthly drum 'n' bass night, which is a rare thing in Dubai. The club is cosy, with a bar downstairs and snug gallery areas upstairs. A garden area is being reclaimed for the winter.

Arts & leisure

Al Ahli Club Experimental Theatre

Al Ahli Club, Al Qusais (04 298 8812). Map p61 E5 **62**

The Al Ahli Club Experimental Theatre has been running since 1981 and exists to promote a lively and progressive programme of Arabic-language productions. The theatre runs workshops and summer schools for local children, encouraging a broad and progressive approach to drama.

Akaru Spa

The Aviation Club (04 282 8578/ www.akaruspa.com). **Open** 10am-10pm daily. **Admission** Dhs265 1hr massage. Map p61 B5 **63**

This pleasant, warmly decorated spa offers facials, massages and body wraps; but for pure, lulling, dreamlike ambience, opt for one of their signature packages. We particularly like Relax, which consists of a body scrub, aromatic body massage and a facial. At Dhs475 it's an expensive treatment, but as indulgences go, it's a wonderful one.

Aviation Club

Next to Tennis Stadium (04 282 4122/www.aviationclub.ae). **Open** 6am-11pm daily. Map p61 B5 **64**

Home to Dubai's prestigious tennis tournament, and one of the few clubs to establish itself on the Deira side of the Creek, the Aviation Club is incredibly popular. It boasts an impressive list of facilities, namely ten floodlit tennis courts, a swimming pool with 25m lap lanes, two squash courts, a dedicated spinning studio, a sauna, a steam room, plunge pools and a fully equipped gym. Non-members should call for day prices.

Dubai Creek Golf & Yacht Club

Opposite Deira City Centre (04 205 4646/www.dubaigolf.com). **Open** 7am-6pm daily. Map p61 B4 **65**

The Dubai Creek Golf & Yacht Club's own 10m (32ft) single cabin yacht *Sneakaway* is available for trips for up to six people. The price – from Dhs2,550 for four hours to Dhs3,550 for eight – includes tackle, bait and fuel, as well as a good supply of soft drinks. If you prefer something a bit racier, you can hire the *Princess* sports boat.

Grand Cineplex

Next to Wafi City mall (04 324 2000). **Admission** Dhs30. Map p61 A4 **66**

This 12-screen cinema is one of the city's better known cineplexes, and tends to show safe US imports alongside one or two Asian films. It occasionally gets first screenings a few days before other cinemas in the city.

Griffin's Health Club

JW Marriott (04 607 7755/www. marriott.com). **Open** 6am-11pm daily. **Admission** Dhs77 Mon-Thur, Sun; Dhs99 Fri, Sat. Map p61 C3 **67**

There are two squash courts, an outdoor swimming pool, a spa and a jacuzzi, as well as a gym with a separate cardio room at this reasonably priced health club. Classes (Dhs30) include aerobics, spinning and step.

Spa InterContinental

InterContinental Dubai Festival City (04 701 1257). **Open** 8am-10pm daily. **Admission** Dhs400 1hr massage. Map p61 A6 **68**

The Spa InterContinental is minimal in design, but the treatments on offer are quite the opposite. They soothe and replenish skin that has been suffering from Dubai's harsh desert environment. The spa is home to the only Natura Bissé treatments (we recommend the Natura Bissé Diamond Facial, Dhs1,150) in the emirate, and the treatment rooms boast some great views over the Creek. The organic range Just Pure and the local brand Shiffa are also available.

Abra crossing point

Bur Dubai

As Dubai was settled, a residential area developed along the sandy southern banks of the Creek, and became known as Bur Dubai. It was here that the emirate's rulers made their home, in sea-facing fortifications, and the district remains the seat of the Diwan ('ruler's office'), Dubai's most senior administrative body. As the city grew, the area acquired embassies and consulates, creating an atmosphere of diplomatic calm, with commercial activity centred on the mouth of the Creek.

Today, the situation is changing fast, and although the banks of the Creek are still free of development, Bur Dubai has sprawled inland, with tower blocks springing up on practically every inch of sand. As the residential community has grown, so commerce has developed to meet local demand. The once tiny souk has expanded dramatically, supermarkets and shopping malls have opened, and dual carriageways cross the area. **Dubai Museum** makes a good starting point for exploration of Bur Dubai, and it's possibly the best part of town to explore by foot.

Sights & museums

Abra crossing point
End of Al Seef Road, nr entrance of Bastakia souk, Dubai Creek.
Map p80 D2 ①
The cheapest way to view the Creek is on one of the abras (traditional wooden water taxis) that cross the Creek day and night. These rickety but watertight boats have been ferrying people across the Creek since Dubai was first settled; originally they were rowing boats, but today they're powered by smelly diesel.

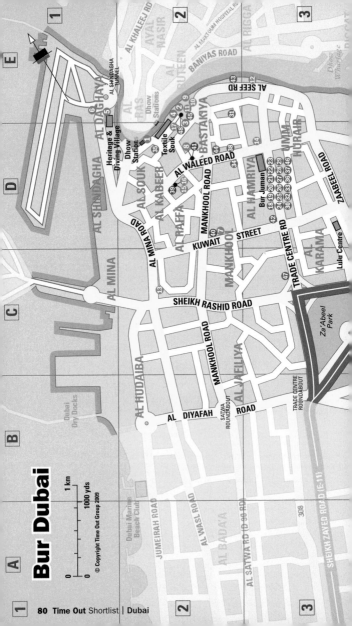

Bur Dubai

Heritage & Diving Village

Even now, around 15,000 people cross the Creek by abra every day. The abras are commuter vehicles for low-paid workers, and boarding can be chaotic at peak times. You're likely to find yourself pulled across the decks of several boats by helpful abra captains, who are quick to extend welcoming hands to anyone hesitating or looking for a space on the bench seating. The basic crossing lets you take in the atmosphere of the Creek and gives a good insight into how the city operated in the past. For a more comprehensive tour it's worth hiring your own abra – simply ask a boat captain and agree a price and the length of the tour before you set out. A journey up and down the Creek should cost no more than Dhs50.

Bastakia

Between Al Fahidi Street & southern bank of the Creek. **Map** p80 E2 ❷
One of Dubai's most picturesque heritage sights, Bastakia is being carefully renovated and turned into a pedestrianised conservation area. The name Bastakia comes from the first people to settle the area, traders from Bastak in southern Iran. The ruler of

Dubai encouraged immigration in the early 1900s by granting favourable tax concessions; many people came and stayed, which explains why so many Emiratis are of southern Iranian descent. Walking through the narrow alleyways can feel like a step into Dubai's past, even though few of the buildings and wind towers are original.

Dubai Museum

Al Fahidi Fort, Bastakia (04 353 1862/www.dubaitourism.co.ae). **Open** 8.30am-8.30pm Mon-Thur, Sat, Sun; 2.30-8.30pm Fri. **Admission** Dhs3; Dhs1 reductions. **Map** p80 D2 ❸
Considered by many residents to be a must for visitors, Dubai's museum is indeed worth a visit. The Al Fahidi Fort was built in 1787 as Dubai's primary sea defence, and also served as the ruler's residence. In 1970 it was renovated so the museum could be housed within its walls. Inside, the displays are creative and imaginative, allowing you to peek into an Islamic school, walk through a 1950s souk and watch video of traditional craftsmen at work.

Grand Mosque

Nr Dubai Museum. **Open** 24hrs daily. **Map** p80 E2 ❹
Although it may look like a restored historical building, the Grand Mosque was only built a little over ten years ago. However, it was constructed and styled to resemble the original Grand Mosque that was built around 1900 in the same location and doubled as a religious school. Sadly, the first Grand Mosque was torn down in the '60s.

Heritage & Diving Village

Al Shindagha (04 393 7151/ www.dubaitourism.co.ae). **Open** 8.30am-10pm Mon-Thur, Sun; 4-10pm Fri, Sat. **Admission** free. **Map** p80 E1 ❺
This 'living' museum by the Creek, staffed by guides, potters, weavers and other craftspeople, focuses on Dubai's maritime past and depicts the living conditions of original seafarers, who farmed the waters of the Gulf for pearls and fish. A tented village gives a

Antique Bazaar

glimpse into the Bedouin way of life, which remained unchanged until well into the 20th century. During religious holidays, such as Eid Al Fitr and Eid Al Adha, and throughout the Dubai Shopping Festival (Jan-Feb), traditional ceremonies are laid on, including sword dancing and wedding celebrations. At these times old pearl divers are often on hand to recount tales of adventure and hardship.

Sheikh Saeed Al Maktoum House

Al Shindagha (04 393 7139/ www.dubaitourism.co.ae). **Open** 7.30am-9pm Mon-Thur, Sat, Sun; 3-10pm Fri. **Admission** Dhs2; Dhs1 reductions; free under-7s. **Map** p80 E1 ⑥

Built in 1896 out of coral covered in lime and sand plaster, this traditional house was the home of Dubai's ruler until his death in 1958 (hence its strategic position at the mouth of the Creek). Now restored and converted into a museum, it hosts small exhibitions of old documents, stamps, currencies and a collection of old photographs of Dubai and its ruling family. Guided tours are available.

Eating & drinking

Aangan

Dhow Palace Hotel, Kuwait Street (04 359 9992). **Open** 12.30-3.30pm, 7.30pm-1am daily. **$$**. **Indian**. **Map** p80 D2 ⑦

The flurry of fussy attention that greets you as you set foot in the dimly lit, wood-finished restaurant can be overwhelming, but persevere and start with the jhinga kandhari, with its absurdly large, torrentially juicy tiger prawns, seared to unworldly perfection in tandoori spices. The main courses are also excellent, especially the saag gosht with tender lamb in a rich sauce of puréed spinach, coriander and onions. Aangan is one of the city's finest Indian restaurants.

Antique Bazaar

Four Points by Sheraton (04 397 7444). **Open** 12.30-3pm, 7.30pm-2am daily. **$$**. **Indian**. **Map** p80 D2 ⑧

Walk into Antique Bazaar and you're likely to find a restaurant full of diners enraptured by the musicians performing Indian music. The audience will probably be enjoying their food too. The shami kebab appetisers are tidy

THE MUSIC ROOM

Featuring 2 resident bands, **Flipside** and **The Rockspiders,** the Music Room is Dubai's signature live music venue.

These talented musicians take to the stage from 7 pm every nig and will ensure an unforgettable evening with their renditions of rc songs from the 60's til today.

LIVE MUSIC
EVERY NIGHT

Open
12:00 NN - 3:00 AM

MAJESTIC
Hotel Tower Dubai

P.O. Box 122235 | Mankhool Rd | Bur Dubai | Dubai
04 501 2631 | 04 359 8888
www.dubaimajestic.com

Bastakiah Nights

packages of soft minced lamb and chickpeas infused with boldly flavoured coriander. The dark, rich minced lamb of the Hyderabadi kheema makes for a fine main course; the flavour of the soft, juicy meat is every bit as pleasing as its appearance. All in all, this is a reliably good mid-range restaurant.

Bait Al Wakeel
Bur Dubai (04 353 0530).
Open noon-midnight daily. **$**.
Arabian. Map p80 E2 ❾
The Creek location makes for spectacular views, smells and spectacles as abras, dhows and water taxis crisscross the busy waterway. What about the food? Well, it's perfectly passable and reasonably priced, especially given the location: think dishes of mutabbal, tabbouleh, hummus and falafel. Order a spread of these along with zesty Arabian salad and some very good meat dishes. The shish taouk and lamb chops are delightfully spiced and marinated – tear off strips of warm bread, and dig in. Finish your meal with sweet mint tea and shisha to complete the Arabian dining experience.

Basta Art Café
Bastakia, Bur Dubai (04 353 5071).
Open 8am-10pm daily. **$**. **Café**.
Map p80 E2 ❿
At the far end of the Bastakia quarter, twinkling fairy lights lead to courtyard, shaded by leafy trees and decorated with fountains and Arabian lanterns. Basta Art Café has long been a favourite lunch spot with residents and visitors, serving healthy dishes in romantic surroundings. The food has improved in the last year. Try a freshly squeezed juice and a jacket potato with sweet souk salad, finished by a tangy pot of Moroccan tea and a delightful plate of Arabian sweets.

Bastakiah Nights
Bastakia, Bur Dubai (04 353 7772).
Open 12.30-11.30pm daily. **$$**.
Arabian. Map p80 E2 ⓫
Step inside this restaurant and prepare for your romantic Arabian fantasies to be fulfilled. The flickering torches and grand, heavy wooden doors – intricately carved and studded with vast iron nails – immediately transport the unsuspecting guest into old-world Arabia. Sadly, the service and food don't quite live up to the setting. Truckloads of mezze and grilled meats arrive when you order the set menu, but nothing really stands out, and service can be slightly grumpy.

Bateaux Dubai
Bur Dubai, Al Seef Road, opposite the British Embassy (04 399 4994).
Open boarding 7.30pm (departs 8.30pm) daily. **$$**. **International**.
Map p80 E3 ⓬

DUBAI BY AREA

Player's Lounge

A dinner cruise on the Creek couldn't be enjoyed on a better vessel – the boat's huge glass windows offer superb views of the city's skyline and the air-conditioning offers respite during the scorching summer months. The dinner cruise costs Dhs275 per person, which is significantly more expensive than its competitors, but on Bateaux Dubai you get canapés, and a four-course à la carte meal. There's even an onboard pianist and violinist, making Bateaux Dubai by far the most sophisticated option on the water.

Player's Lounge

Country Club Hotel (formerly Chelsea Hotel), Sheikh Rashid Road (04 398 8840). **Open** noon-3am daily. **Bar**. Map p80 C2 ⓯

Sink into the dining booth seating and you would be forgiven for thinking you're back in Blighty. Still, this windowless boozer with tasteless carpets is a popular destination among Bur Dubai expats who love football, rugby, basketball and ice hockey, or enjoy the comedy night – the Laughter Factory – that's sometimes held here. There is greasy pub grub too, but the loud, clichéd house bands might drive you back out the door.

Rock Bottom Café

Regent Palace Hotel, Bur Dubai (04 396 3888). **Open** noon-3am daily. **Bar**. Map p80 D3 ⓮

Although it's officially a bar and a restaurant rather than a club, the Rock Bottom Café only really comes alive as other boozers kick out. Something of a cattle market, it pulls in an impressive crowd with its bullfrogs (a highly potent cocktail that uses all the white spirits plus Red Bull) and a resident DJ and live band, who pump out the crowdpleasers until closing time. There's even an in-house shawarma joint for dancers with the munchies.

Troyka

Ascot Hotel, Bank Street (04 352 0900). **Open** 12.30-2.45pm, 8pm-2.45am daily. **$$**. **Russian**. Map p80 D2 ⓯

This is a great place for a big group of friends to go to for a lively night out. Don't bother arriving before 11pm, as the restaurant will be empty and the entertainment, which comes in the form of a hilarious, camp Russian cabaret, starts at around 10.30pm. You could try the Troyka steak, which contains cow's tongue, but it's not to all tastes. The borscht is tasty, but the beef's a little tough. We love the potato to dumplings, but the last time we had them, they were lukewarm.

Waxy O'Conner's

Ascot Hotel, Khalid Bin Al Waleed Road, 'Bank Street' (04 352 0900/ www.ascothoteldubai.com). **Open** noon-2am Mon-Wed, Sat, Sun; noon-3am Thur, Fri. **Pub**. Map p80 D2 ⓰

In no way affiliated to the popular UK chain, Waxy O'Conner's is a bustling Irish pub on the equally frantic Bank Street. The reason for the dark bar's success is simple: the proprietors have lined up a deluge of deals to pull in the budget-conscious drinker. The biggest bargain is the Friday brunch, when Dhs70 will get you a full Irish breakfast, five drinks and a roast dinner later in the day. Try the Yorkshire pudding, with a lake of steaming beef casserole. Waxy's has all the style of a gastropub.

XVA Café

Bastakia, Bur Dubai (04 353 5383).
Open 9am-9pm Mon-Thur, Sun;
9am-6pm Fri; 9am-9pm Sat. **$. Café**.
Map p80 D2 **⑰**

XVA's clandestine hiding place in the middle of Bastakia makes it one of the most atmospheric spots in the city. The trees and canopies in its sun-dappled courtyard also help. Prices are high in the little café, but where else can you find a pretty, historic courtyard surrounded by art galleries, with regular film nights and old world charm, all a stone's throw from the Creek?

Shopping

Agent Provocateur

Saks Fifth Avenue, BurJuman Centre (04 351 5551/www.agentprovocateur.com). **Open** 10am-10pm Mon-Thur, Sat, Sun; 4-10pm Fri. **Map** p80 D2 **⑱**

Agent Provocateur serves up decadent sauciness without descending into sleaze. As a brand, it's a well executed and well oiled machine, from the pretty packaging and perfume to the lingerie itself. This is a good place at which to pick up stockings.

Aldo

BurJuman Centre (04 351 2787/www.aldoshoes.com). **Open** 10am-10pm Mon-Thur, Sat, Sun; 11am-11pm Fri. **Map** p80 D2 **⑲**

This Canadian shoe chain is hard to beat for sheer choice – a dazzling array of styles for men and women at surprisingly cheap prices. Aldo is pretty hot on the (forgive us) heels of the latest trends, and sells a great selection of bags, belts and beads.

Arabian Oud

BurJuman Centre (04 352 9988/www.arabianoud.com). **Open** 10am-10pm Mon, Tue, Sun; 10am-11pm Wed, Thur; 3-11pm Fri. **Map** p80 D2 **⑳**

This Saudi perfume chain's eastern ambience is balanced by a contemporary interior and a wide range of oils and potions. You can create your own mix of scents and choose the intricate bottle it will end up in.

Burberry

BurJuman Centre (04 351 3515/www.burberry.com). **Open** 10am-10pm Mon-Thur, Sun; 2-11pm Fri; 10am-11pm Sat. **Map** p80 D2 **㉑**

At Burberry, customers can wander across acres of plush carpet to lay their hands on cashmere scarves, desirable updates on the classic Burberry trench, and plenty of chequered tartan on bags, skirts and accessories.

BurJuman Centre

Trade Centre Road (04 352 0222/www.burjuman.com). **Open** 10am-10pm Mon-Thur, Sat, Sun; 2-10pm Fri. **Map** p80 D2 **㉒**

Much improved following an extension, the BurJuman Centre is a subdued, chic mall with plenty of designer brands, including Burberry, Donna Karan, Christian Lacroix and Tiffany & Co as well as a good selection of high street stores, such as Zara, Mango, Diesel and Massimo Dutti. Saks Fifth Avenue makes it stand out from the crowd. There are plenty of upmarket cafés in which to relax.

Christian Lacroix

BurJuman Centre (04 351 7133/www.christian-lacroix.fr). **Open** 10am-10pm Mon-Thur, Sat, Sun; 2-10pm Fri. **Map** p80 D2 **㉓**

This hoity-toity designer range has a small but wildly elegant selection in its Dubai branch. With plenty of eccentric pieces, this is the place for people who view fashion as art.

Diesel

BurJuman Centre (04 351 6181/www.diesel.com). **Open** 10am-10pm Mon, Tue, Sat, Sun; 10am-11pm Wed, Thur; 2-11pm Fri. **Map** p80 D2 **㉔**

Chock-full of hipster must-haves that ooze attitude, this is a veritable warehouse of jeans and accessories. Well cut jeans and retro tops will leave you looking too cool for school.

Donna Karan

BurJuman Centre (04 351 6794/www.donnakaran.com). **Open** 10am-10pm Thur, Sat; 2-11pm Fri. **Map** p80 D2 **㉕**

DUBAI BY AREA

Ohm Records

At Donna Karan's first-floor BurJuman outlet, you'll find many of her signature tailored pieces, together with plenty of sumptuous coats and brilliant red dresses. For dressed down – and more affordable – clothing, look no further than the DKNY diffusion range that's available on the ground floor.

Faces
BurJuman Centre (04 352 1441). **Open** 10am-10pm Mon, Tue, Sun; 10am-11pm Wed, Thur; 2-11pm Fri. **Map** p80 D2 ❻

Beauty magazines come to life when you step inside this shop. With a combination of designer fragrances, pretty cosmetics and mid-range brands such as Bourjois, Urban Decay and Benefit, it's a favourite among fashionable women in their 20s and 30s.

Golf House
BurJuman Centre (04 351 4801). **Open** 9.30am-10pm Mon, Tue, Sun; 9.30am-11pm Wed, Thur; noon-10pm Fri. **Map** p80 D2 ❼

Catering for the flourishing golf scene in Dubai, Golf House is a great stop-off before you hit the green. With top-of-the-range clubs, sports clothing and all the essentials, it has plenty to keep both the novice and the seasoned professional happy.

Hermès
BurJuman Centre (04 351 1190/ www.hermes.com). **Open** 10am-10pm Mon-Wed, Sun; 10am-11pm Thur-Sat. **Map** p80 D2 ❽

Liberally sprinkled in the credits of all the major fashion magazines, Hermès has become known as a symbol of Gallic elegance and style. Push through the intimidating doors and you'll find scarves of every hue and design, a great range of glamorous tote bags, and purses made from the skins of a variety of deceased exotic animals.

Mango
BurJuman Centre (04 355 5770/www.mango.com). **Open** 10am-10pm Mon, Tue, Sat, Sun; 10am-11pm Wed-Fri. **Map** p80 D2 ❾

Dubai's Mango outlets are as well stocked and as reasonably priced as those in Europe. As well as the usual range of carefully chosen clothes, expect some bejewelled and flowing styles to fit in with local tastes.

Max Mara
BurJuman Centre (04 351 3140). **Open** 10am-10pm Mon, Tue, Sat, Sun; 10am-11pm Wed-Fri. **Map** p80 D2 ❿

If there is one thing Max Mara does well, it's coats. Not wildly flamboyant ones, but simple, good quality classics;

Saks Fifth Avenue

the Italian fashion house has a long-standing reputation for creating couture lines. You'll also find SportMax stocked here too, a slightly cheaper line of knits and outdoor wear.

Ohm Records

Opposite BurJuman Centre (04 397 3728/www.ohmrecords.com). **Open** 2-10pm daily. **Map** p80 E2 ③

Ohm Records claims it was the first shop in the Middle East to sell vinyl shipped in from overseas. Although this seems unlikely, the store prides itself on introducing the masses to electronic music, and all its records come from independent labels. Professional and bedroom DJs gather at the weekends to play on the decks for free. The shop also sells record bags, turntables and a small line of streetwear.

Promod

BurJuman Centre (04 351 4477/ www.promod.com). **Open** 10am-10pm Mon-Thur, Sat, Sun; 2-10pm Fri. **Map** p80 D2 ③

This Spanish store's vibe is definitely bohemian. There's a vast range of daywear and covetable extras like beaded necklaces, bangles, hats, scarves and bags. With Promod's casual clothes, you can rejuvenate your wardrobe without breaking the bank.

Saks Fifth Avenue

BurJuman Centre (04 351 5551/ www.saksfifthavenue.com). **Open** 10am-10pm Mon-Thur, Sun; 2-10pm Fri; 10am-10pm Sat. **Map** p80 D2 ③

The epitome of New York designer chic, this store has not lost any of its sassiness through being transplanted to the Middle East. On two levels you'll find an array of top-end labels, including Prada, Alberta Ferretti, Philosophy and Dior. You can also splurge on Manolo Blahnik here.

Sun & Sand Sports

Khalid Bin Al Waleed Road 'Bank Street' (04 351 6222/www.sunand andsports.com). **Open** 10am-10pm Mon-Thur, Sat, Sun; 2-10pm Fri. **Map** p80 D2 ③

One of the biggest sports shops in Dubai, Sun & Sand Sports stocks everything from the latest tennis gear and swimwear to gym equipment. Clothing prices are reasonable, and although you won't find the best selection of footwear in the city, the sheer quantity of everything else more than makes up for this.

Textile Souk

Al Fahidi Street (no phone). **Open** 9am-1pm, 4-10pm Mon-Thur, Sat, Sun; 4-10pm Fri. **Map** p80 D2 ③

DUBAI BY AREA

Pool of rock

Mosh away at Dubai's only metal night.

Alternative music has always been thin on the ground in Dubai, which is why Bur Dubai's burgeoning rock and metal scene is such a rare treat. **Rock Nation**, which spins big tunes, is held at Touch (Four Points Sheraton, 04 397 7444) on most Wednesdays and Sundays. Original live music, a rarity in these parts, is also booked. Expect local legends like Sandwash to prance around the stage as though it's their last performance and belt out cheeky schoolboy-esque lyrics. The organisers behind the night are Hook, Line and Sinker, and they also throw together the occasional metal night at the same venue, again with live bands.

The **Strong South** is an evening of similar music mayhem at Submarine (p91). It costs a reasonable Dhs30 on the door, and takes place on Fridays or Saturdays. Submarine has been host to a number of alternative nights since it opened its doors last year, and the music isn't limited to moshing metal madness. Mondays see Doktor Pepper take to the decks, and give thirtysomethings the chance to reminisce about their teenage years, and the days they spent gazing through long sloppy hair and swaying to the likes of psychedelic rock band Inspiral Carpets in their flared jeans. The trip down memory lane is aptly, although not originally, called Happy Mondays.

The shops on this street have a good variety of materials, in designs that range from very plain to incredibly elaborate. Most of the textiles come from India and Pakistan, and haggling is expected here. If you intend to get something made up by a tailor, check how much fabric you will require to avoid any unnecessary revisits. A man's shirt, for example, will need two to two and a half yards of cloth, depending on sleeve length and the girth of the gent in question.

Versace

BurJuman Centre (04 3514 7792/ www.versace.com). **Open** 9.30am-10.30pm Mon, Tue, Sun; 9.30am-11.30pm Wed-Fri; 9.30am-10.30pm Sat. **Map** p80 D2 ③⑥
Figure-hugging dresses, the skinniest of trousers, leather jackets and lashings of fur and gold are the order of the day at this designer store. Alongside the ostentatious creations are lots of very wearable clothes.

Vincci

BurJuman Centre (04 351 7246). **Open** 10am-10pm Mon-Thur, Sat, Sun; 2-10pm Fri. **Map** p80 D2 ③⑦
This upmarket store stocks one of the city's finest ranges of footwear. The quality of the shoes is excellent, and there are some interesting details in the mainstream styles. Delicate pumps sit alongside suede slouch boots and glam sky-high heels.

V.V. & Sons

Al Fahidi Street (04 352 2444/www.vvsons.com). **Open** 9am-1pm Mon-Thur, Sat, Sun; 4.30-9.30pm Fri. **Map** p80 D2 ③⑧
This is the shop for the serious audiophile. A vast range of speakers is displayed at the back of the store, catering for everything from home cinema to outdoor gigs. Upstairs there's a selection of high-quality DVD players and amps for heavy-duty home cinema. Lesser-known brands such as Jamo and Sherwood Electronic Labs sit alongside international favourites like JBL in V.V.&Sons.

Nightlife

Elegante

*Royal Ascot Hotel, Bur Dubai
(04 352 0900).* **Open** 10.30pm-3am
Tues-Fri. **Map** p80 D2 ❸
A relative newcomer to the Bur Dubai
club scene. There have been some big-
name DJs to get you through the door.

Submarine

*Dhow Palace Hotel, Bur Dubai
(04 359 9992).* **Open** 6pm-2.30am
daily. **Map** p80 D2 ❹
The Dhow Palace, Bur Dubai's flashiest
boat-shaped hotel, is swimming the
nautical theme with its new stylish
club, Submarine. Featuring an impressive interior, this particular underwater vessel boasts some excellent local
DJ talent. They also have retina-scorch-
ing laser shows and fireman-frighten-
ing smoke machines.

Touch

*Four Points Sheraton, Khalid Bin
Al Waleed Road, 'Bank Street',
Bur Dubai (04 397 7444).* **Open**
7pm-3am daily. **Map** p80 D2 ❹
This small, dark and faintly gothic club
will never be one of Dubai's glamorous
venues. We don't imagine that the management cares, though, since the hugely varied nights (everything from down
and dirty drum 'n' bass DJs to indie rock
bands) pull in the punters regardless.

Arts & leisure

Bagash Art Gallery

*Kuwait Street, nr Centrepoint
Apartments (04 351 5311/www
.bagashartgallery.com).* **Open**
10am-7pm Mon-Wed, Sat, Sun.
Admission free. **Map** p80 D3 ❹
Bagash is a vibrant space that regularly
hosts fresh and challenging exhibitions
from the subcontinent and Far East.

Bluesail

*Dubai Creek, Al Seef Road, opposite the
British Embassy (04 374 5145/www.
bluesailyachts.com).* **Open** 9am-5pm
daily. **Map** p80 E2 ❹
The highest qualified Royal Yachting
Association (RYA) sailing school in the

Submarine

Middle East runs certified training at all
levels, from novice to RYA Yachtmaster.
It offers powerboat, sailing yacht and
motorcruising courses on the latest
vessels. There are 13m (42ft) sailing
yachts available for charter, or you can
go on a Speed Boat Blast. Prices start
at Dhs200 for one hour and go up to
Dhs2,500 per hour for a 15m (50ft)
powerboat. It costs Dhs4,000 to charter
a sailing yacht for half a day.

Colosseum Muay Thai Health & Fitness Club

*Montana Building, Zabeel Road,
Karama (04 337 2755/www.colosseum
uae.com.* **Open** 6am-midnight
Mon-Thur, Sat, Sun, 9am-9pm Fri.
Admission Dhs40. **Map** p80 D2 ❹
Martial arts practitioners tend to be
fanatical, and can't live without a few
kicks while on holiday. If you count
yourself among them, take a trip to
this dedicated martial arts centre. The
Colosseum Muay Thai Health & Fitness
Club has five boxing studios, an outdoor swimming pool and a sauna and
Jacuzzi. Classes in karate, Thai boxing,
aikido and kick boxing are all available
to keep your eye in.

DUBAI BY AREA

Majlis Gallery

Majlis Gallery
Al Fahidi roundabout, Bastakia
(04 353 6233/www.majlisgallery.com).
Open 9.30am-8pm Mon-Thur, Sat, Sun.
Map p80 E2 ⓭
With its appealing location in Bastakia,
Dubai's old town, this is a great place
in which to stop off for a bit of shopping as you wander the winding alleys.
Small sculptures and Arabian ornaments are often on display, and if you
don't mind paying top dirham, the
gallery has a deserved reputation for
its original on-canvas creations.

N.Bar
BurJuman Centre (04 359 0008).
Open 10am-10pm Mon, Tue, Sat, Sun;
10am-11pm Wed, Thur; 2-10pm Fri.
Map p80 D2 ⓮
N.Bar is light and airy with white walls
and chrome fittings, although it stops
just short of being clinical. The staff
are friendly, helpful and efficient.
Treatments include waxing, massage,
manicures, pedicures, acrylic, silk, gel
and fibreglass nail enhancements, plus
a number of luscious-sounding treatments for pampered hands and feet.

Scubatec
Sana Building, Karama (04 334 8988).
Open 9am-1.30pm, 4-8.30pm Mon-
Thur, Sat, Sun. **Map** p80 C3 ⓯

Scubatec is a PADI dive centre offering diving charters. The PADI Discover
Scuba Diving experience costs Dhs450,
and Open Water costs Dhs1,900.

XVA
Behind Majlis Gallery, Bastakia
(04 353 5383/www.xvagallery.com).
Open 9am-7pm daily. **Admission**
free. **Map** p80 E2 ⓰
This Dubai institution has revitalised
itself with a number of strong recent
shows focusing on contemporary
Middle Eastern art. A definite must-
see, this picturesque space also has a
café and a tiny, romantic guest house.

Oud Metha

Sights & Museums

Al Khor Wildlife Sanctuary
*Ras Al Khor industrial area (04 223
2323).* **Open** 9am-4pm Mon-Thur, Sun.
Admission free. **Map** p81 B6 ⓱
Managed by WWF and the Emirates
Wildlife Society, this is the only protected urban area in Dubai. Located at
the beginning of the Creek (and encir-
cled by highways) the marshy ground
is home to thousands of flamingoes,
waders and other birds, many of which
migrate to Dubai seasonally.

Three hides are open to the public. The first viewing area, Flamingo, is situated opposite the Emarat garage on the Oud Metha road. From here it is a short walk to the Lagoon sanctuary, a quieter hide. If you return to the Oud Metha Road and travel away from the city, then take the left turn to Ras Al Khor, you'll find the Mangrove hide. Although located further away from the wildlife, this wooden shack enjoys superb views across the wetlands towards the city. Admission to the hides is free, but a maximum of ten people are permitted at one time, and groups which are larger than four must apply for an entry permit from the municipality (04 221 5555). Forms can be downloaded from their website, www.environment.dm.gov.ae.

Al Khor Wildlife Sanctuary

Eating & Drinking

Aroma Garden Caffe

Garden Home Building, Oud Metha (04 336 8999). **Open** 10am-2am daily. **$$**. **Café**. Map p81 D4 ⑩

The Aroma Garden Caffe is a vast theme park of a café. On one side of the complex you'll be caressed by dangling fronds creeping into the seating area from the virulent vegetation; on the other, a dismal purple ceiling looms ominously above. The food is reasonable albeit pricey, but people come to puff on shisha, not for a three-course meal.

Asha's

Wafi (04 324 0000). **Open** noon-3pm, 7-11pm daily. **$$**. **Indian**. Map p81 D5 ㊶

The first branch of music icon Asha Bhosle's planned global chain is getting better all the time, although in a city blessed with an abundance of great Indian restaurants, it's not yet quite at the top of the league. For mains, the machli masala is delicious, with perfectly cooked hammour in onion and tomato gravy. There's no doubt it's good fun to dine at such an atmospheric and friendly restaurant; the food just needs a little more edge and it'll be a serious contender.

Crossroads Cocktail Bar

Raffles Dubai (04 324 8888/ www.dubai.raffles.com). **Open** 5pm-2am daily. **Bar**. Map p81 D5 ㊷

Finally, a cocktail has been named after this fair city. A trip to the Crossroads is essential, not only to get your lips round a Dubai Sling, but also to sample the panoramic views of the city skyline.

Fire & Ice

Raffles Dubai (04 324 8888). **Open** 7pm-midnight daily. **$$$$**. **Steakhouse**. Map p81 D5 ㊸

Fire & Ice is all about drama, from the moment you strut through the imposing hotel lobby. Perhaps the main courses are delayed to create theatrical tension, but when they step into the limelight, they shine like stars. The Tasmanian salmon is enough to make you burst into applause, but the wagyu beef tenderloin threatens to stop the show with its rich, marbled, crimson flesh, which returns encore after encore of intense meat flavours.

The Fish Basket

Opposite Mövenpick Hotel, Oud Metha (04 336 7177). **Open** 10am-1am daily. **$$**. **Seafood**. Map p81 D4 ㊹

This Lebanese seafood joint shuns showiness in favour of the straightforward. Pick the customary collection of

DUBAI BY AREA

Some fin to consider

Should you go to the dolphin show?

Dubai Dolphinarium

The Dubai Dolphinarium (www.dubaidolphinarium.ae) at Creek Park is a new Dhs33 million project funded by a private backer with the support of Dubai's municipality, which granted the space. It has all the usual bells and whistles: bottlenose dolphins catching fish and jumping through hoops, seals waving their paws and giving a honk on cue, and the shows are very popular with families. But such displays are not without controversy, and Dubai does not have a great record in areas of conservation; the zoo, for example, is retro in hardly the best sort of way.

At the time of going to press, all dolphins at the dolphinarium had been transported to Dubai in line with the rules of CITES (Convention on International Trade in Endangered Species), even though bottlenose dolphins are not actually endangered. However, although some of the dolphinarium's dolphins were born in captivity, others were captured from the wild.

The management claims that the dolphinarium will have a 30m (98ft) tank, a circular oceanarium called Gatorville, where people can learn about reptiles, a fish farm that explains husbandry techniques and a marine science institute.

The main argument in favour of such plans is that they introduce people to dolphins and pique the curiosity of young minds. Every future marine biologist needs a resource to spark their interest in the mysteries of the deep.

The counter argument is that these young minds are being fed misinformation. Flying through hoops doesn't happen in the wild. Spectators see animals performing unnatural tricks. There are health concerns, as the means of transport (usually air freight) to a pool smaller than their natural environment can cause the animals stress, which can shorten their lifespan and lead to abnormal behavioural patterns.

The Dolphinarium emphasises its concern for its charges, but bear their care in mind before coming to watch flipper on a family outing.

mezze, including a passable hummus, a vigorous fattoush and an unorthodox muhammra. The fried fish roe delivers crashing ocean flavours among its roughly textured eggs. Plump and perfectly grilled, the shrimps showcase what the Fish Basket does best.

Iz

Grand Hyatt Dubai (04 317 1234).
Open 12.30-3pm, 7-11.30pm daily.
$$$. Indian. Map p81 D5 ⑤⑤
The concept here involves picking a number of small tandoori dishes from the menu, which arrive in the order they are cooked – something like Indian tapas. After a deluge of warm and wondrous mini naan breads of various hues, try the sensuous masala sauce with a fine catch of podgy prawns. The salmon tikka, vegetable biryani with apricot, cashew nuts and figs, and the raan leg of lamb can also be recommended.

Jimmy Dix

Mövenpick Hotel (04 336 8800).
Open 6pm-3am daily. **Bar.**
Map p81 D4 ⑤⑥
Dark and dingy, with a mixture of flashing brand names around the bar area, Jimmy Dix is a popular haunt with anyone missing the grit of alternative bars in the Western world. The venue gets busy on the weekends, and it regularly lines up bands.

Khazana

Al Nasr Leisureland (04 336 0061).
Open 12.30-2.30pm, 7-11.30pm daily.
$$. Indian. Map p81 D5 ⑤⑦
Celebrity chef Sanjeev Kapoor's Khazana serves up arguably the best Masala popadoms in town. The murgh makhani – the simplest and mildest dish on the menu – is a medley of rich tomato sauce, with a hint of tandoor, the occasional touch of chilli and rounded off with fluffy basmati rice. Although the odd urchin running about could ruin a romantic soiree, as you tuck into a plate of sheer-e-zannat Indian desserts and a mug of masala tea, you'll probably feel it all adds to the homely ambience of the place.

Lan Kwai Fong

Oud Metha, opposite Mövenpick Hotel (04 335 3680). **Open** 11.30am-3.30pm, 6.30-11.30pm daily. **$$. Chinese.**
Map p81 D4 ⑤⑧
Lan Kwai Fong captures a genuine sense of a Chinese dining hall, with its authentic decor and a largely Chinese clientele. Massive portions at rock-bottom prices are the order of the day. The appetiser platter is a great way to start, with crispy spring rolls and prawn toast. However, the distinction between 'starter' and 'main course' is blurred to the point that everything is served at the same time, which makes dining a bit cramped, but does encourage sharing. If you only order one meal, make sure it's the juicy, meaty, slow-cooked barbecued duck.

Lemongrass

Nr Lamcy Plaza, Oud Metha (04 334 2325). **Open** noon-11.15pm daily. **$. Thai. Map** p81 D4 ⑤⑨
This is one of the most authentic and tasty Thai restaurants in the city. It's awash in sleek yellow and dark wood, and moodily appointed with carved Thai antiques and reed vases, resulting in a sleek yet immensely warm and welcoming atmosphere. The food is exquisite: heady aromas usually only found in Bangkok leap off dishes laden generously with peppercorns, lime leaves and other such Thai essentials. Chu chi is a signature dish, with juicy tiger prawns swimming in a pool of red curry sauce. A delightful place.

Manhattan Grill

Grand Hyatt Dubai (04 317 1234).
Open 12.30-3pm, 7-11.30pm daily. **$$$$.**
Steakhouse. Map p81 D5 ⑥⓪
The steaks are Manhattan Grill's biggest draw: mighty fine Nebraskan cuts served on the bone that melt like sorbet in the summer sun. The decor – a mismatch of booths, grand tables, side rooms and a mini veranda – might not be to everyone's taste; think impressive business dinners rather than romantic soirées. Still, the staff are knowledgeable, polite and welcoming.

DUBAI BY AREA

Medzo

Wafi (04 324 0000). **Open** 12.30-3pm, 7.30-11.30pm daily. **$$. European. Map** p81 D5 ➄

Wafi's much-loved Mediterranean restaurant continues to show off its considerable strengths. The food is very good, the decor is spot on and the service is excellent. A buffalo mozzarella and beetroot salad makes a beautifully delicate starter and mains also impress. Smoked duck with foie gras is a highlight, as are the herb gnocchi. With its cool monochrome prints, soft leather chairs, billowing white tablecloths and affable staff, Medzo's got the formula just right.

The Noble House

Raffles Dubai (04 324 8888). **Open** 7-11.30pm daily. **$$$$.** **Chinese. Map** p81 D5 ➅

From the welcome ritual – a ridiculously limber chap literally bending over backwards to deliver piping hot green tea from a long-spouted pot – you know you're in for something special. The main courses come in pairs, which means you're invited to enjoy the ginger and spring onion wok-fried lobster at the same time as the dreamy, creamy black pepper wagyu beef. Even the side dishes look like a labour of love that you have to slash open with your knife. Every bite in this wonderful restaurant feels like an act of exquisite vandalism.

Thai Chi

Wafi, Oud Metha (04 324 0000). **Open** 12.30-3pm, 7-11.45pm daily. **$$. Thai/Chinese. Map** p81 D5 ➆

With tasteful decor, an impressively varied menu and attentive service, Thai Chi is a solid bet for good Thai and Chinese food, just like the name suggests. Once you've navigated the bridge over the burbling river and ducked under the pagoda, there's a range of rooms to sit in, so you can either enjoy a private meal or savour the bustling atmosphere. Main courses of sweet and sour chicken and Thai red chicken curry are served in generous portions and are very tasty, but connoisseurs of Chinese or Thai food probably wouldn't come to Thai Chi to sample their favourite dishes.

Vintage

Pyramids, Wafi, Oud Metha Road (04 324 4100/www.waficity.com). **Open** 6pm-1am Mon-Wed, Sat, Sun; 4pm-1am Thur, Fri. **Wine bar. Map** p81 D5 ➃

There is something about the chic interior and stupendous cellar of Vintage that soothes the soul. The wine bar is constantly buzzing with sophisticated chatter, and there is a good cheese board on hand to help you soak up excess alcohol.

Shopping

Chanel

Wafi (04 324 0464/www.chanel.com). **Open** 10am-10pm Mon-Thur, Sat, Sun; 2-10pm Fri. **Map** p81 D5 ➄

This shop is the epitome of chi-chi French chic, and has a small but select range of the label's latest items. In among the classy suits are a few gems from the couture eveningwear range. There is also an excellent selection of affordable accessories.

Etoile La Boutique

Wafi (04 327 9132). **Open** 10am-10pm Mon-Thur, Sat, Sun; 2-10pm Fri. **Map** p81 D5 ➅

The floor is swathed in custom-made burgundy carpet, the walls are adorned with 350 gold leaves, the lights are Swarovski and upholstery is imported from Denmark. The current line-up includes John Galliano, Christian Dior, Christian Lacroix and Valentino. It's also the only boutique in town with a hospitality lounge, serving a raft of fanciful brews in grandiose Paris crockery.

Fashion Factory

Lamcy Plaza, Oud Metha (04 336 2699). **Open** 9am-10.30pm Mon-Wed, Sat, Sun; 9am-midnight Thur, Fri. **Map** p81 D4 ➆

Don't let Fashion Factory's location deter you from visiting. Lurking at the back of Lamcy Plaza, it's easy to miss, but with almost every item in the store priced under Dhs100, you'd do well to seek it out. There are bargains to be had on major high street brands, including Monsoon and Camaïeu.

Five Green

Behind Aroma Garden Caffe, Oud Metha (04 336 4100/www.fivegreen. com). **Open** 10am-10pm Mon-Thur, Sat, Sun; 4-10pm Fri. **Map** p81 D4 ⑱
The perfect antidote to the acres of identikit boutiques and stores that smother the city, Five Green is an elegant and tasteful repository of loveliness. Part clothes store, part art space, part music store (think Soul Jazz Records and Jazzanova releases), it stages art shows while stocking items from the likes of 2K, Aei:Kei, Paul Frank, Gsus and Upper Playground, as well as fashion by Dubai-based designers.

GapKids

Wafi (04 327 9197). **Open** 10am-10pm Mon-Wed, Sat, Sun; 10am-11pm Thur, Fri. **Map** p81 D5 ⑲
Whenever there's a niece or nephew to spoil, GapKids is a safe port of call. Everything from its cute hoodies, at Dhs110, to its *Little House on the Prairie* frocks brings out the parent in us all. Like the grown-up range, it's conservative casual wear in natural fabrics.

Ginger & Lace

Wafi (04 324 5699). **Open** 10am-10pm Mon-Wed; 10am-midnight Thur-Sun. **Map** p81 D5 ⑰
Funky decor, sugar-pink walls, ornate hanging rails and Fashion TV on loop; the surroundings are almost as flamboyant as the stock. Items from the likes of Betsey Johnson, draped fluid tops and dresses by Lotta Stensson and Anna Sui, and jewellery from Johnny Loves Rosie are just a few of the avant-garde fashions on sale.

Jashanmal

Wafi (04 324 4800/www.jashanmal-uae.com). **Open** 10am-10pm Mon-Wed, Sun; 10am-midnight Thur, Fri; 10am-10pm Sat. **Map** p81 D5 ⑰

Tiger Lily p98

The UAE's answer to the UK's John Lewis, this store has a fine selection of well-stocked departments. The household section is particularly strong: you'll find everything from Disney sandwich boxes to kettles, vacuum cleaners, Le Creuset pans, bedding and crockery.

Kitson

Wafi (04 324 2446/ www.shopkitson.com). **Open** 9.30am-10.30pm Mon-Wed, Sat, Sun; 9.30-10.30pm Thur; 2pm-midnight Fri. **Map** p81 D5 ⑰
The selection of T-shirts is probably the best thing about this store (look out for the men's tees by a brand called Smash). If you know the LA store, don't get too excited, because many of the labels stocked there aren't on the rails at this shop.

Lamcy Plaza

Oud Metha (04 335 9999/www. lamcyplaza.com). **Open** 9am-10pm Mon-Wed, Sat, Sun; 9am-midnight Thur, Fri. **Map** p81 D4 ⑰
Seemingly lost in a strange time warp, Lamcy certainly doesn't keep up with the obsession with cutting-edge modernity in evidence at other malls. The interior is dated, there's a bizarre and tacky replica of Tower Bridge, and an

DUBAI BY AREA

Ginseng

unrealistic-looking waterfall. But if you're looking for bargains, this might just be the perfect place. You can stock up on cut-price clothes from Fashion Factory and handy Dhs510 knick-knacks at the extraordinary Japanese discount store Daiso.

I Pinco Pallino
Wafi (04 324 4944/
www.ipincopallino.it).
Open 10am-10pm Mon-Wed, Sun;
10am-midnight Thur; 5pm-midnight
Fri. **Map** p81 D5 ⓴
This upmarket Italian brand's formal range includes pastel-coloured gowns in luxurious natural fibres with coordinated accessories; clothes for babies and casual wear are also available. But I Pinco doesn't come cheap, and Park Avenue princesses-to-be can expect to shell out a small fortune.

Salam
Wafi (04 324 5252/www.salams.com).
Open 10am-11pm Mon-Thur, Sat, Sun.
Map p81 D5 ⓵
This department store can kit out your whole family – including the kiddies – with designer gear from a plethora of brands, including Armani, Citizens of Humanity, Dolce & Gabbana, Escada, Lacoste, Moschino and Versace.

Sell Consignment Shop
Ground floor, Sultan Business Centre,
next to Lamcy Plaza (04 334 2494).
Open noon-9pm Mon-Thur, Sat, Sun.
Map p81 D4 ⓶
This second-hand treasure chest has racks of designer clothes, shoes, jewellery and bags, with new stock arriving weekly. We spotted a cute printed Anna Sui dress (Dhs600), a Valentino evening gown (Dhs4,000) and an Alessandro Dell'Acqua handbag (Dhs1,300). Tops can cost as little as Dhs200. Other brands to keep an eye out for include Louis Vuitton, D&G, Prada and Chanel.

Tiger Lily
Wafi (04 324 8088). **Open** 10am-10pm
Mon-Wed, Sun; 10am-midnight Thur;
5-10pm Fri. **Map** p81 D5 ⓷
Shopping here is akin to rummaging through a stylish celebrity's wardrobe. Rails hung with flowing, feminine dresses vie for your attention, and kitsch accessories catch the eye. Look for pieces by Australia's hottest exports Sass & Bide, as well as UK talent Julien MacDonald.

Wafi
Oud Metha Road (04 324
4555/www.wafi.com). **Open** 10am-
10pm Mon-Wed, Sat, Sun; 10am-10pm
Thur, Fri. **Map** p81 D5 ⓸
With a new extension to the already massive mall, Wafi continues to attract fashion-conscious shoppers keen to keep up with the latest trends. Chanel, Lancel Paris, Givenchy and Jaeger are some of the names that share floor space with local designer labels. On the first floor of the old Wafi mall are shops with more affordable price tags, such as Miss Sixty, Jumbo Electronics and Marks & Spencer.

Nightlife

Chi
Al Nasr Leisureland, Oud Metha
(04 337 9470/www.lodgedubai.com).
Open 9pm-3am daily. **Map** p81 D5 ⓹
Once a dilapidated meat market of a club, the former Lodge was overhauled

in early 2007, becoming a jolly plush and incredibly spacious four-roomed venue. The gargantuan garden area is hugely popular during winter months, and benefits from an adventurous booking policy. Inside there's an all-white room that hosts hip hop, funk and soul, and the lavish VIP area is home to champagne-wielding dandies. Make sure that you get down here early as the queues can be long.

Ginseng

Pyramids, Wafi, Oud Metha Road (04 324 8200/www.ginsengdubai.com). **Open** 7pm-1am Mon, Sat, Sun; 7pm-2am Tue-Fri. **Map** p81 D5 ⑩

A cosy, Asian-themed venue that can't quite work out whether it's a bar, a restaurant or a nightclub. Ginseng has a large array of cocktails, and although it's stylish, it's not as pretentious as many similar bars in the city. Once inside, you can enjoy one of the most eclectic record boxes in town, with chill out mixes throughout the week.

Mix

Grand Hyatt Dubai (04 317 1234). **Open** 10pm-3am Mon-Fri, Sun. **Map** p81 D5 ⑪

Since Deep started putting on DJs such as Erick Morillo, Kurd Maverick, Angello & Ingrosso and Tom Novy, the club has risen back to its old popular status. Housed in the huge Grand Hyatt hotel by Garhoud Bridge, it is an excellent choice if you're looking for big-name DJs that play big beats.

Arts & leisure

Al Nasr Leisureland

Behind the American Hospital, Oud Metha (04 337 1234/www.alnasrll. com). **Open** 9am-11.45pm daily. **Admission** Dhs10; Dhs5 reductions. **Map** p81 D5 ⑫

Ice skating, ten-pin bowling, tennis, squash, swimming, fitness training and mini bumper cars are on offer in a kid-friendly atmosphere at Leisureland. Group bookings are taken, but you must fax your reservation details to 04 337 6832 in advance.

Cleopatra's Spa

Wafi (04 324 7700/www.waficity.com). **Open** 8am-8pm daily. **Admission** Dhs325/1hr massage. **Map** p81 D5 ㉝

For the ultimate in spa treatments, you can't go far wrong with the luxurious Cleopatra's. The usual facials, massages and wraps complement some very different treatments. Among these is the gorgeous aroma stone massage, in which the body is massaged with exotic oils and hot 'batu' stones from Indonesia.

Five Green

Behind Aroma Garden Caffe, Oud Metha Road (04 336 4100/ www.fivegreen.com). **Open** 10am-10pm Mon-Thur, Sat, Sun; 4-10pm Fri. **Admission** free. **Map** p81 D4 ㉞

Although this boutique isn't strictly a gallery, it displays cutting-edge art. The venue frequently plays host to quirky exhibitions and performances by local and visiting artists, musicians and cultural activists.

Pursuit Games Paintball

Next to Wonderland Theme & Water Park, by Garhoud Bridge (050 651 4583/www.paintballdubai.com). **Open** 10am-10pm daily. **Admission** Dhs80 2hr session; Dhs30 extra 50 paintballs; Dhs50 extra 100 paintballs. No credit cards. **Map** p81 D5 ㉟

At this park, groups are divided into opposing teams before being given protective overalls, face masks, guns and paint balls, followed by a safety demonstration. The organisers claim that they will open at any time of the day or night to accommodate visitors. Discounts are available for group bookings (minimum of six people, 30 to take over the whole park).

Raffles Amrita

Raffles Dubai (04 314 9869/ www.dubai.raffles.com). **Open** 9am-9pm daily. **Map** p81 D5 ㊱

Try the Romantic Retreat package, Dhs1,199 per couple, for you and your partner: it offers 90 minutes of bath, massage and utter relaxation.

DUBAI BY AREA

Jumeirah Mosque

Satwa, Jumeirah & Sheikh Zayed Road

Just half a century ago, Jumeirah was a fishing village some way outside Dubai. Today it is one of the most high-profile areas of the city, and Western residents often jokingly refer to it as the Beverly Hills of Dubai. A few original villas survive, and are much sought after by expats as (almost) affordable beachside homes.

The area commonly referred to as **Jumeirah** – although Jumeirah is only a part of it – stretches along Dubai's southern coast for a good distance. It is serviced by two main roads: Jumeirah Beach Road, which runs along the coast, and Al Wasl Road, which runs parallel to it a few blocks inland. A haphazard network of streets lined with luxury villas links the two. Jumeirah developed southwards from Satwa's borders, and the oldest part, known as Jumeirah 1, remains one of the most desirable addresses in Dubai. It was here that the first chic malls and coffee shops grew up, and it's a popular choice for people in search of a latte or manicure. At this end of the Jumeirah Beach Road, the **Jumeirah Mosque** is one of the city's most picturesque, and the only mosque that allows non-Muslims to have a peek inside as part of a guided tour.

Neighbouring **Satwa** is one of the few remaining parts of Dubai that feels like a 'normal' city, with street life, vibrant restaurants, and a mish-mash of nationalities making up the community. Unfortunately it's not going to be like this for long, because this prime real estate is to be flattened to make way for another big property development (box p118).

These areas are bordered inland by Sheikh Zayed Road. Although this highway runs for hundreds of kilometres, the stretch here, with its skyscrapers set up like giant dominos, is the most famous spot. Set back from this main strip is the city's grandest landmark, the Burj Dubai. Although the world's tallest building hadn't opened as this book went to press, the area around it (known as Downtown) was becoming an increasingly important shopping and social hub.

Satwa & Jumeirah

Sights & museums

Dubai Zoo

Jumeirah Beach Road, Jumeirah 1 (04 349 6444). **Open** 10am-5pm Mon, Wed-Sun. **Admission** Dhs3. **Map** p103 D1 ❶

The animals at the Dubai Zoo are the survivors of a private collection now owned by the Dubai Municipality. The conditions are somewhat shabby and the animals enjoy limited freedom. There are plans to relocate, but despite many promises over several years, there has been little action. There are lions, tigers, giraffes, bears, reptiles and birds, but it's up to your conscience as to whether you'd enjoy visiting them here.

Jumeirah Mosque

Jumeirah Beach Road, Jumeirah 1. **Open** 10am Tue, Thur, Sat, Sun. **Admission** Dhs10. **Map** p103 E1 ❷

Arguably the most beautiful mosque in Dubai, this stands at the northern end of the Jumeirah Beach Road. The Sheikh Mohammed Centre for Cultural Understanding (04 353 6666, smccu@ emirates.net.ae) organises visits here (no children under five). You'll walk through the mosque with a small group before putting questions to your guide about the building and the Islamic faith. You must wear modest clothing (no bare legs or arms, and women must cover their heads).

Majlis Ghorfat Um Al Sheef

Jumeirah Beach Road, Jumeirah 4; look for nearby brown heritage signposts (04 394 6343). **Open** 8.30am-1.30pm, 3.30-8.30pm Mon-Thur, Sat, Sun; 3.30-8.30pm Fri. **Admission** Dhs1. **Map** p102 A2 ❸

Built in traditional style from coral and stone, this was used by the late Sheikh Rashid bin Saeed Al Maktoum, the founder of modern Dubai. The fact that many of the plans for modern Dubai were probably hatched in such a simple structure, by a man who had known nothing of 20th-century luxury for most of his life, is remarkable. That said, the majlis only merits a fleeting visit.

Eating & drinking

Boston Bar

Jumeirah Rotana Hotel, Al Diyafah Street (04 345 5888). **Open** noon-2am Mon, Tue, Fri-Sun; noon-3am Wed, Thur. **Bar**. **Map** p103 F2 ❹

Based on the bar in the American sitcom *Cheers*, this unpretentious expat boozer can get very lively during football matches. It's typically full of Brits, but occasionally attracts other nationalities. The food is hit and miss.

Flooka

Dubai Marine Beach Resort & Spa, Jumeirah Beach Road (04 346 1111). **Open** 12.30-2.45pm, 7.30-11.45pm Mon-Thur, Sun; 12.30-11.45pm Fri, Sat. **$$**. **Seafood**. **Map** p103 E1 ❺

All contemporary pine, clean lines and nautical rope adornments, this Lebanese seafood restaurant is a pleasant place for an evening of feasting. The mezze innovatively includes fish; the makanek samak are spicy little seafood sausages, the kibbeh samak emit gusts of ocean flavour from their crispy wheat shells, and the samke nayyeh consist of fragile morsels of hammour carpaccio that disintegrate in the mouth. The main courses are straightforward but excellent, and Flooka is a major hit with the city's seafood eaters.

DUBAI BY AREA

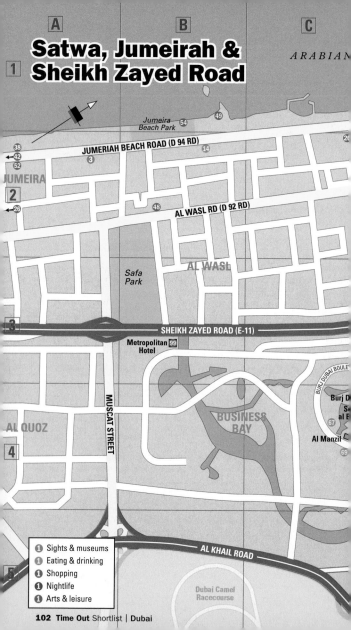

Satwa, Jumeirah & Sheikh Zayed Road

A
B
C

1

ARABIAN

Jumeira
Beach Park 54
49

38
42
52

JUMEIRAH BEACH ROAD (D 94 RD) 14

3

JUMEIRA

2

26

48 AL WASL RD (D 92 RD)

AL WASL

Safa
Park

3 SHEIKH ZAYED ROAD (E-11)

Metropolitan 99
Hotel

BURJ DUBAI BOULE

Burj D
Se
al E

AL QUOZ

BUSINESS
BAY

57

Al Manzil

4

69

MUSCAT STREET

AL KHAIL ROAD

5

❶ Sights & museums
❶ Eating & drinking
❶ Shopping
❶ Nightlife
❶ Arts & leisure

Dubai Camel
Racecourse

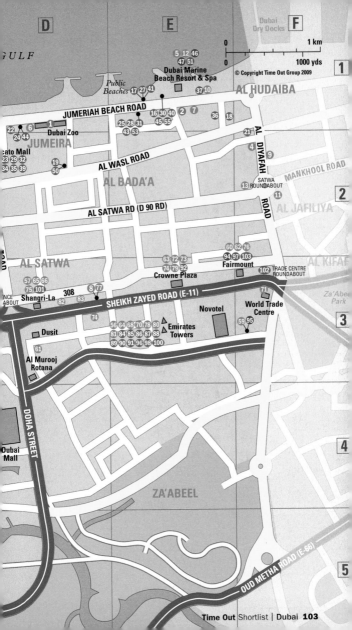

D | E | F

GULF

Dubai Dry Docks

0   1 km
0   1000 yds
© Copyright Time Out Group 2009

1

5 12 46
47 51

Dubai Marine
Beach Resort & Spa

Public Beaches 17 27 41

37 10

AL HUDAIBA

JUMEIRAH BEACH ROAD

16 30 40
45 55

2 7

36 18

22 6
24 44
1

Dubai Zoo

JUMEIRA

25 28 31
43 53

21

AL WASL ROAD

4

DIYAFAH

9

cato Mall
23 29 32
34 35 39

19 50

MANKHOOL ROAD

AL BADA'A

13 SATWA ROUNDABOUT

AL SATWA RD (D 90 RD)

11 AL JAFILIYA

ROAD

2

60 62 76
94 97 103

63 72 73
74 79 92

Fairmount

AL KIFAF

AL SATWA

Crowne Plaza

102 TRADE CENTRE ROUNDABOUT

57 65 66
75 101

8 77

71

Za'Abeel Park

NCE ABOUT

Shangri-La

308

82   83

SHEIKH ZAYED ROAD (E-11)

World Trade Centre

74

Novotel

59 95

3

Dusit

56 64 68 70 78 80
81 84 85 86 87 88
89 90 91 96 98 100

Emirates Towers

61

Al Murooj Rotana

DOHA STREET

ZA'ABEEL

4

Dubai Mall

OUD METHA ROAD (E-66)

5

The Royal Court has changed.
Feeling Royal hasn't.

At THE MONARCH DUBAI, we believe in old fashioned ways of treating our guests like royalty. Our sophisticated amenities are completed with old world refinement and we take great pride in our majestic levels of personalised service. THE MONARCH DUBAI invites you to hold court in regal luxury.

THE
MONARCH
DUBAI

One Sheikh Zayed Road

Tel. +971 4 501 8888
welcome@themonarchdubai.com
www.themonarchdubai.com

Fudo

Next to Mercato Mall, Jumeirah Beach Road (04 349 8586). **Open** 9am-3am daily. **$$**. **Café**. Map p103 D1 **6**

One of the most eccentrically, and perhaps inappropriately designed places in Dubai, Fudo places large images of war refugees and African children alongside chandeliers, goldfish in uncomfortably tiny bowls and cosy colourful sofas. The menu is eclectic, spanning several continents and hundreds of dishes, most of which are fairly good. The Thai appetiser plate is a safe way to start, with tender battered cuttlefish and a garlicky chicken skewer, and the goods from the sushi bar are well sliced and impressively fresh.

Lime Tree Café

Nr Jumeirah mosque, Jumeirah Beach Road (04 349 8498). **Open** 7.30am-6pm daily. **$$**. **Café**. Map p103 E1 **7**

The Beach Road branch, with its leafy plants, trickling water and shady courtyard and upstairs balcony, offers some of the most sought-after seating in the city. The menu changes daily and the food is fresh, wholesome and well priced. You can't go wrong with the olive-studded focaccias, healthy wraps and chunky, delicious salads. The dairy-free smoothies and freshly squeezed juices are excellent. Indulge in the rich chocolate brownies and the huge slices of legendary carrot cake. The café can get very busy.

Long's Bar

Towers Rotana Hotel, Sheikh Zayed Road (04 312 2202/www.rotana.com). **Open** noon-3am daily. **Bar**. Map p103 D3 **8**

Long's is one of those places ruddy-faced expats refer to, with a crinkly grin, as being a 'Dubai institution'. Certainly, some of the punters here could do with being removed to a facility of some sort, but the reason it's such a longstanding favourite is because it's a fairly authentic reproduction of a spit 'n' sawdust British pub. Expect TV football, good-value drinks and predictable albeit tasty food.

Al Mallah

Al Diyafah Street, Satwa (04 398 4723). **Open** 6am-4am Mon-Thur, Sun; noon-4am Fri; 6am-4am Sat. **$**. No credit cards. **Arabian**. Map p103 F1 **9**

An old stalwart on the bustling Al Diyafah Street scene, Al Mallah is the place to go to for simple Arabian fast food. Skip the mezze (they're better elsewhere) and munch on winning shawarmas and falafel sandwiches. The lamb and chicken shawarmas are small, but among the tastiest in the city, and the falafel drips with tahini. Al Mallah is a prime people-watching spot, especially on weekend evenings, when young men drive in circles around Satwa, showing off their cars.

The One Café

Next to Jumeirah mosque, Jumeirah Beach Road (04 345 6687). **Open** 9am-9pm Mon-Thur, Sat, Sun; 2-9pm Fri. **$$**. **Café**. Map p103 E1 **10**

We've yet to be disappointed by the fresh and inventive food served at the café of this popular furniture store. Try the raspberry and halloumi salad with sunflower seeds and quail eggs, or tuck into the One ravioli stuffed with braised rosemary lamb and marinated mushrooms. The soups are standouts here too; the chunky beef and vegetable served with a cheese-topped soft roll is a satisfying affair, and the spicy miso with prawns, accompanied by prawns on a skewer and a green bean salad, is one of our favourites.

Pars

Behind Satwa roundabout, beside Rydges Plaza. (04 398 4000). **Open** 7pm-1am daily. **$**. **Iranian**. Map p103 F2 **11**

Although the food at all the Pars outlets is uniformly excellent, you will want to visit the Satwa branch in particular, which is almost entirely open-air. The kash-e-bademjan, a dish of soft, smoky, puréed aubergine mixed with whey, is a great place to start from. As you finish your starters, the smoke billowing from the grill will already be whetting your appetite for

DUBAI BY AREA

One of a kind

Independent shops are making their mark along the Jumeirah Beach Road.

Ayesha Depala

Some of the city's best independent retailers are based on Jumeirah Beach Road. Consequently, discerning shoppers flock here at weekends to drop some dirhams. There can be few things less *de rigueur* than turning up at an event where another woman is wearing your dress, but that's less likely to happen if you come here. Dubai's multitude of malls is generally fairly unimaginative, with the same big brands predominating. But, for a little of something different, this stretch of calm consumerism between the Jumeirah Mosque and the tumble-down Jumeirah Zoo is well worth investigating.

First stop is the Village mall, home to S*uce (04 344 7270), one of the most cutting-edge retailers in the city. You will salivate over their expensive designs. If your purse convulses at the prices, cross the road to Jumeirah Centre Mall. S*uce Lite (04 344 4391) lives here, and sells last season's leftovers.

You're likely to spot cool labels such as Sass & Bide, Antoni & Alison, Citizens of Humanity, See (the Chloé concession) and Johnny Loves Rosie. You can save yourself anything from 40 to 80 per cent by rummaging around. Next door to the original S*uce are sophisticated dresses by Dubai's favourite designer, Ayesha Depala (04 344 5378). Also worth a look, in the same mall, is Luxecouture (04 344 7933) for avant-garde labels.

Over at Jumeirah Plaza, Le Stock (04 342 0211) should be your first stop, with Tiger Lily, Matthew Williamson, Joseph, Chloé and Victor & Ralph all on the shelves. Fleurt (04 342 0906), at Mercato Mall, stocks the show-stopping dresses that you would expect the cast of *Sex and the City* to step out in. Betsey Johnson and Dina Bar-El are also represented. If you're expecting a baby, make sure that you check out Mamas & Papas (04 344 0981), which is also in Mercato Mall.

the impressively sized main courses. Reasonable prices, polite service and an Iranian crowd complete the relaxing, authentic picture.

Al Qasr

Dubai Marine Beach Resort & Spa (04 346 1111). **Open** 12.30-3.30pm, 7.30pm-2am Mon-Wed, Sun; 12.30-3.30pm, 7.30pm-3am Thur; 12.30-3.30pm, 7.30pm-2am Fri, Sat. **$$. Arabian. Map** p103 E1 ⑫

Al Qasr doesn't do things by half. Opt for the set menu and a dizzying deluge of mezze arrives with all the commotion of a flash flood. The banquet then continues with a verdant tabouleh, kibbeh nayyeh (raw lamb), lamb sausages and a tremendous mixed grill. While the band plays and the belly dancer does her thing, you finish with a mountainous stack of fresh fruit, cakes and shisha. You might not be able to stand up after an evening here, but it is fantastic fun.

Ravi Restaurant

Between the new mosque & Satwa roundabout, Satwa (04 331 5353). **Open** 5am-3am daily. **$. Pakistani. Map** p103 F2 ⑬

Ravi Restaurant focuses on Punjabi food from Pakistan. Try the haleem, which is a slow-cooked dish of wheat, lentils and meat (usually lamb), the consistency of porridge. Its digestibility makes it popular as a fast-breaker during Ramadan. Nihari is also popular in Pakistan's cities, though it originates in Delhi's Muslim communities. Made with beef (and therefore taboo to Hindus), this slow-cooked meat is so tender it falls from the bone, and is served in a delicately aromatic sauce.

Shu

Nr Imart Hospital & Jumeirah Beach Park (04 349 1303). **Open** 10am-4am Mon-Fri, Sun; 10am-3am Sat. **$$. Arabian. Map** p102 B2 ⑭

With its eccentric red and grey fascia, lizard-eye oval window and splashy fountain, this contemporary Lebanese restaurant looks like the abode of one of Roger Hargreaves' Mr Men. Among the offerings from the menu (which features stunning photographs of the Earth from the skies above), are delicious fatayer pastries, vibrant and fresh-tasting stuffed vine leaves and a brilliant signature dish – fried sparrow drizzled in pomegranate syrup.

Shopping

Armani Junior

Mercato Mall, Jumeirah Beach Road (04 342 0111/www.armanijunior.com). **Open** 9am-10pm Mon-Thur, Sat, Sun; 2-10pm Fri. **Map** p103 D1 ⑮

Armani Junior stocks a colourful range of kids' clothing for boys and girls from the age of two to 14. As well as T-shirts, hats and jeans, denim separates for girls are available along with trousers and jackets for cooler climes. For the label-conscious young man, a range of trousers, hoodies and trainers completes the collection.

Ayesha Depala

The Village, Jumeirah Beach Road (04 344 5378). **Open** 10am-10pm Mon-Thur, Sat, Sun; 4.30-10pm Fri. **Map** p103 E1 ⑯

This talented young Indian designer's first boutique in Dubai is awash with silk, chiffon, tulle and lace, all in soft, serene colours. Her collections are the epitome of femininity – as is the store itself. With lilac walls, sparkling chandeliers and an elegant chaise longue, browsing is a treat. From long evening gowns to baby-doll dresses and delicate cardigans, each garment is beautifully cut, and so timelessly stylish it will never go out of fashion.

Blue Cactus

Jumeirah Centre, Jumeirah Beach Road (04 344 7734). **Open** 10am-9pm Mon-Thur, Sat, Sun; 4.30-9pm Fri. **Map** p103 E1 ⑰

Quality, not quantity, is what's on offer at Blue Cactus. The store may be small, but the stock consists of top-notch chain-store labels and designer womenswear. Expect to find Kay Unger dresses and other desirable brands at a fraction of their usual retail price.

DUBAI BY AREA

"An ingredient so powerful it didn't just change the taste of our dishes, it even changed the name of our restaurant."

Rhodes
Mezzanine

Book World

Al Hudaiba Street, Satwa (04 349 1914). **Open** 9.30am-9.30pm Mon-Thur, Sat, Sun; 4-9.30pm Fri. No credit cards. **Map** p103 E1 ⓭

Crammed with over 45,000 second-hand books and thousands of magazines, this book store operates on a pile-them-high-sell-them-cheap policy. Everything from gluts of Ian Rankin to the odd Khaled Hosseini is available, and few items cost over Dhs25.

Al Boom Diving Club

Al Wasl Road, by Iranian Consulate (04 399 2278/www.alboomdiving.com). **Open** 8am-9pm Mon-Thur, Sat, Sun; 8-4pm Fri. **Map** p103 D2 ⓳

Al Boom offers diving lessons and all the equipment that you'll need to get started. It has unbeatable facilities (including a swimming pool for beginners), a wide range of PADI courses, full equipment rental and a shop stocking the latest from top brands in diving.

Creative Art Centre

Behind Choithram supermarket, Jumeirah Beach Road (04 344 4394). **Open** 8am-6pm Mon-Thur, Sat, Sun. **Map** p102 C2 ⓴

Spanning over two pristine villas, this centre brings together souvenirs, art and antiques. As a result it's a haunt for people who want to add a splash of panache to their homes, as well as a great spot for visitors to find some interesting keepsakes from their trip. Among the array of Arabian knick-knacks are several collector's items, including wooden chests, old Omani doors turned into coffee tables and plenty of Bedouin silver.

Dethar

Al Ghazal Mall, Satwa (04 345 4403). **Open** 10am-10pm Mon-Thur, Sat, Sun; 4-10pm Fri. **Map** p103 F2 ㉑

Dethar is a unique shop, with its entire collection hailing from a handful of Lebanese artisans. The embellished bags are the highlight, but the metallic pumps, crochet cardigans and plethora of costume jewellery are all hard to leave behind. Bring a big bag.

Dubai Desert Extreme

Beach Centre, Jumeirah Beach Road (04 344 4952/www.dubai desert extreme.com). **Open** 10am-7.30pm Mon-Thur, Sat, Sun. **Map** p103 D1 ㉒

This is where skateboarding kids get their decks, trucks, wheels and spare rails. If you're looking for some chilled-out skate fashions, then Dubai Desert Extreme is a good bet, with T-shirts from Shorty's and Independent the pick of the bunch.

Fleurt

Mercato Mall, Jumeirah Beach Road (04 342 0906). **Open** 10am-10pm Mon-Thur, Sat, Sun; 2-10pm Fri. **Map** p103 D1 ㉓

A selection of the highly desirable and glamorous Dina Bar-El dresses, colourful leather handbags and stylish modern jewellery is what's on offer at this sassy little store. We defy you to leave empty handed.

Heat Waves

Town Centre Mall, Jumeirah Beach Road (04 342 0445). **Open** 10am-10pm Mon-Thur, Sat, Sun; 2-10pm Fri. **Map** p103 D1 ㉔

For straightforward swimsuits and bikinis in a range of plain, flattering colours, head to Heat Waves. While most of the swimwear on offer does lean towards the conservative, if you are prepared to have a root around, then you should come across more fashionable styles.

House of Prose

Jumeirah Plaza, Jumeirah Beach Road (04 344 9021). **Open** 9am-8pm Mon-Thur, Sat, Sun; 5-8pm Fri. No credit cards. **Map** p103 E1 ㉕

This Dubai institution has a simple policy: buy any one of the reasonably priced books, read it, and either keep it or return it and get 50 per cent of your money back. This ensures that the books stay in circulation, you save money and you get to see what the bookworms of the city are reading. If you rummage through the shelves for long enough, you're guaranteed to find something for everyone.

DUBAI BY AREA

House of Prose p109

IF Boutique
Umm Al Sheif Street (04 394 7260).
Open 10am-9pm Mon-Thur, Sat, Sun.
Map p102 A2 26
With its art deco-style façade and front terrace of cast iron statues, it's no surprise that this store is home to labels such as Comme des Garçons, Emma Hope, Undercover and Milia M. One of the few boutiques to move out of the malls, it's situated in an ideal location beside a string of cafés and within walking distance of the beach.

Jumeirah Centre
Jumeirah Beach Road (04 349 9702/ www.gmgdubai.com). **Open** 10am-9pm Mon-Thur, Sat, Sun; 4-9pm Fri.
Map p103 E1 27
This attractive mini-mall is popular with local residents and has compact outlets interspersed over its two floors. Benetton, The Nike Store and The Body Shop all feature, as well as Blue Cactus, which sells discounted designer gear. At the handicraft store Sunny Days, you can splash out on beautiful textiles and Persian rugs. Alternatively sit back in one of the alfresco cafés with a cappuccino and relax.

Jumeirah Plaza
Jumeirah Beach Road (04 349 7111).
Open 9am-10pm Mon-Thur, Sat, Sun; 4-9.30pm Fri. **Map** p103 E1 28

There are no big brands to be found when shopping in the Jumeirah Plaza, but this pretty centre is home to a number of smaller outlets, including the gift store Susan Walpole and the excellent second-hand bookshop House of Prose. For creative browsers, there is a T-shirt design shop, and for interior fanatics, there are a few well stocked craft shops on the upper level.

Kas Australia
Mercato Mall, Jumeirah Beach Road (04 344 1179/www.kasaustralia. com.au). **Open** 10am-10pm Mon-Thur, Sat, Sun; 2-10pm Fri. **Map** p103 D1 29
Kas Australia is a master purveyor of the soft, fluorescent and frilly. Citrus-coloured pillows plump up against extravagantly textured throws and brightly coloured furnishings in this snug Aussie outlet.

Luxecouture
The Village, Jumeirah Beach Road (04 344 7933). **Open** 10am-10pm Mon-Thur, Sat, Sun; 3-10pm Fri.
Map p103 E1 30
Stocked with chic New York labels, this compact shop focuses on niche designers and classics rather than frivolous items of clothing. You can find everything for your wardrobe, from comfortable T-shirts to slick work attire and breathtaking gowns.

Magrudy's

*Jumeirah Plaza, Jumeirah Beach Road
(04 344 4193/www.magrudy.com).*
Open 9am-9pm Mon-Thur, Sat, Sun;
2-10pm Fri. **Map** p103 E1 ③①

A Dubai institution, Magrudy's now
has shops throughout the city, although
this original outlet on Jumeirah Beach
Road remains its spiritual home. The
chain has had to improve to keep up
with the likes of Borders and Virgin,
but it is holding its own with particularly impressive education, business
and children's sections, and a good
selection of audiobooks.

Mamas & Papas

*Mercato Mall, Jumeirah Beach Road
(04 344 0981).* **Open** 10am-10pm
Mon-Wed, Sun; 10am-11pm Thur, Fri.
Map p103 D1 ③②

Mamas & Papas is the ultimate place
to meet all your high-end kiddie needs.
Everything from the gift hampers
(which include an array of exquisite
rabbit toys, bibs and clothes) to the
maternity wear (which even non-
maternal types would happily don)
smacks of luxury.

Mercato Mall

*Jumeirah Beach Road (04 344
4161/www.mercatoshoppingmall.com).*
Open 10am-10pm Mon-Thur, Sat, Sun;
2-10pm Fri. **Map** p103 D1 ③③

Italian-designed and inspired, Mercato
is a light and airy mall decorated with
stonewash murals and alleys. Although
there is not quite the range here you'll
find in bigger malls, there's a good mix
of stores, including Mango, Massimo
Dutti, a Virgin Megastore and Topshop.
Check out the sprinkling of little boutiques, including the funky swimwear
and lingerie store Moda Brazil.

Moda Brazil

*Mercato Mall, Jumeirah Beach Road
(04 344 3074).* **Open** 10am-10pm Mon-
Thur, Sat, Sun; 10am-midnight Fri.
Map p103 D1 ③④

This lush Latino boutique stocks one
of the widest selections of fashionable
beachwear in town, from racy cut-out
swimsuits to tropical-coloured bikinis.

End of the road

The city's coolest, quirkiest, best-loved neighbourhood is about to get flattened.

Satwa is a kooky neighbourhood
that mixes Arabian, Indian,
Pakistani and Filipino in the
heart of Dubai. Its ramshackle
buildings and streets (some
as much as 30 years old) are
a delightful contrast to the
relentless towers and highways
in the rest of the city. But it's
also prime real estate, and soon
to be demolished. Any night of
the week, it's worth stopping at
the cafés on **Al Diyafah Street**
for a freshly squeezed juice, to
watch flash cars cruise by and
local residents promenade; from
young Filipino men done up like
surf dudes to Emirati families in
search of ice cream. At the top
of this strip, and near Pars
Iranian restaurant, are municipal
basketball courts that stay busy
even through July and August.
You'll find dozens of Filipino,
Asian and Arabian peoples
playing, in the kind of community
scene not often found in Dubai.

Around the corner from Diyafah
is **Al Satwa Road**, which, with its
flashes of neon colour, is the
heart of an area that is part
Manila, part Islamabad and part
'old' Dubai. But you'll notice that
some of the textile shops are
now empty, the shisha cafés
are being boarded up, and the
communities are starting to
move out. Explore while you still
can; it is easily the most vibrant
area of the city to walk around.

DUBAI BY AREA

Sizes are on the small side, but the designs are cutting edge and will make you feel as though you have just stepped off the catwalk.

Nayomi

Mercato Mall, Jumeirah Beach Road (04 344 9120/www.nayomi.com.sa). **Open** 10am-10pm Mon-Thur, Sat, Sun; 2-10pm Fri. **Map** p103 D1 ③⑤

One of the leading Middle Eastern retailers of quality lingerie, Nayomi stocks lacy dressing gowns and rather less sexy nightdresses at about Dhs300.

The One

Next to Jumeirah Mosque, Jumeirah Beach Road (04 345 6687). **Open** 9am-10pm Mon-Thur, Sat, Sun; 2-10pm Fri. **Map** p103 E1 ③⑥

This Dubai company is almost as famous for its colourful ad campaigns and publicity stunts as it is for its often splendid contemporary furniture. The secret to its success is its design-led product range, which neatly marries ethnic accessories (think incense burners, Buddha heads and textured photo frames) with bold, contemporary furniture that wouldn't look out of place in an interior designer's home.

Palm Strip

Jumeirah Beach Road (04 346 1462). **Open** 10am-10pm Mon-Thur, Sat, Sun; 1.30-10pm Fri. **Map** p103 E1 ③⑦

Set by the beach, this whitewashed mall is one of the very few open-air shopping strips in the city. Shops are set back from the road and arranged across two levels. The lower level is dominated by eateries, including Starbucks and Japengo Café, in addition to a well stocked branch of Zara Home. Upstairs you can opt for a bit of preening in the N.Bar nail salon, browse through a few home stores, or check out a great haunt for mothers, Favourite Things Mother & Child.

Picnico

Al Bahr Marine, Jumeirah Beach Road (04 394 1653). **Open** 9am-9pm Mon-Thur, Sat, Sun; 4.30-9pm Fri. **Map** p102 A2 ③⑧

Picnico is an eclectic camping emporium on Jumeirah Beach Road (on the edge of the petrol station forecourt). It's better suited to seasoned rather than inexperienced campers, specialising in GPS systems as well as tents, sleeping bags, gas stoves and barbecue sets.

Pretty FIT

Mercato Mall, Jumeirah Beach Road (04 344 0015/www.prettyfit.com.sg). **Open** 10am-10pm Mon-Thur, Sat, Sun; 2-10pm Fri. **Map** p103 D1 ③⑨

Pretty FIT is a reliable shop selling flats, heels, strappies and slip-ons in a variety of colours. Styles are often adorned with stripes, polka dots, checks or flowers that may not be to everyone's taste, but there is a range of beautifully simple styles that will work with any outfit. Prices are an absolute bargain too.

S*uce

The Village, Jumeirah Beach Road (04 344 7270/www.shopatsauce.com). **Open** 10am-10pm Mon-Thur, Sat, Sun; 4.30-10pm Fri. **Map** p103 E1 ④⓪

S*uce is a true fashion cocktail of flirty cult labels, including Anna Sui and 3.1 philip lim; the latest collections by young designers like Mira, La Petite Salope and Third Millennium; and established brands such as Vanessa Bruno and See by Chloe. As well as a mishmash of colourful dresses, handmade jewellery and spangly belts and bags, there's a well stocked gift section. S*uce also sells Chamaille handcrafted clothes for children.

S*uce Lite

1st floor, Jumeirah Centre, (04 344 4391). **Open** 10am-9pm Mon-Thur, Sat, Sun; 4.30-9pm Fri. **Map** p103 E1 ④①

Basically, everything that doesn't sell at S*uce gets shipped across the road to S*uce Lite. The collection of clothes, accessories and cute little gifts such as the Very London Style Guide are fantastic – and unbelievably good value. When we visited, they had just put out a few Alice Temperley dresses with a price tag of Dhs1,000. And there were also disco-style Felix Ray belts for

Dhs100, Willow dresses for Dhs600 and Cacharel dresses for Dhs250. The selection of accessories was also wonderfully quirky, and prices averaged at around Dhs100 for a ring or necklace. Utter bliss.

Showcase Antiques, Art & Frames

Jumeirah Beach Road (04 348 8797/www.showcasedubai.com). **Open** 9am-6pm Mon-Thur, Sat, Sun. **Map** p102 A2 ㊷

Three storeys of antiques, artefacts and art make Showcase Antiques a store that's well worth a visit. There are plenty of items hailing from Oman; you can pick up a rosewood chest from around Dhs1,800, and 19th-century firearms from Dhs900. The beautiful Arabian pots that line the stairs are hard to resist, and will set you back around Dhs700 a piece. A range of framed tribal jewellery, knives and khanjars about 100 years old will appeal to customers looking to purchase a small slice of history.

Le Stock

Jumeirah Plaza, Jumeirah Beach Road (04 342 0211). **Open** 10am-1.30pm, 2.30-9pm Mon-Thur, Sat, Sun; 5-9pm Fri. **Map** p103 E1 ㊸

The items that didn't find an owner at fashion store Tigerlily (in Wafi City) come to Le Stock for a last chance. Some of the pieces date back to 2001, so feel a little dated. That said, if you are prepared to rummage about, you can find some great bargains. They offer 50 to 90 per cent off the original price, so a Vanessa Bruno top will cost you around Dhs150, an Alessandro Dell'Acqua dress Dhs1,000 and an Anna Sui skirt Dhs100. Other great brands include Matthew Williamson and Sass & Bide. Worth a look.

Town Centre

Jumeirah Beach Road (04 344 0111). **Open** 10am-10pm Mon-Thur, Sat, Sun; 2-10pm Fri. **Map** p103 D1 ㊹

Situated next to Mercato Mall, this boxy centre seems slightly dated. But Feet First offers top-notch reflexology,

the SOS salon provides affordable beauty treatments, and the Kaya Skin Clinic can tackle any skin woes. Visiting families should check out the innovative Café Céramique, where you can paint your own crockery while snacking on healthy food.

The Village

Jumeirah Beach Road (04 342 9679/www.thevillagedubai.com). **Open** 10am-10pm Mon-Thur, Sat, Sun; 4-10pm Fri. **Map** p103 E1 ㊺

Attracting boutiques rather than high street outlets, the Village is an avant-garde shopper's dream. S*uce is a girly fashionista's treasure, Luxecouture is packed with New York's finest designer pieces, and Ayesha Depala boasts a range of wonderfully chichi designs.

Nightlife

Boudoir

Dubai Marine Beach Resort & Spa, Jumeirah Beach Road (04 345 5995). **Open** 7.30pm-3am daily. **Map** p103 E1 ㊻

This swanky, Parisian-style club ranks as one of the most exclusive venues in the city. Different nights play host to various music genres, accompanied by bottles of bubbly. Boudoir attracts a predominantly Lebanese crowd, and if you want to get past the door staff you should be dressed to impress and preferably in a couple.

Sho Cho

Dubai Marine Beach Resort & Spa, Jumeirah Beach Road (04 346 1111/ www.dxbmarine.com). **Open** 7pm-3am daily. **Map** p103 E1 ㊼

With a gorgeous terrace overlooking the Gulf and Manga movies projected onto the fish tank-studded walls, Sho Cho is a super-hip Japanese-themed bar. Sophisticated, classy and trendy, this is where the beautiful people go to play, pose and look pretty: you will not see an ounce of spare body fat in the place. Tuesday and Sunday nights are crammed, so phone ahead for reservations or arrive as a couple – the door policy is notoriously anti single males.

DUBAI BY AREA

Arts & leisure

1 x 1 Art Space
*Villa 1023, Al Wasl Road
(04 348 3873).* **Open** 11am-8.30pm
Mon-Thur, Sat, Sun. **Admission** free.
Map p102 B2 **48**
This Jumeirah-based enterprise is ded-
icated to showing some of the best con-
temporary Indian art.

Alasalla Spa
*Dubai Ladies Club (04 349 9922/
www.dubailadiesclub.com).* **Open**
8am-10pm daily. **Map** p102 B1 **49**
Treatments are Arabian-inspired and
specifically for women. Choose one of
their hammam sessions; once you've
indulged, you'll want to go regularly.

Al Boom Diving
*Nr Iranian Hospital, Al Wasl Road.
(04 342 2993/www.alboomdiving.com).*
Open 10am-8pm daily.
Map p103 D2 **50**
Al Boom is a five-star PADI dive cen-
tre offering courses suitable for divers
from beginner to instructor, as well as
daily diving and snorkelling trips in
Dubai, Fujairah and Musandam. The
PADI Discover Scuba Diving experi-
ence costs Dhs550, the Scuba Diver
course costs Dhs1,500 and the Open
Water course costs Dhs2,000.

Dubai Marine Beach
Resort & Spa
*Beach Road. (04 346 1111/
www.dxbmarine.com).* **Open**
7am-sunset daily. **Map** p103 E1 **51**
The resort, which is a favourite with a
handful of supermodels, features two
pools, a kids' pool, a private beach and
a tennis court; non-members can only
book the court for tennis lessons.

Dubai Offshore
Sailing Club
*Jumeirah Beach Road, by Miraj Gallery,
KFC & Hardees (04 394 1669/www.
dosc.ae).* **Open** 8am-10pm daily.
Map p102 A2 **52**
This non-profit club is usually abuzz
with eager sailors. Recognised by the
Royal Yachting Association, the DOSC

offers courses all year round in opti-
mists, lasers and toppers (the Friday
and Saturday Cadet Club is popular
with younger enthusiasts). There are
races every Friday, mooring facilities
are provided, and the club runs a full
social calendar.

Elche Natural
Beauty Retreat
*Villa 42, Street 10, behind Jumeirah
Plaza (04 349 4942/www.elche.ae).*
Open 10am-8pm Mon-Thur, Sat, Sun.
Map p103 E1 **53**
This idiosyncratic spa offers organic
skincare treatments for women by
trained Hungarian therapists, with
facials starting at Dhs325. Herbalists
hand-pick the ingredients, and the company's founder, Ilcsi Molnar, a beauti-
cian and herbalist, makes up the
lotions and potions.

Jumeirah Beach Park
*Jumeirah Beach Road (050 858
9887/349 2555).* **Open** 8am-11pm
daily (ladies only Mon).
Map p102 B1 **54**
There aren't that many facilities at the
beach, but if you're after some relaxation, pack your beach bag, grab a sun
lounger and chill out for the day. This
is one of the cheapest beaches in town,
meaning that it's always busy. There's
also a café selling junk food, a barbecue area, a children's playground and
changing rooms.

SensAsia Urban Spa
*1st floor, the Village, Jumeirah
Beach Road (04 349 8850/
www.sensasiaspas. com).* **Open**
10am-10pm Mon-Thur, Sat, Sun;
12.30-9pm Fri. **Map** p103 E1 **55**
An exotic, Eastern-style spa for women
who like their shops, services and spas
to be a little more independent, this is
the best non-hotel-based spa in town.
The treatments are well tailored for
women (and women only) looking for
relaxation and pampering. There are
no swimming pool and gym facilities
waiting for you after your session, but
there is a small relaxation area if you
want to unwind for a little longer.

Hoi An p117

Downtown & Sheikh Zayed Road

Eating & drinking

The Agency

Jumeirah Emirates Towers,
Sheikh Zayed Road (04 319 8780/
www.jumeirahemiratestowers.com).
Open noon-3am Mon-Thur, Sun;
3pm-3am Fri, Sat. **$$. Wine bar.**
Map p103 E3 ⑤⑥

An upmarket wine bar, the Agency
attracts affluent, well dressed profes-
sionals looking to drink away the
stresses of the day. The exterior is
uninspiring: sat on patio furniture and
flanked by potted plants, you gaze out
towards a pair of escalators. If it's
alfresco ambience you're after, the
branch at Souk Madinat Jumeirah is a
better bet, although it can be practical-
ly impossible to get a seat there many
nights of the week.

Amwaj

Shangri-La Hotel Dubai (04 343 8888).
Open 1-3pm, 7pm-midnight Sun-Fri.
$$$. Seafood. Map p103 D3 ⑤⑦

The arrival of chef Matthias Diether
has turned Amwaj into a gastronomic
heavyweight. The raw wagyu beef
with asparagus is tremendous, the scallops bathed in lemongrass sauce are

cooked to perfection, and the foie gras
and veal tenderloin is astoundingly
tender and tasty. The chink in Amwaj's
armour is its setting – one of the few
fine dining restaurants in Dubai without any view. However, it's home to
a chef talented enough to let the food
satisfy all the senses.

Asado

The Palace Old Town, Downtown
Burj Dubai. (04 428 7888). **Open**
noon-3pm, 7pm-midnight daily. **$$.**
Steakhouse. Map p102 C4 ⑤⑧

Asado – the Palace Hotel's Argentine
grill – offers a little more than most
steakhouses. The meat is beautifully
marbled, sensationally tender and
tasty, as it should be, but the soups are
also worth a look. Devour a thick,
creamy and rustic mushroom broth
with a drop of herby olive oil. You can
take a table on the terrace and marvel
at the Burj Dubai standing more than
800m (2,625ft) high.

Blue Bar

Novotel, Sheikh Zayed Road, behind
Dubai World Trade Centre (04 332
0000/www.novotel.com). **Open** 2pm-
2am Mon-Thur, Sun; 4pm-2am Fri.
Bar. Map p103 F3 ⑤⑨

Located on the ground floor of the
businesslike Novotel, the Blue Bar
combines fashionable decor with an

DUBAI BY AREA

Marrakech

unusually good selection of draught Belgian beers to potent effect. The bar organises a popular jazz night every Wednesday, Thursday and Friday.

Cin Cin

Fairmont Dubai, Sheikh Zayed Road (04 332 5555/www.fairmont.com). **Open** 6pm-2am daily. **Wine bar**. **Map** p103 E3 ⑥⓪
Curved around an enormous central pillar, this horseshoe-shaped wine bar is a favourite among the post-office crowd. The floor-to-ceiling wine racks house over 250 varieties, and the selective use of lighting, languid soundtrack and adjoining cigar bar all impress.

Double Decker

Al Murooj Rotana Hotel & Suites Dubai, Defence roundabout, nr Dusit Dubai (04 321 1111/www.rotana.com). **Open** noon-3am daily. **Bar**. **Map** p103 D3 ⑥①
From the grandiose coats of armour adorning the walls to the hordes of sunburnt punters, Double Decker is a home away from home for the British expatriate crowd. It might not harbour the most adventurous atmosphere, but with great service and a resident DJ armed with party tunes, it's a packed pub. The Friday brunch followed by a raucous karaoke contest will either be your idea of heaven or hell on earth.

The Exchange Grill

Fairmont Dubai (04 311 5999). **Open** 7pm-midnight daily. **$$$**. **Steakhouse**. **Map** p103 E3 ⑥②
The Exchange Grill is one of the region's finest steakhouses, and the food speaks for itself. A starter of blue swimmer crab cakes with pineapple and vanilla relish and a tarragon mustard aioli may look a little like a tarted-up collection of potato croquettes, but the chunky meat responds electrically to its sweet, fruity accompaniment. Follow up with a filet mignon steak – an utterly luscious slab of beef, alive with flavour and bursting with character. Teamed up with delicately steamed asparagus and some exquisite steak fries, it's a poem of a meal.

Fibber McGee's

Behind the Crowne Plaza, Sheikh Zayed Road (04 332 2400/www. fibbersdubai.com). **Open** noon-2am daily. **Bar**. **Map** p103 E3 ⑥③
Tucked away behind a coterie of glass-fronted skyscrapers on Sheikh Zayed Road, this independent boozer is not one for people seeking a beautiful sunset. A lack of windows means that the place is perpetually dark, although in Fibber's defence, the closed-in feeling helps create a great atmosphere, particularly on the nights that the football is on. The food is well put together, with fish and chips, and the green curry among the highlights.

Harry Ghatto's

Jumeirah Emirates Towers, Sheikh Zayed Road (04 330 0000/ www.jumeirahemiratestowers.com). **Open** 8pm-3am daily. **Bar**. **Map** p103 E3 ⑥④
Nestled in the back room of the Tokyo@The Towers sushi restaurant, karaoke bar Harry Ghatto's cosiness and twin microphone set-up inspires a brothers-in-song ambience. Dutch courage comes courtesy of imported Japanese beer and sake. But don't worry if you're still a little nervous: the staff are always on hand to show you exactly how it's done.

Hoi An

Shangri-La Hotel Dubai (04 343 8888).
Open 7pm-midnight daily. **$$.**
Asian. Map p103 D3 ⑥⑤
Hoi An offers customers a wily fusion
of French and Vietnamese cuisine. Try
the soup with delicate flakes of fresh-
water eel, fried onion and slender shi-
take mushrooms in a thick, intensely
flavoured stock. You might like to
order the escargots with ground garlic
and coriander, as they're particularly
scrumptious. The atmosphere can be
cold, literally, due to the strong air con,
as well as the predictable new-age
Asian music; but nevertheless, Hoi An
offers an impressive dining experience.

Marrakech

Shangri-La Hotel Dubai (04 343 8888).
Open 6.30pm-1am Mon-Thur, Sat, Sun.
$$. North African. Map p103 D3 ⑥⑥
This upmarket Moroccan joint is effort-
lessly elegant. The decor is clean-cut
North African – graceful arches, subdued lighting, plenty of pottery, and an
imposing, tiled and tomblike central
feature bedecked with artfully arranged
twigs. Two gentlemen in burnouses
(hooded cloaks) sit in an alcove, one
with an oud, the other toting a violin,
soulfully singing. The food is a perfect
match, with a huge pigeon pastilla,
mountainous couscous dishes, and
note-perfect lamb and chicken tagines.

Mezza House

*Yasoon Building, Old Town Burj Dubai
(04 420 5444).* **Open** 11am-midnight
daily. **$$. Middle Eastern**.
Map p102 C4 ⑥⑦
This restaurant by the Burj Dubai is a
tribute to the traditional cuisine of the
Levant region, showcasing the age-old
delights of Lebanon, Jordan, Syria and
Palestine. The tabouleh (from Lebanon)
is full of zest, and the mohamara (a
spicy Syrian dip of blitzed peppers and
walnuts) is a thick paste brimming
with matured flavours. The raw lamb,
also known as kibbeh nayyeh, is a
smooth spread of uncooked meat,
ground with spices and bulgur wheat
that perfectly accompany the salads.

Al Nafoorah

*Jumeirah Emirates Towers (04 319
8088).* **Open** 12.30-3pm, 8pm-midnight
daily. **$$. Lebanese** Map p103 E3 ⑥⑧
Nafoorah welcomes streams of discern-
ing foodies through its elegant doors.
The Lebanese staples are excellent:
light and fluffy houmous that you dive-
bomb with squadrons of flatbread; a
baba ganoush salad of aubergine, onion,
tomatoes and fragrant herbs; and a lip-
stick-pink mound of kibbeh – a carpet
of minced lamb with bulgur wheat. Al
Nafoorah offers good food in stately
surroundings, or on a beautiful terrace
in the shadow of skyscrapers above.

Double Decker

Reaching for the stars

What will be in the world's tallest building?

Burj Dubai

Dubai is an architect's dream, with exciting projects announced daily. Local residents read about crazy new developments with open mouth, and Burj Dubai has been the most talked about of all. In May 2008, it reached 636 metres in height, and became the tallest man-made structure on earth, surpassing the KVLY-TV mast in Dakota, USA. The developers – Emaar – aren't announcing the finished height of the structure. Rumours that the building will be as tall as 940 metres are probably exaggerated, but it's expected to rise above 700 metres. So what's it all about? In a ghastly bout of real estate marketing-speak,

the tower's website says it is simply 'monument. Jewel. Icon.' When the structure is completed in around September 2009, it will actually contain a mix of shops, bars and restaurants, a hotel and apartments.

The hotel will have 160 rooms on the first floors of the building, two restaurants, a nightclub and a spa. Private apartments will occupy floors 17 to 108, and according to the spiel, all 800 units were sold within eight hours of going on sale. Floor 78 has the outdoor pool. There will be a total of 144 Armani residences, decorated, of course, by the Armani Casa range, and other facilities will include four pools, a cigar lounge, a library, residents' room and a gym. These flats are selling for about $3,500 per square foot. Most of the remaining upper floors will be offices. The exception is the 124th, which will feature an indoor and outdoor observatory. The time-poor (and cash-rich) residents and workers can access their swanky addresses via one of the world's fastest elevators: it travels at 18 metres per second, or 40 miles per hour. The area surrounding Burj Dubai includes the huge Dubai Mall, Souk al Bahar and other hotels and restaurants.

But the priapic one-upmanship is unlikely to end here. Another developer, Nakheel, is planning Al Burj near Ibn Battuta to be 1.4 kilometres high, and the proposed Mile-High Tower in Jeddah is expected to reach 1.6 kilometres and be true to its name.

Nezesaussi

*Al Manzil Hotel, Burj Dubai Boulevard
(04 428 5888).* **Open** 3pm-1am
Mon-Thur, Sun; 1pm-2am Fri, Sat.
Bar. Map p102 C4 ⑥⑨
The name may be utterly unpro-
nounceable, but Nezesaussi is usually
buzzing with animated punters. The
curved bar should be generously populated by sports fans, and the restaurant full of favourite dishes from New
Zealand, South Africa and Australia.
The 'Ref's Advocate' offers three giant
skewers of tender beef, juicy chicken
and flavoursome lamb, and the
Australian CAAB steak is butter-soft.

The Noodle House

*The Boulevard at Jumeirah Emirates
Towers (04 319 8757).* **Open** noon-
midnight daily. **$$. Asian.**
Map p103 E3 ⑦⓪
The food, a mixture of Asian styles, is
reliably good, service is cheery, the
atmosphere is buzzy, and prices are
reasonable. The Noodle House creates
glassy crystal shrimp dumplings and
sweet and doughy chicken siew mai
that should be the envy of a Hong Kong
street café. Thai chicken with cashew
abounds with a rich nutty flavour and
the Singapore noodles are delightfully
slurpy with plenty of prawns. Even the
broccoli on the side strikes a balance
between crunchy and soft. This is a
great bet for a quick eat.

Options

World Trade Centre (04 329 3293).
Open noon-3pm, 7-11.30pm daily. **$$.**
Indian. Map p103 F3 ⑦①
Take your seat in plush, crimson-cush-
ioned comfort as the DJ bounces a few
eastern vibes around the soft furnishings. The menu's show-stealing dish
arrives in a torrent of orange flames, as
the magnificent raan buzkazi blazes
into fire with a splash of rum. The service is efficient and helpful throughout,
and Options lives up to its name with
its dessert selection, which includes a
few of the usual subcontinental sus-
pects alongside a selection of tempting
international favourites.

Oscar's Vine Society

*Next to Crowne Plaza, Sheikh Zayed
Road (04 331 1111/ www.ichotels
group.com).* **Open** 6pm-2am daily.
Bar. Map p103 E3 ⑦②
A noted addition to Dubai's small wine
bar scene. The food includes oysters,
cheese, cold cuts, and a truly splendid
black pudding with roasted apples and
mashed potatoes. Oscar's serves decent
food, and has a good range of wines.

Sakura

*Crowne Plaza Hotel Dubai (04 331
1111).* **Open** noon-3pm, 7-11.30pm
daily. **$$. Japanese.**
Map p103 E3 ⑦③
This Japanese restaurant at the
Crowne Plaza is great fun, with clangs
of knives, clatters of saltshakers and
roars of laughter greeting guests upon
their arrival. The food is a little hit
and miss, although the wonderful
samurai teppanyaki, which is tossed,
twirled and juggled about with great
dexterity, makes up for the rather aver-
age sushi and sashimi.

Shakespeare & Co

*Al Attar Business Tower, Sheikh Zayed
Road (04 331 1757).* **Open** 7am-
12.30am daily. **$$. Café.**
Map p103 F3 ⑦④
A world away from the soulless, identikit coffee empires that are taking over
the world, Shakespeare & Co – with its
granny-chic interiors, mix-and-match
furniture and stunning outdoor terrace
– radiates warmth. The food is reasonable rather than impressive – try the
mushroom soup – and the service is
very erratic; but they could be serving
up stewed tea and scones that bounce,
and we'd still return just to soak up the
languid ambience.

Shang Palace

*Shangri-La Hotel Dubai, Sheikh Zayed
Road (04 343 8888).* **Open** 12.30-3pm,
8pm-midnight daily. **$$$. Chinese.**
Map p103 D3 ⑦⑤
The Beijing duck at Shang Palace
offers contrasting textures and flavours
that surpass all the ceremony of its
preparation. The main courses are also

DUBAI BY AREA

superb – the beef tenderloin with green peppers in black bean sauce is excellent, and the scallops are tender and as light as dandelion fluff. Although the staff tend to be friendly and helpful, the restaurant is nudged into the corner of the mezzanine floor overlooking the cold marble foyer, which doesn't help the atmosphere. But it's still one of the best Chinese restaurants in Dubai.

Spectrum on One

Fairmont Dubai (04 332 5555).
Open 6.30-11.45pm daily. **$$**.
European. Map p103 E3 ⑦⑥
The appeal of Spectrum on One lies in its sheer variety. The chefs at each cooking station communicate via Madonna-esque headphones and microphones, coordinating every table's meals to within five seconds, regardless of whether the dishes hail from the mountains of India or the heart of rural France. Most of them are very good, such as the rich king scallops with buttery cauliflower purée. The large wicker basket of dim sum is also a hit.

Teatro

Towers Rotana Hotel (04 343 8000).
Open 6-11.30pm daily. **$$**.
International. Map p103 D3 ⑦⑦
A permanent fixture on Dubai's restaurant leader board for over five years, Teatro consistently works its magic on the hearts and taste buds of a loyal crowd of regulars. The choice of food is excellent, with options from around the globe: Thailand, China, Italy and India. They even have a sushi menu, and the standard is consistently high. Lately the service has greatly improved, and Teatro is now a fun, buzzy and friendly place for an evening meal.

Tokyo@TheTowers

Jumeirah Emirates Towers (04 319 8088). **Open** 12.30-3pm, 7.30pm-midnight Mon-Thur, Sun; 1-3pm, 7.30pm-midnight Fri; 12.30-3pm, 7.30pm-midnight Sat.
$$. **Japanese**. Map p103 E3 ⑦⑧
The menu at Tokyo seems expensive, and the decor is a bit of a letdown with an awkward layout. Thankfully, the food is superb. The oyster ponzu consists of shellfish ingeniously deep-fried, the saba sashimi are tiny but potently smoky slices of blanched mackerel, and the sushi is always perfectly fresh. It's one of the city's better Japanese restaurants; just be sure to request one of the tables in the main room.

Trader Vic's

Crowne Plaza Hotel Dubai, Sheikh Zayed Road (04 331 1111/www. tradervics.com). **Open** noon-midnight Mon-Thur, Sat, Sun; 7pm-midnight Fri.
Bar. Map p103 E3 ⑦⑨
Trader Vic's combination of a cheerful Polynesian-style band and some of the most potent cocktails in the UAE creates a wonderfully carefree atmosphere. But seating is limited and the bar is frequently crowded, so ensure that you arrive early to make the most of the happy hours (times at which prices drop from the astronomical to the merely expensive).

Vu's

Jumeirah Emirates Towers (04 319 8088). **Open** 12.30-3pm, 7.30-11.30pm daily. **$$**. **European**. Map p103 E3 ⑧⓪
From up here, you can look down across Satwa and up along Sheikh Zayed Road, but the food is wonderful as well. On the starter front, get stuck into the sea scallop beignet, stunningly presented on a doughy blob of shellfish with creamed sweetcorn and citrus crème fraîche. For the main course, the veal steaks are a good choice, perfectly pink, tender and flavoursome, with a hint of Asian sweetness and a mound of creamed potatoes.

Vu's Bar

Jumeirah Emirates Towers Hotel, Sheikh Zayed Road (04 330 0000/ www.jumeirahemiratestowers.com).
Open midnight-2am daily.
Bar. Map p103 E3 ⑧①
Head up to this classy, 51st-floor bar for one of the finest views in Dubai. Arrive early in the evening to watch the sun go down and the lights go up across the city, an experience which is enhanced by dipping into the sweet

Vu's

cocktail list. Make sure that you wear a collar and smart shoes, or you won't be able to enter this elegant bar.

Zaatar W Zeit
Sheikh Zayed Road (04 800 922 827). **Open** 24 hours daily. **$. Lebanese. Map** p103 D3 ③②
The funky atmosphere and friendly service in this chain lend themselves best to groups of friends and casual late-night snacks. Zaatar W Zeit specialises in saj – Lebanese pizza made with flatbread, served piping hot from the oven and usually dripping with gooey cheese. Try the lahme beajine, a rolled-up baked flatbread full of nicely spiced minced meat and tomatoes, or the jebneh halloumi, stuffed full of fresh cheese. Unlike other Lebanese saj bakeries, they also serve sweet dishes.

Zyara
Sheikh Zayed Road (04 343 5454). **Open** 8am-midnight daily. **$$. Café. Map** p103 D3 ③③
There's a bohemian atmosphere well suited to the smoky espresso and Lebanese mezze on offer here. The real draw of Zyara, however, is its stylish shisha. The relaxed ambience draws a trendy crowd of women and men at work on their laptops while puffing from the elegant shisha pipes on the large outdoor patio.

Shopping

Boulevard at Emirates Towers
Sheikh Zayed Road (04 330 0000/ www.jumeirahemiratestowers.com). **Open** 10am-10pm Mon-Thur, Sat, Sun; 4-10pm Fri. **Map** p103 E3 ③④
Set at the base of the Jumeirah Emirates Towers' office block, this swanky shopping mall offers a sophisticated spread of designer stores across its two floors. Gucci, Giorgio Armani, Yves Saint Laurent and Bottega Veneta dominate the ground floor, and upstairs you'll find Jimmy Choo.

Boutique 1
The Boulevard at Jumeirah Emirates Towers (04 330 4555). **Open** 10am-10pm Mon-Thur, Sat, Sun; 2-10pm Fri. **Map** p103 E3 ③⑤
Formerly known as Villa Moda, Boutique 1 has more than 150 brands under one roof, from established names such as Chloé, Blumarine, Elie Saab and Missoni to emerging designers. Ideal for menswear, it offers sharp suits by Cesare Attolini and classic shoes by Harrys of London, as well as streetwise styles from Maharishi and Y-3 by Yohji Yamamoto. With a bountiful supply of jeans and eveningwear, and everything in between, it combines luxury with youthful energy.

DUBAI BY AREA

Cartier

The Boulevard at Jumeirah Emirates Towers (04 330 0034/ www.cartier.com). **Open** 10am-10pm Mon-Thur, Sat, Sun; 5-10pm Fri. **Map** p103 E3 🟤

This branch of Cartier swarms with dazzling charms, links and delicate pieces. Sometimes the service can be a bit snooty, but the place is still superior to most of the other jewellery houses in Dubai. With prices as they are, expect a quiet shopping experience.

Coach

Jumeirah Emirates Towers (04 330 1020/www.coach.com). **Open** 10am-10pm Mon-Thur, Sat, Sun; 2-10pm Fri. **Map** p103 E3 🟤

There's certainly plenty to choose from at Coach. The Slim Tote, a sleek bag trimmed with embossed alligator skin, has a casual sophistication and is perfect for everyday use. Other models in Legacy canvas include the Carly, Slim Flap, Shoulder Bag and Satchel. Even more perfect for wearing in Dubai is the Straw Collection. Coach's iconic straw baskets inspired Krakoff to design a collection of handwoven accessories, lined with a quirky, lighthearted Legacy Watercolour Stripe fabric. Bags cost around Dhs2,000.

Giorgio Armani

Boulevard at Jumeirah Emirates Towers (04 330 0447/ www.armani.com). **Open** 10am-10pm Mon-Thur, Sat, Sun; 2-10pm Fri. **Map** p103 E3 🟤

A slick store that oozes style thanks not only to the high-end fashion, but to the minimally decorated surroundings. Sparkling black marble floors, dark walls and spotlights draw you to the colourful rails of clothes. Women will discover a mind-boggling selection of flattering skirts, smart jackets and funky party pieces, and men will leave in perfectly fitting suits.

Gucci

Boulevard at Jumeirah Emirates Towers (04 330 3313/www.gucci.com). **Open** 10am-11pm Mon-Thur, Sat, Sun; 5-9.30pm Fri. **Map** p103 E3 🟤

Gucci has long been synonymous with high-octane glamour and sex appeal, and this has been maintained despite Tom Ford's departure a few years back. You'll find the best of the best in this two level outlet. The womenswear, menswear and accessory departments are all brimming with luxurious but expensive buys.

Jimmy Choo

Boulevard at Jumeirah Emirates Towers (04 330 0404/www. jimmychoo.com). **Open** 10am-10pm Mon-Thur, Sat, Sun; 2-10pm Fri. **Map** p103 E3 🟤

The king of shoemaking, Jimmy Choo has a swanky branch in the sleek Jumeirah Emirates Towers. You can load up with ornate sandals, strappy kitten heels, spectacular evening shoes and leather books, but don't be surprised if you see well-dressed women in Dubai sporting the same design.

Juicy Couture

Boulevard at Jumeirah Emirates Towers (04 330 0018). **Open** 10am-10pm Mon-Thur, Sat, Sun; 2-10pm Fri. **Map** p103 E3 🟤

Juicy Couture's first ever store in the Middle East is ridiculously bling. As well as the trademark velour tracksuits, there are necklaces jingling with faux pearls and gold crown charms. For a teenage girl, Juicy Couture has the qualities of a shopping fairytale. You'll also find swimwear, sunglasses and shoes for men and women. The menswear is subtler, and a metrosexual man in his 20s or 30s will probably find something he'll like.

Music Chamber

Crowne Plaza Shopping Centre (04 331 6416). **Open** 10.30am-11pm Mon-Thur, Sat, Sun. **Map** p103 E3 🟤

The philosophy of the Music Chamber is 'we are musicians, not merchants'. This ethos means that prices are kept low on instruments from handmade guitars to pianos. There are 15 practice rooms that you can hire to play the piano or rehearse with your band in. Lessons are available: choose from flute,

Mandara Spa p124

guitar, kanoun, oud, percussion, piano, sax, singing, trumpet and violin, you'll pay Dhs540 for four one-hour lessons, plus a one-off registration fee of Dhs100.

Souk Al Bahar

By the Palace, the Old Town Hotel, Al Burj area (04 367 5588/ www.emaar.com). **Open** 10am-10pm Mon-Thur, Sat, Sun; 2-10pm Fri. **Map** p103 C4 ❸

This is a new shopping mall, designed like a traditional souk, and very nice it is too. There's a mix of high street retailers like Ted Lapidus, local boutiques such as 50°C, selling hip homeware and accessories, and touristy trinket shops, which sit alongside a few restaurants, bars and cafés. So once you're all shopped out, you can stop for a light lunch at New York's favourite deli, Dean & Deluca, or unwind over dinner at the Meat Company.

Nightlife

The 400 Club

Fairmont Dubai, Sheikh Zayed Road (04 332 5555/www.fairmont dubai.com). **Open** 11pm-3am Tue, Thur, Fri. **Map** p103 E3 ❹

A superexclusive club catering for an upmarket, well-dressed, posy crowd. Expect people to be more interested in keeping up with the Joneses than having a good old knees-up on the dance floor. Music policy is a mix of Arabian, house and R&B beats.

Lotus One

Next to Novotel, Sheikh Zayed Road (04 329 3200/www.lotus1.com). **Open** noon-2.30am daily. **Map** p103 F3 ❾❺

A swanky Thai fusion restaurant/ bar/ club, Lotus One is a popular weekend hangout. With occasionally slow bar service and plenty of knocks and nudges from sunglasses-toting posers, it can be a little frustrating, but with suspended decks and chairs, cow-print leather cushions and a glass floor showcasing a river and rubble scene underneath, there's plenty to keep your eyes busy.

Arts & leisure

1847

The Boulevard at Jumeirah Emirates Towers, Sheikh Zayed Road (04 330 1847). **Open** 9am-10pm daily. **Admission** Dhs220 1hr massage. **Map** p103 E3 ❾❻

One for the gents. 1847 offers a range of high-end services from shaves and facials to manicures, pedicures and massages. This is certainly one of the best places in town for men to head to for a spot of grooming.

DUBAI BY AREA

Art Space

9th floor, Fairmont Dubai (04 332 5523/www.artspace-dubai.com).
Open 10am-8pm Mon-Thur, Sat, Sun.
Admission free. **Map** p103 E3 **57**

Art Space is a sleek and contemporary art space, with a clean and functional layout. It excels in sourcing artwork by young female artists from across the Middle East and subcontinent. This is one of the most popular galleries in town, partly because it's easier to find than its counterparts.

The Big Apple

Boulevard at Jumeirah Emirates Towers, Sheikh Zayed Road (04 319 8661/www.jumeirahemirates towers.com). **Open** 6am-11pm daily.
Admission Dhs50 day; Dhs530 month. **Map** p103 E3 **98**

Tucked away in the lower levels of the Jumeirah Emirates Towers, the Big Apple is a highly polished chrome and steel affair, the epitome of modern urban fitness centres. It lacks swimming, sauna or steam room facilities, but is armed to the teeth with state-of-the-art equipment, meaning you probably won't find yourself hanging around to use the treadmill or stepper.

Grand Metroplex

Metropolitan Hotel, Interchange 2, Sheikh Zayed Road (04 343 8383).
Admission Dhs30. **Map** p102 B3 **99**

One of the older cinemas in the city, with eight screens. It's worth a visit if they're showing something you can't get into elsewhere. If you do go, make sure that you have a look at the hotel lobby – it's like stepping into 1970.

H2O Male Spa

Jumeirah Emirates Towers (04 319 8181/www.jumeirahemirates towers.com). **Open** 9am-11pm daily.
Admission Dhs350 55min massage.
Map p103 E3 **100**

H2O provides a range of therapies for men, including manicures, pedicures, tanning, waxing, facial therapy and massage. For something a bit different, give the Flotation Pool (Dhs300) and Oxygen Lounge (Dhs75-Dhs300) a try.

The first is a relaxation treatment that involves spending an hour inside a salt-water tank, floating in privacy while listening to soothing music, said to be as refreshing as eight hours of deep sleep.

Health Club & Spa

Shangri-La Hotel, Sheikh Zayed Road (04 405 2441/www.shangri-la.com).
Open 6am-midnight daily.
Admission Dhs180 Mon-Thur, Sun; Dhs220 Fri, Sat. **Map** p103 D3 **101**

Despite its upmarket location, this is a distinctly average hotel-based gym. If you prefer classes to gym workouts, it's possible to go along to a wide range of hatha yoga, martial art and salsa classes (Dhs40) on offer.

Mandara Spa

The Monarch Dubai, Trade Centre roundabout (04 501 8888/www.themonarchdubai.com). **Open** 9am-10pm daily. **Admission** Dhs465 1hr massage. **Map** p103 F3 **102**

One of the most Zen-like spas to hit these shores, the Mandara is the ideal bolt-hole for the vexed and stressed. The therapists mix traditional Asian and Arabian therapies with modern spa techniques to create a zone of total urban relaxation. The facilities include a sauna, a steam room and a jacuzzi. Try the signature Mandara Massage, Dhs950 for 95 minutes, which involves two therapists working on you at the same time in a unique blend of styles.

Willow Stream Spa

Fairmont Dubai, Sheikh Zayed Road (04 332 5555/www.fairmont.com).
Open 6am-midnight daily.
Admission Dhs320 1hr massage.
Map p103 E3 **103**

Expect high-quality pampering at the sublime Willow Stream Spa, which covers a vast amount of floor space. As well as separate whirlpools, saunas and steam rooms for men and women, it has two large outdoor swimming pools, situated to catch the morning and afternoon sun. Signature treatments are based on aromatherapy. There is a wading pool for children and a lounge that is open to all.

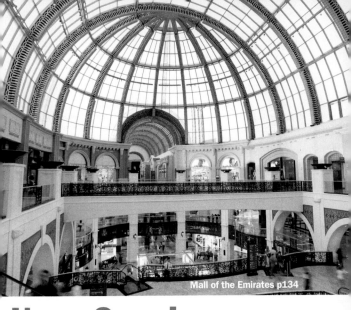
Mall of the Emirates p134

Umm Suqeim

Umm Suqeim is the stretch of town that runs south along the coast from Al Safa and Jumeirah 3, and along Sheikh Zayed Road to the vast Mall of the Emirates. Along the coast here are the **Burj Al Arab** and **Jumeirah Beach Hotel**. These were once quite isolated spots, but with the development of **Souk Madinat Jumeirah**, this part of town has become a significant social hub. Confusingly, a number of places tag the word Jumeirah on to their name, to try to gain a little cachet from Dubai's most desirable area.

To the east runs **Al Quoz** industrial zone, a rather desolate slab of factories, warehouses and workers accommodation; but, in true postmodern style, this dated industrial wasteland is becoming a new centre for arts in the city.

Eating & drinking

Almaz by Momo
Harvey Nichols, Mall of the Emirates (04 409 8877). **Open** 10am-midnight Mon-Thur, Sun; 10am-1.30am Fri; 10am-midnight Sat. **$$. North African.** Map p126 A3 **①**
With its multicoloured, low-hanging lamps, a ceiling that glitters like a desert sky and a soundtrack of frantic zithering beats, the dusky Almaz by Momo certainly isn't short on atmosphere. The food is impressive as well: tiny, golden nuggets of lamb kibbeh, aromatic pan-fried liver, spicy merguez sausages, zesty Moroccan salad and chocolate moelleux with vanilla ice-cream are among the highlights of the menu. Almaz arrived here in 2006, courtesy of the restaurateur Mourad 'Momo' Mazouz, whose outlet in London provides the blueprint for this excellent restaurant.

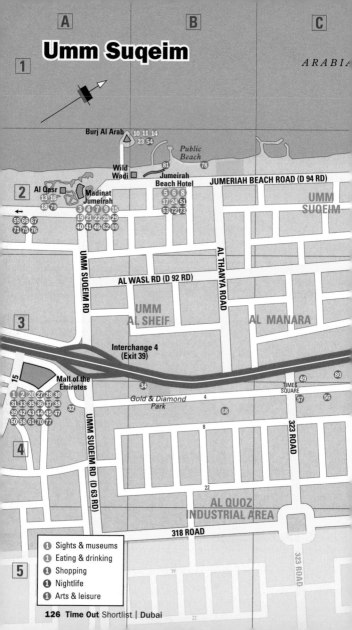

Umm Suqeim

A
B
C

1

ARABIA

2

Burj Al Arab
Wild Wadi
Al Qasr
Madinat Jumeirah

Public Beach

Jumeirah Beach Hotel
JUMERIAH BEACH ROAD (D 94 RD)

UMM SUQEIM

10 11 14
23 54
81
78

13 16
18 79
3 4 7 9 15
19 21 22 25 29
40 41 46 62 69
5 6 8
17 24 51
53 72 73

59 66 67
71 75 76

UMM SUQEIM RD

AL THANYA ROAD

AL WASL RD (D 92 RD)

3

UMM AL SHEIF

AL MANARA

Interchange 4
(Exit 39)

15

Mall of the Emirates

1 2 20 27 28 30
31 33 35 36 37 38
39 42 43 44 45 47
50 58 61 70 77
32

34

Gold & Diamond Park

4

68

8

49
80

TIMES SQUARE

57
56

UMM SUQEIM RD (D 63 RD)

323 ROAD

4

22

AL QUOZ
INDUSTRIAL AREA

318 ROAD

323 ROAD

5

19

1 Sights & museums
1 Eating & drinking
1 Shopping
1 Nightlife
1 Arts & leisure

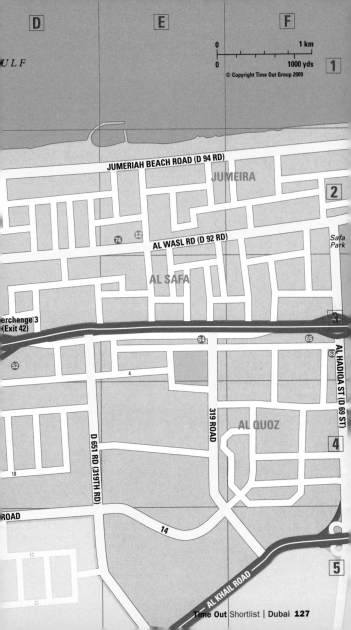

D E F

0   1 km

0   1000 yds

© Copyright Time Out Group 2009

1

ULF

JUMEIRAH BEACH ROAD (D 94 RD)

JUMEIRA

2

74   12

AL WASL RD (D 92 RD)

Safa
Park

AL SAFA

3

erchange 3
(Exit 42)

64   65

63

52

AL HADIQA ST (D 69 ST)

4

319 ROAD

AL QUOZ

4

D 651 RD (319TH RD)

18

ROAD

14

AL KHAIL ROAD

5

Après

Mall of the Emirates (04 341 2575).
Open noon-1am daily. **Bar**.
Map p126 A3 ❷

Après is an unlikely compromise between alpine resort and contemporary nightspot. Armed with every conceivable drink under the sun, the staff claim to be able to make a cocktail to suit anyone's tastes. With connoisseur choices made from ingredients as diverse as cucumber, tobacco-infused rum, sage and coriander, they should satisfy the discerning customer. The food is reasonably good too; try the spectacularly tasty fondue. The sight of cartwheeling skiers through the large slope-facing windows, along with the cocktail waiters' impressive juggling, should keep you entertained.

BarZar

Souk Madinat Jumeirah (04 366 6197/www.madinatjumeirah.com).
Open 5pm-2am Mon-Wed, Sat, Sun; noon-3am Thur, Fri. **Bar**.
Map p126 A2 ❸

BarZar's languid waterside terrace is one of the most popular drinking spots in the city. Located in the Madinat's bustling souk, the bar pulls in patrons with a variety of drink promotions. The place is huge, with two indoor floors plus the aforementioned terrace. Big-screen TVs play a mix of muted MTV and sports events.

Caviar House & Prunier

Souk Madinat Jumeirah (04 368 6282).
Open 3pm-1am daily. **$$$$**.
Seafood. **Map** p126 A2 ❹

As should be expected, the caviar is excellent. The 'palette duo' tasting plate consists of two superb quenelles of Prunier caviar alongside a sliced blini and a smidgen of crème fraîche; the oysters are delightful and the maki platter is expertly prepared. Sample the salmon in the 'gourmande palette' – the exquisitely smooth fillets dissolve in the mouth. Although far from cheap, we would heartily recommend Caviar House & Prunier for an occasional taste of the finer things in life.

Der Keller

Jumeirah Beach Hotel (04 348 0000).
Open 6pm-1am daily. **$$**. **European**.
Map p126 B2 ❺

Thankfully, Der Keller isn't one of those German establishments that trumpets its existence with maddening oom-pah music. There are no waiters in lederhosen heartily plonking frothing beer steins onto your table. Instead, it's so unpretentiously German that it's like being a schnitzel's throw from the Rhine. The classic Berlin-style soup is full of soft potato and chunky pork, but a better bet is the marinated salmon, which comes curled up like rose petals on crisp potato blinis in a dense forest of salad sprayed with basil foam.

Dhow & Anchor

Jumeirah Beach Hotel (04 348 0000/ www.jumeirahbeachhotel.com).
Open noon-midnight daily. **Bar**.
Map p126 B2 ❻

Falling somewhere between an old-fashioned British bar and a vibrant Mediterranean tavern, the Dhow & Anchor is a lively place where residents and tourists knock back drinks and talk nonsense at an increasing volume. However, beyond the fog of cigarette smoke is a snug dining room and a lovely open terrace where decent anglocentric pub fare can be sampled reasonably cheaply.

JamBase

Souk Madinat Jumeirah (04 366 6914/www.madinatjumeirah.com).
Open 7pm-2am Mon-Thur, Sat, Sun.
Bar. **Map** p126 A2 ❼

JamBase is the best venue for nightly live music in the city, although it's hardly up against strong competition. The furniture here is artfully angular, the decor is calculated art deco chic, and the food – with dishes inspired by the southern states of America – is very tasty too. The in-house jazz and blues band is one of Dubai's finest.

Al Khayal

Jumeirah Beach Hotel (04 348 0000).
Open 7pm-2am daily. **$$$**.
Arabian. **Map** p126 B2 ❽

Al Mahara

Al Khayal does good set menus with all the Arabian trimmings: fattoush, tabouleh, sambusak and fatayer. The grilled halloumi, falafel and potato harra are all worthy mentions and the mixed grill with a tender combination of lamb, beef, kibbeh and chicken hit the spot. Portions are very generous, so pace yourself. The distracted and occasionally vacant service will help. Entertainment comes in the form of belly dancing and an Arabian singer.

Left Bank
Souk Madinat Jumeirah (04 368 6171/ www.madinatjumeirah.com). **Open** noon-2am daily. **Bar**. Map p126 A2 ❾
Neon lighting, low seating and minimalist decor is the order of the day here. Left Bank's All Bar One-esque interior won't be to everyone's taste, but it's darker and cooler than the UK chain and the bar staff know their cocktails well. The waterside terrace is also a popular venue.

Al Mahara
Burj Al Arab (04 301 7600). **Open** 12.30-3pm, 7pm-midnight daily. **$$$$**.
Seafood. Map p126 A2 ❿
Getting to Al Mahara involves a trip in a pretend submarine with outrageously corny visuals and sound effects. Inside

the restaurant, there's an aquarium filled with freaky-faced fish, sharks, turtles and eels, and mid-meal a diver feeds the fish, which might just distract you from a fantastic (if wallet-crunching) dinner. The wagyu carpaccio is a particularly tasty starter: the mains are equally impressive and the halibut served in creamy mushroom and champagne sauce offers a lesson in how to prepare fish. This is a highly memorable dining experience, and reservations are essential.

Majlis Al Bahar
Burj Al Arab (04 301 7777).
Open 7pm-midnight daily. **$$$$**.
European. Map p126 A2 ⓫
If the first bite is with the eye, then Majlis Al Bahar offers a full banquet before you've even taken your seat. Flickering candles and uplit palm trees fringe the alfresco dining area while the Gulf and its bobbing crowd of yachts, tankers and cruisers glisten in the moonlight just beyond. The Burj Al Arab completes the scene, proudly displaying its chameleon-with-a-complex lightshow. The food might be unremarkable and hugely expensive, but for the impressive setting, you can just about justify the cost.

DUBAI BY AREA

Maria Bonita's Taco Shop

Near Spinneys Umm Sequim,
Al Sheif Road (04 395 4454).
Open noon-11.30pm daily. **$$**.
Mexican. Map p127 E2 ⑫

Maria Bonita's Taco Shop continues to exude its authentic charm with its fresh, traditional Mexican food, homely and comfortable feel and reasonable value for money. To the sound of chirping parrots and Mexican pop music, try the excellent fajitas and burritos, which are the best in Dubai by some distance. Kick back with a pitcher of iced horchata (a cinnamon drink made with rice milk), and soak up the laid-back atmosphere for a while.

MJ's Steakhouse

Al Qasr, Madinat Jumeirah (04 366 8888). **Open** 7-11.30pm daily. **$$$$**.
Steakhouse. Map p126 A2 ⑬

In its previous incarnation as a modern Californian restaurant, this place served good dishes, but there was room for improvement. Now it has re-emerged as a steakhouse, beach-side carnivores are in luck. While the high ceilings and bright lights mean that the atmosphere

is a little cold, and the giant Alice In Wonderland chairs create an imposing feel, the menu rethink is far more successful. The immaculate beef carpaccio melts in the mouth and the pan-seared beef fillet is a triumph, an intense hunk of smoky flavours. One of the best steakhouses in town.

Al Muntaha

Burj Al Arab, Jumeirah (04 301 7600).
Open 12.30-3pm, 7pm-midnight daily.
$$$$. **European**. Map p126 A2 ⑭

Al Muntaha's location, at the peak of the Burj Al Arab, with sweeping views of man-made archipelagos and sky-scraping towers, demands you dress up to the nines. The menu is slathered in luxuries such as oysters, caviar, lobster and foie gras; the prices are steep, but the flavours are worth it, and the goat's cheese espuma starter and steamed barramundi are notable highlights. Though the ambience is a bit stiff, the resident jazz band, along with the rumble of the neighbouring Sky View bar, lightens things a touch. Merely mentioning you're off to the Burj make the trip worthwhile.

Maria Bonita's Taco Shop

P2

Souk Madinat Jumeirah (04 366 8888).
Open noon-3pm, 7-11.30pm daily.
$$$$. Seafood. Map p126 A2 ⑮

This informal outdoor brasserie opened in the spring of 2007, and is every bit as good as you'd expect the younger sibling of Pisces to be. The fresh oysters arrive on a crystalline bed of ice with dishes of piquant sauce and citrus slices; the duck confit is delicately crisp yet succulent; and the crème brûlée is light and fluffy. Diners will inevitably draw comparisons between the food downstairs at Pisces and the fare at this algebraically named restaurant, but P2 is worth a visit alone.

Pai Thai

Al Qasr, Madinat Jumeirah (04 366 8888). **Open** 7-11.30pm daily. **$$$.**
Thai. Map p126 A2 ⑯

Accessible via artificial waterways on an inauthentic-looking abra, Pai Thai is a wonderfully peaceful restaurant serving good Thai food. Start your feast with crunchy spring rolls or Thailand's famous papaya salad (big enough for two), before moving to mains. Standards like the red or green curry are served with clumps of sticky steamed rice and don't disappoint, and the pad thai also impresses; it's not overly greasy as it can be elsewhere. For a taste of Thailand in the heart of the desert, head here.

La Parrilla

Jumeirah Beach Hotel (04 348 0000).
Open 6.30pm-1am daily. **$$$$.**
Steakhouse. Map p126 B2 ⑰

The tango show at this Argentinean restaurant is full of red-blooded passion, but the real drama unfolds on your plate. You can warm up with the succulent chilli prawns and sweetcorn nuggets with guacamole and salsa. The tenderloin is a superb main course, and the flambé margarita is tossed in a flaming combination of strawberries and crêpes at your table. It will make you want to open the windows and loudly extol La Parrilla's virtues from the 25th floor.

Pierchic

Al Qasr, Madinat Jumeirah (04 366 8888). **Open** noon-2.30pm, 7-11.30pm daily. **$$$$. Seafood.**
Map p126 A2 ⑱

If you can get a seat on the terrace, Pierchic is Dubai's most romantic restaurant. After a gentle meander down the pier, you can dine with an uninterrupted view of the neon Burj Al Arab sails, the Palm Jumeirah and the Madinat Jumeirah. The poached trout is as close to perfect as is imaginable: despite being flown in, it is as firm, flaky and pink a specimen as the most discerning piscatologist could wish for. Elsewhere, the roasted John Dory is solid, chunky and imbued with a whiff of autumnal smokiness.

Pisces

Souk Madinat Jumeirah (04 366 8888). **Open** noon-2.30pm, 7-11.30pm daily. **$$$$. Seafood. Map** p126 A2 ⑲

The food at Pisces is glorious. Ask them to deliver the king crab, in all its rich, meaty glory, and you'll be chowing down on the delicious crustacean in under five minutes. Move onto the confit of grey snapper – which comes teetering on a bed of creamy mash bolstered by squid ink breadsticks – and you'll be hooked. By the time the chocolate marquise swishes by for dessert, it's a done deal. Fine dining.

Salmontini

Mall of the Emirates (04 347 5844).
Open noon-11.30pm daily. **$$.**
Seafood. Map p126 A3 ⑳

Salmontini, as you may guess, specialises in salmon. The tasting platter – served with rye bread rolls and the standard-issue hard butter – is ample as a starter for two. A sort of salmon greatest hits, it comprises sashimi, briney gravadax and smoked salmon (all pleasantly cool if a trifle monotonous), plus a ramekin of deliciously herby salmon tartare. Grilled king prawns, meanwhile, are the size of salt-shakers and beautifully firm. A dedicated salmon restaurant with a view of an indoor ski slope: only in Dubai.

DUBAI BY AREA

Saluna

Mina A'Salam (04 366 8888). **Open** 4.30-11pm Sat. **Bar. Map** p126 A2 ㉑

Here's an odd one: six nights a week the voluminous Layali Tent hosts an Arabian restaurant, but each Saturday it's transformed into Saluna, a beachside bar that attracts a mix of pretty, rich types and intrigued tourists. The atmosphere is relaxed, with the bar being more of a hang-out-and-chat joint than a dancing venue – and with the sea literally a stone's throw away and the sun setting behind the nearby Burj Al Arab, it's hard to imagine a nicer place at which to chill out.

Segreto

Malakiya Villas, Souk Madinat Jumeirah (04 366 8888). **Open** noon-3pm, 7-11.30pm daily. **$$$. European. Map** p126 A2 ㉒

It's clear that the owners here are going all out for the lovers' dirham: there's even a cheeky Petrus on the wine list for couples who are prepared to blow Dhs40,000. The starters are on the steep side, but are innovative and very tasty: the pumpkin-stuffed ravioli justifies the Dhs70 price tag. For mains, the Barolo-braised beef short rib with truffle potato gnocchi and sautéed root vegetables is excellent, the beef melting in the mouth and the truffle gnocchi proving to be the highlight of the entire meal. Though expensive, the food at Segreto is faultless and the service is impeccable.

Skyview Bar

Burj Al Arab (04 301 7777/www.burj-al-arab.com). **Open** 11am-2am daily. **Bar. Map** p126 A2 ㉓

Certainly not the place for a swift drink (there's a minimum spend of Dhs250 per person, reservations are essential and the evening dress code is strict). The Skyview Bar's position atop the famous 'seven-star' hotel Burj Al Arab ensures its popularity. The decor is garish, to say the least, with a carpet and colour scheme to shame the most outlandish '80s discotheque, but the views are superb.

Villa Beach Restaurant

Jumeirah Beach Hotel (04 348 0000). **Open** noon-4.30pm, 7-11pm daily. **$$$$. European. Map** p126 B2 ㉔

Some of the most postcard-perfect views in the emirate can be found at this beachside restaurant, including the Burj, in all its alien glory, flickering in the night sky. Unfortunately, too many of the tables don't enjoy a view, which can make a visit a bit of an anticlimax. The pick of the menu is a wondrously tender beef fillet with a bundle of oxtail served with wild mushroom mash and green peppercorn sauce. Ultimately it's a solid experience, but if you haven't got the view it's difficult to justify the high price.

Zheng He's

Mina A'Salam, Madinat Jumeirah (04 366 8888). **Open** noon-2.30pm, 7-11.30pm daily. **$$$$. Asian. Map** p126 A2 ㉕

Beyond this restaurant's inimitable sense of style, there's substance in abundance. Get stuck into prawn and caviar or squid ink dumplings; the Beijing duck is a classic, the meat is tender and not too dry. If you want to venture away from duck, try the beef tenderloin with wild mushrooms, which is spectacular. Scallops with black truffle and white asparagus are a winner, and although the vegetable dishes can be a little watery, the sautéed french beans with garlic and dried prawns are a good alternative bet. It's evidence enough that Zheng He's has the culinary prowess to match its beautifully elegant interior.

Shopping

Antique Museum

3rd Interchange, Al Quoz Industrial Area (04 347 9935). **Open** 9am-8.30pm Mon-Thur, Sat, Sun; 9am-11.30am, 3.30-8.30pm Fri. **Map** p126 C4 ㉖

Al Quoz may appear to be a deserted industrial estate, but tucked away behind the bleak exteriors are some of Dubai's best antique haunts. Though the Antique Museum is not an actual gallery, the warehouse is a diamond in the rough: once you get past the giant wooden doors you are transported into a secluded cave of lost treasures. The narrow aisles are packed with a diverse range of handicrafts, shisha pipes, pashminas, furniture and the odd belly dancing costume.

Areej

Mall of the Emirates (04 340 5223/ www.altayer.com). **Open** 10am-midnight daily. **Map** p126 A3 ㉗

As well as plenty of designer names including Dior and Chanel, you'll find funkier labels such as Smashbox at branches of Areej. New fragrances tend to arrive here promptly, which means that you're bound to find the latest products. One of the most popular beauty shops in the city.

Bershka

Mall of the Emirates (04 341 0223/ www.bershka.com). **Open** 10am-10pm Mon-Wed, Sun; 10am-11pm Thur-Sat. **Map** p126 A3 ㉘

Bershka produces an exciting collection of funky casual clothes and sassy going-out gear. Thumping trance music accompanies customers around the store and gets them in a foot-stomping festival mood. People looking for shops like Miss Selfridge should head here.

Bonpoint

Souk Madinat Jumeirah (04 368 6212/ www.bonpoint.com). **Open** 10am-11pm daily. **Map** p126 A2 ㉙

A store with its finger firmly on the fashion pulse, Bonpoint has cornered a niche market, showcasing a children's collection inspired by high fashion and celebrity culture. Thoughtfully laid out, Bonpoint's collection features cute, yet terribly chic outfits.

Boom & Mellow

Mall of the Emirates (04 341 3993). **Open** 10am-10pm Mon, Tue, Sat, Sun; 10am-midnight Wed-Fri. **Map** p126 A3 ㉚

This is the Aladdin's cave of the accessory world, where bags line the walls, chunky necklaces hang temptingly

from silver pegs, and crystal-encrusted earrings sparkle alluringly behind glass cabinets. Sometimes there's a bit of vintage in stock too.

Carolina Herrera

Mall of the Emirates (04 341 5095). **Open** 9.30am-10pm Mon-Wed, Sun; 9.30am-midnight Thur-Sat. **Map** p126 A3 ㉛

Featuring walls adorned with photos of the lady herself, and scented candles scattered around, this store feels like a chic living room. Carolina Herrera's gowns are popular on the red carpet, and, should you have the funds, are well worth investing in.

Chocoa

Al Barsha, behind Mall of the Emirates (04 340 9092). **Open** 10am-11pm Mon, Tue, Sat, Sun; 10am-midnight Wed-Fri. **Map** p126 A3 ㉜

Wonderful chocolate-covered dates and dried apricots are piled high in this sugar-scented showroom. It's enough to ensure that you leave more hopped-up on cocoa than a giddy toddler at a birthday party. It's a shame that the shop isn't in the mall: you have to cross a busy road to get to chocolate heaven.

Gallery One

Mall of the Emirates (04 341 4488). **Open** 9.30am-10pm Mon-Wed, Sun; 9.30am-midnight Thur-Sat. **Map** p126 A3 ㉝

With its beautifully bold prints and one-offs, this compact exhibition space is rapidly gaining popularity among the art-lovers of Dubai. The outlet has oil prints and photography, including limited-edition original prints of the Beatles, Bob Marley and Jimi Hendrix.

Gold & Diamond Park Museum

Gold & Diamond Park, Interchange 4, Sheikh Zayed Road (04 347 7788/ www.goldanddiamondpark.com). **Open** 10am-10pm Mon-Thur, Sat, Sun; 4-10pm Fri. **Admission** free. **Map** p126 B4 ㉞

The Gold & Diamond Park features examples of Arabian, Italian and Indian

DUBAI BY AREA

Chocoa p133

jewellery, and conducts guided tours to the manufacturing plant, showing visitors how diamonds are cut and gold is produced. In the central atrium of shops, there are plenty of opportunities to make purchases. Pinctada Pearls, and white, yellow and purple golds are available. However, you will probably get a better deal in the souks.

Goldenpoint

Mall of the Emirates (04 341 0834). **Open** 10am-midnight Mon-Thur, Sat, Sun; noon-10pm Fri. **Map** p126 A3 ⑤
Sporty labels from Speedo to Rip Curl are stocked here. As well as more frivolous styles, avid sporty types will be able to pick up items that won't fly off in the crashing waves.

Harvey Nichols

Mall of the Emirates (04 409 8888/ www.harveynichols.com). **Open** 10am-10pm Mon-Wed, Sun; 10am-midnight Thur-Sat. **Map** p126 A3 ⑥
The third venture for Harvey Nichols on foreign soil after Riyadh and Hong Kong, this store filled a gap in Dubai's shopping market. With high-end brands, luxury accessories and the cult juice bar Fushi, the department store is certainly sleek, with a clientele to match.

Jeff de Bruges

Mall of the Emirates (04 341 0960/ www.jeff-de-bruges.com). **Open** 10am-11pm Mon, Tue, Sat, Sun; 10am-midnight Wed-Fri. **Map** p126 A3 ⑦
Chocolate-lovers will adore the scrumptious offerings at Jeff de Bruges. With the finest Belgian chocolates on sale this side of Wallonia, it is replete with truffles, marzipan, fruit jellies and pralines. Of course, these will make the perfect gift, but don't leave without picking up some for yourself too.

Mall of the Emirates

Interchange 4, Sheikh Zayed Road (04 409 9000/www.mallotheemirates. com). **Open** 10am-10pm Mon-Wed, Sun; 10am-midnight Thur-Sat. **Map** p126 A3 ⑧
Staggeringly big and horrifically busy at weekends, this Mall of the Emirates is Dubai's main hive of shopping activity, bringing together designer, high street, boutique and craft outlets under one enormous roof. The ground level is lined with high street names and a huge Carrefour, whereas the upper level caters for exclusive brands. Take time off and catch a film at the multiplex, or cool off after all that window-shopping by getting on the piste at Ski Dubai.

Oil & Vinegar

*Harvey Nichols (04 409 8961/
www.oilandvinegar.com).* **Open**
10am-10pm Mon-Wed, Sun; 10am-
midnight Thur-Sat. **Map** p126 A3 ③⑨
Ordinary bottles of oil and vinegar
might suit you fine, but if you have a
fine taste in condiments and you're a
sucker for pretty packaging, then you'll
find solace here. Situated on the top
floor of Harvey Nichols, Oil & Vinegar
offers an elaborate selection of oils,
from olive to truffle.

Ounass

*Souk Madinat Jumeirah (04 368 6167/
www.altayer.com).* **Open** 10am-11pm
daily. **Map** p126 A2 ④⓪
The best thing about Ounass is the fact
that it brings together an eclectic mix
of labels and clothing styles such as
Hale Bob and Juicy Couture, alongside
sleek lingerie, pretty dresses and a
great range of footwear.

Patchi

*Souk Madinat Jumeirah (04 368 6101/
www.patchi.com).* **Open** 10am-11pm
daily. **Map** p126 A2 ④①
Renowned for its high-quality selection
of chocolates, Patchi, a Lebanese brand,
is undoubtedly the Rolls Royce of luxury treats in the region. The wondrous
sweets range from classic perfetto to
chocolate espresso beans and pista-
chios. For a quick fix, they'll let you
pick 'n' mix from the counter.

Pixi

*Mall of the Emirates (04 341 3833/
www.pixibeauty.com).* **Open** 10am-
10pm Mon-Wed, Sun; 10am-midnight
Thur-Sat. **Map** p126 A3 ④②
A treasure trove of cosmetic variety,
Pixi is bursting with rainbow-coloured
make up, natural skincare and all the
beauty tools that you need to keep
yourself immaculately groomed. As
the name suggests, the vibe is fun,
cheeky and definitely quirky.

Praias

Mall of the Emirates (04 341 1167).
Open 10am-midnight Mon-Wed, Sun;
noon-10pm Thur-Sat. **Map** p126 A3 ④③

The fashion-conscious will love Praias:
it has the sexiest bikinis in town. And
it's not just for model figures, since a
good handful of the bikinis are under-
wired and offer excellent support. This
is the perfect place to head to if you've
forgotten to pack your swimwear.

Rage

Mall of the Emirates (04 341 3388).
Open 10am-midnight daily.
Map p126 A3 ④④
This boasts the best range of skate-
boards in the city, and the place is full
of personality too; expect to find punk
tunes blasting out and smashed-up
boards decorating the ceiling. Whether
you're after a pair of Etnies trainers, a
funky bikini or the latest Flip skate-
board, you won't leave disappointed.

Reiss

*Mall of the Emirates (04 341 0515/
www.reiss.co.uk).* **Open** 10am-10pm
Mon-Wed, Sun; 10am-midnight Thur-
Sat. **Map** p126 A3 ④⑤
This is a gorgeous shop where the
clothes have a designer feel. There are
full and pleated skirts with unusual
stitching details and abstract patterns
in the weave, plus light, cotton tops in
contemporary shapes and plenty of
well-tailored suits. Although Reiss is
more expensive than your average
chain, it's worth the splurge.

Souk Madinat Jumeirah

*Al Sufouh Road (04 366 6546/
www.madinatjumeirah.com).* **Open**
10am-11pm daily. **Map** p126 A2 ④⑥
One of Dubai's most popular spots, the
Madinat's souk has been created to
resemble a traditional Arabian market-
place. With its maze of dimly lit, iden-
tical corridors, it's easy to find yourself
walking in circles past the colourful
outlets selling crafts, homeware, jewellery and souvenirs. Although there is
a handful of branded stores, including
Bonpoint and Ounass, most shops cater
for tourists, and prices are accordingly
high. Connected to a huge hotel complex, the souk has plenty of licensed
bars and restaurants, which means it
always has bags of atmosphere.

DUBAI BY AREA

Tape à l'Oeil

Mall of the Emirates (04 341 0480).
Open 10am-11pm Mon-Wed, Sun;
10am-midnight Thur-Sat.
Map p126 A3 ❼

If your children fancy themselves as
Monte Carlo high rollers, this fashion
brand from France should match their
aspirations, so long as they're under
12 years old. In this town, the kids are
dressed as immaculately as catwalk
models; can your plastic handle it?

Total Arts

*The Courtyard, between Interchange
3 & 4, Sheikh Zayed Road, Al Quoz
(04 228 2888/www.courtyard-uae.com).*
Open 9am-7pm Mon-Thur, Sat, Sun.
Map p126 C4 ❽

A welcome surprise in the middle of
dreary Al Quoz, the Courtyard is a self-
enclosed street (dimly) reminiscent of
New York's SoHo. It offers an eclectic
hotchpotch of art stores and cafés.
Tribal weavings and rugs from Iran
are available, and every piece is clearly
labelled with details of age and origin.

Twisted

*Times Square Centre Mall
(04 341 8746/www.twistedco.com).*
Open 10am-10pm Mon-Wed, Sat,
Sun; 10am-midnight Thur, Fri.
Map p126 C3 ❾

This is a great place to visit if you're
shopping for jeans and T-shirts, and
it won't cost you a fortune: T-shirts are
Dhs55, jeans Dhs149. All the accessories are designed in-house, so every
item is unique. Army-green T-shirts
and shirts fill the racks for men and
women; the fabrics have been washed
to give that worn-in look, and there are
also some rock chic belts and cool
leather and canvas bags.

Yves Saint Laurent

Mall of the Emirates (04 341 0113).
Open 10am-10pm Mon-Wed, Sun;
10am-midnight Thur-Sat.
Map p126 A3 ❺⓿

Yves Saint Laurent's modern collection
ranges from expensive jackets right
down to reasonably priced dress shirts.
Although it's not cheap, you should
consider that in 1999 Gucci bought the
YSL brand, so the standards will be
high, and the prices remain cheaper
than at the parent company.

Nightlife

360°

*Jumeirah Beach Hotel (04 348 0000/
www.jumeirahbeachhotel.com).* **Open**
4pm-2am daily. **Map** p126 B2 ❺❶

360° is where the beautiful, young and
affluent go to show off. With comfortable sofas and excellent shishas, you
can relax to the chilled-out electronica
played by DJs. Situated at the end of its
own pier, this alfresco venue overlooks
the ever-expanding coastline of the
Arabian Gulf and the Burj Al Arab, so
always pulls a big crowd.

Arts & leisure

4 Walls Art Gallery

*Al Quoz, opposite Knotika (04 338
8892/www.4walls-dubai.com).* **Open**
10am-1pm, 4-7pm Mon-Thur, Sat, Sun.
Map p127 D3 ❺❷

In this art space, a collection of Middle
Eastern work is displayed by the ebul-
lient Sawsan Mahmoud. Creatives can
dip into regular painting and sculpture
workshops. The gallery is one of several in the Al Quoz area, and worth
a visit if you're doing an art crawl. As
it's set apart from most of the other galleries, it can be tricky to find. Entering
Al Quoz from Exit 3, head towards
Home Centre, do a U-turn at the traffic
lights, take the first right, first left, then
follow the road to the right.

Art Marine

*Jumeirah Beach Hotel (04 348
0000/www.artmarine.net).* **Open**
7am-6pm daily. **Map** p126 B2 ❺❸

Art Marine runs one of the biggest fishing operations in Dubai, and offers a
friendly, flexible service. There are various boats available for hire (which will
take six to 12 passengers per fishing
trip), and multiple fishing lines ensure
that you're trawling for sharks while
catching some rays.

Assawan Spa & Health Club

Burj Al Arab Hotel, Beach Road (04 301 7338/www.burj-al-arab. com/spa). **Open** 6.30am-10.30pm daily. **Map** p126 A2 ㊄
This lavishly decorated club is on the 18th floor of Dubai's iconic landmark, which provides spectacular views of the Gulf. There are separate men's and women's areas, a total of eight spa treatment rooms, a sauna, a steam bath, a plunge pool, a jacuzzi and a solarium. Espa and La Prairie facials are available, as well as wraps, massages and hot stone treatments. Don't expect all this to come cheap – a one hour basic massage will set you back Dhs600 – but for a once-in-a-lifetime experience, this is the place to come to.

Ayyam Gallery

Al Quoz 1, nr Kanoo (050 115 5358/ www.ayyamgallery.com). **Open** 6.30am-10.30pm daily. **Admission** free. **Map** p126 C4 ㊅
The world-renowned Syrian gallery is now open in Dubai, and exhibits an impressive range of contemporary art.

B21

Al Quoz 3, nr The Courtyard (04 340 3965/www.b21gallery.com). **Open** 11am-7pm Mon-Thur, Sat, Sun. **Admission** free. **Map** p126 C4 ㊇
B21 is the place to visit for provocative, in-your-face and (as far as the term can be applied to Dubai) cutting-edge art. The focus is on contemporary works by Syrian artists. If you manage to find this place, you'll easily discover the excellent Third Line gallery, which is on the opposite side of the road.

Basement Gallery

Street 8, behind Times Square, Al Quoz 3 (04 341 4409). **Open** 11am-7pm Mon-Thur, Sat, Sun. **Admission** free. **Map** p126 C4 ㊆
A recently opened gallery that seeks to raise the profile of unseen talents and explore the role of art in daily life. Basement promises to show a varied line-up of international painters, film directors and fashion designers.

CineStar at Mall of the Emirates

Mall of the Emirates (04 341 4222). **Admission** Dhs30; Gold Class Dhs100. **Map** p126 A3 ㊈
One of the best cinemas in town. Don't be surprised to find teenagers talking throughout the film; you might also find the film has been cut to fit in with the local culture – violence is generally fine, swearing, kissing (and anything more) is generally cut. The Gold Class seats at the front are popular.

Club Mina

Le Méridien Mina Seyahi Hotel, Al Sufouh Road (04 399 3333/ www.lemeridien-minaseyahi.com). **Open** 9am-7pm daily (members only Fri, Sat). **Map** p126 A2 ㊉
One of the trendier clubs in town, Mina has a private beach that stretches for about a kilometre and draws many of the city's beautiful people whenever a powerboating race comes to town. If you can't beat 'em, join 'em. The beachside Barasti restaurant is a terrific place for a meal; its facilities include three large swimming pools and two smaller, shaded pools for children.

Courtyard Gallery & Café

Off Sheikh Zayed Road, between junctions 3 & 4, exit 42, Al Quoz 3. (04 347 9090/www.courtyard gallerydubai.com). **Open** 9am-6pm Mon-Thur, Sat, Sun. **Map** p126 C3 ㉖
Part trendy café, part inspiring modern art gallery, the Courtyard combines a rich selection of international art with a stylish cultural hangout. This is a great place to mosey around when the weather is too hot for outdoor activities.

Dubai Community Theatre & Arts Centre

Mall of the Emirates, Level 2, Magic Planet entrance (04 341 4777/ www.ductac.org). **Open** 9am-10pm Mon-Thur, Sat, Sun; 2pm-10pm Fri. **Map** p126 A3 ㉑
A welcome addition to the cultural scene, the Dubai Community Theatre & Arts Centre (DUCTAC) opened with great expectations in 2006, complete

DUBAI BY AREA

with two purpose-built auditoriums, art galleries, studios and classrooms. There is a reasonably consistent programme of events, which takes in a diverse range of theatrical productions. The anglophone Dubai Drama Group (www.dubaidramagroup.org) and the the Streetwise Fringe (www.streetwise-fringe.com) often perform here.

Dubai Fencing Club
Quay Health Club, Mina A'Salam hotel, Madinat Jumeirah (04 366 8888/www. dubaifencingclub.com). **Open** *Beginners & advanced* 7.40pm Mon. *Advanced* 7pm Wed, Sat. **Map** p126 A2 ⑥²
The head coach of this popular club is Mihail Kouzev, who has represented Bulgaria in the Pentathlon World Championships. Fencers of all ages and standards are welcome.

Dubai International Bowling Centre
Next to Century Mall, Al Barsha (04 296 9222). **Open** 10am-midnight Mon-Wed, Sun; 10am-2am Thur, Fri. **Map** p127 F3 ⑥³
Aside from the 36 lanes of bowling fun, there is an enormous area full of the usual arcade games, pool tables and five-puck air hockey (believe us, it's a real challenge). There's also a sound-proofed room that contains a full drum kit, which visitors are free to play.

Dubai Roadsters
Wolfi's Bike Shop, between 2, 8 and 3 Interchanges on Sheikh Zayed Road (04 339 4453/www.dubairoadsters.com). **Open** 9am-7pm Mon-Thur, Sun. **Admission** free; bike hire Dhs100/day. **Map** p127 E3 ⑥⁴
The Dubai Roadsters meet every Sunday and Tuesday at 7pm at Nad Al Sheba. There's also a longer meet for slightly more experienced riders every Friday at 5.45am (6am in winter) from the Lime Tree Café on Jumeirah Beach Road for two to four hours cycling.

The Flying House
Al Quoz (04 265 3365/www.the-flying house.com). **Open** by appointment only Mon-Thur, Sat, Sun. **Map** p127 F3 ⑥⁵

This new gallery hosts exhibitions by Emirati artists, and for the moment it is the only venue in town to specialise in local art. A trip here should be top of your list if you appreciate interesting works of contemporary art.

Givenchy Spa
One&Only Royal Mirage Hotel, Al Sufouh Road (04 399 9999/ www.oneandonlyresorts.com). **Open** 9am-9pm daily. **Map** p126 A2 ⑥⁶
The magnificent Health & Beauty Institute at the Royal Mirage Spa covers an area of 2,000sq m (21,500sq ft), divided over two levels. On the upper floor, the formal Givenchy Spa has separate areas and opening times for women; the rest of the time, it's mixed. The lower floor has an authentic oriental hammam with a traditional heated marble massage table, plus two steam rooms and two private massage rooms. Two jacuzzis, a whirlpool and a plunge shower are also available.

Hiltonia Beach and Pool
Hilton Dubai Jumeirah Hotel, Al Sufouh Road (04 399 1111/ www.hiltonworld resorts.com). **Open** *Beach* 7am-sunset daily. *Pool* 7am-8pm daily. **Map** p126 A2 ⑥⁷
There's no shortage of things to do here: water sports include parasailing, kayaking, jet-skiing, knee-boarding and fishing trips. Or you could just lie by the pool or on the beach. The pools are surrounded by landscaped gardens, and the beach is fairly pleasant.

The Jam Jar
St. 17a, Al Quoz, behind Dubai Garden Centre on Sheikh Zayed Road (04 341 7303/www.thejamjardubai. com). **Open** 10am-9pm Mon-Thur, Sat, Sun; 2-9pm Fri. **Admission** free. **Map** p126 B4 ⑥⁸
Located in the vibrant artistic hub of the industrial quarter of Al Quoz, the Jam Jar showcases emerging artists and international stars. The studio offers four-hour DIY painting sessions, which include all art supplies. One of the most interactive art spaces in the city, this space is fun for everyone.

Spare arts

Independent art in an industrial zone.

B21 p137

A few years ago, only one or two galleries existed in Dubai, but slowly, a scene is developing. In the tradition of post-industrial creativity, the most interesting shows are to be found in a decrepit, depressing and generally down-at-heel industrial area – Al Quoz, which is just off Sheikh Zayed Road at Interchange 3. Total Arts led the way, setting up shop in 1998; B21 and the Third Line opened in 2005; and Basement, the most recent addition, opened its doors in 2008. Even the more conservative gallery, the Jam Jar (p138), relocated from a central location to jump on the bandwagon. If you do head down to the Jam Jar, you can become an artist yourself by buying a canvas and picking up a brush; make sure you book ahead.

Art is becoming big business in the city, with the likes of Dubai International Financial Centre and Coutts sponsoring shows. If you attend an opening while in town, look out for gallery staff putting red 'sold' dots by dozens of works during the evening. Eclectic artists such as British photographer Martin Parr and colourful mixed media artist Rana Begum have all exhibited at the Third Line (p141).

Galleries have recently begun to specialise in certain genres. You'll find trendy Arabian art at the Third Line, fascinating Emirati works at the Flying House, Iranian and Middle Eastern canvases at B21, and vibrant Syrian artists showing at the recently opened Ayyam Gallery.

There are now a dozen galleries to be found in Al Quoz, with some of the best on the same road: the Third Line is opposite B21 and Basement in Al Quoz 3, near the Courtyard and between Marlin Furniture and Spinneys. It's a difficult area for even seasoned taxi drivers to navigate, so if you're planning a visit, make sure that you go armed with a gallery map and phone number: one commercial unit looks much the same as the next.

DUBAI BY AREA

Madinat Theatre

Souk Madinat Jumeirah (04 366 6546/www.madinattheatre.com).
Open times vary. **Map** p126 A2 ⑥⑨
Set amid the extensive Madinat Jumeirah complex, the theatre offers a busy mix of light and accessible entertainment. The theatre excels in family-friendly fun and is consistently popular, especially among the expatriate crowd; the Dubai Drama Group and Streetwise Fringe regularly put on shows here.

Mondo Arte

Mall of the Emirates (04 341 3001).
Open 10am-10pm daily.
Map p126 A3 ⑦⓪
This minimalist art gallery combines made-to-order art with frequent shows by interesting artists. Send your partner for a look here if they don't want them to traipse around the mall with you. There are a few cafés nearby too.

Ski Dubai

Ocean Explorer Fishing Charters

Le Meridien Mina Seyahi Beach Resort & Marina, Al Sufouh Road, (04 399 3333/www.lemeridien-minaseyahi.com).
Open 8am-noon, 2-6pm daily.
Map p126 A2 ⑦①
Tackle, bait, and drinking water are included in the price of these regular trips to some of the best fishing areas in the Gulf (maximum six people), but you'll be asked for a 50 per cent credit card deposit. Look out for the World development on your way out to sea.

Pavilion Dive Centre

Jumeirah Beach Hotel (04 406 8827).
Open 8am-9.30pm daily.
Map p126 B2 ⑦②
The accredited National Geographic PADI dive centre can have you exploring a real shipwreck in no time. The PADI Discover Scuba Diving experience costs Dhs275, and the Open Water course costs Dhs2,050 for five days.

The Pavilion Marina & Sports Club

Jumeirah Beach Hotel (04 348 0000/ www.jumeirahbeachhotel.com). **Open** 10am-7pm daily. **Map** p126 B2 ⑦③
This upmarket beach club is popular with families, because there are so many activities from which to choose. If you're keen on water sports, wind-surfing, water-skiing, kayaks, banana boats and yacht charters are all available. Alternatively, if you simply feel like lounging by the water, there are four pools. People who prefer their sports to be land-based can book themselves in for a few sets of tennis, or have a go on the mini driving range. And if you feel as though you need a break from the little ones, you can pack them off to Sinbad's Kids' Club.

The Red Gallery

Villa 833b, Al Wasl Road (04 395 5811/050 655 7210). **Open** 9am-9pm daily. **Admission** free. **Map** p127 E2 ⑦④
The first gallery in Dubai dedicated to contemporary Vietnamese fine art, this exciting space exhibits pieces by acclaimed and emerging artists.

The Ritz-Carlton Spa

*The Ritz-Carlton Dubai Hotel,
Al Sufouh Road (04 399 4000/www.
ritzcarlton.com).* **Open** 9am-10pm
daily. **Map** p126 A2 ⑦⑤
The heady Balinese theme at the Ritz-
Carlton Spa is a well-executed concept,
running throughout the decor and artwork and extending to the treatments,
which include a Balinese Boreh massage and a Pumpkin and Cinnamon
Body Glow. There are ten treatment
rooms and a salon dedicated to hair
and beauty treatments, as well as a
jacuzzi, sauna and steam room.

Sheraton Jumeirah Health & Beach Club

*Sheraton Jumeirah Beach Resort,
Al Sufouh Road (04 399 5533/
www.starwoodhotels.com).* **Open**
7am-10pm daily (no pool lifeguards
after 7pm). **Map** p126 A2 ⑦⑥
As well as two swimming pools, two
floodlit tennis courts and two squash
courts, the club has a gym packed with
bikes, steppers, rowing machines and
treadmills. Throw in volleyball, water
sports, a sauna and steam room, and
you won't run out of activities. Or, you
could simply treat yourself to a hot
stone massage (50 minutes Dhs310) or
a vitamin facial (60 minutes Dhs425)
at the Armonia spa.

Ski Dubai

*Mall of the Emirates (04 409 4000/
www.skidxb.com).* **Open** 10am-
midnight daily. **Map** p126 A3 ⑦⑦
Skiing in the desert sounds like a crazy
idea, but it has become one of Dubai's
biggest hits. Ski Dubai is now a firm
favourite among tourists and expatriates, especially as a means of cooling
down over the sultry summer months.
For one incredibly low price, you can
hire the necessary equipment, and on
Mondays a DJ is brought in.

Surf Dubai

*By the Burj Al Arab (050 504 3020/
www.surfingdubai.com).* **Open** by
appointment. **Map** p126 A2 ⑦⑧
Beginner's boards are provided, and
there are normal boards available to

rent by the hour (Dhs50, or Dhs200 for
the whole day). To organise a lesson
you need to sign up to the mailing list
on the website and watch out for the
regular forecasts.

Talise

*Al Qasr, Souk Madinat Jumeirah
(04 366 6818/www.madinat jumeirah.
com/spa).* **Open** 9am-10pm daily.
Map p126 A2 ⑦⑨
Many different treatments are on offer
to rejuvenate travellers, from massages
with exotic oils to more scientific heal-
ing and wellness therapies. The Talise
Pure Awakening is the signature treatment at this superior spa, and includes
a massage, foot acupressure and eye
therapy for Dhs475. There are also
saunas, steam rooms and gardens in
which to relax. Facials and massages
start at Dhs465 for 50 minutes.

The Third Line

*Al Quoz 3, nr the Courtyard, between
Marlin Furniture & Spinneys (04 341
1367/www.thethirdline.com).* **Open**
11am-8pm Mon-Thur, Sat, Sun.
Admission free. **Map** p126 C3 ⑧⓪
Slick and professional, the Third Line
ties with B21 as the destination of
choice for people seeking radical and
groundbreaking Middle Eastern art
in a cool and contemporary setting.
Photographer Martin Parr has shown
here, and many arty types consider it
the best gallery in town.

Wild Wadi

*Next to Jumeirah Beach Hotel (04
348 4444/www.wildwadi.com).* **Open**
11am-9pm daily. **Admission** Dhs195;
Dhs165 reductions. **Map** p126 B2 ⑧①
One of the most popular places in the
city for families, this water park is best
known for the Jumeirah Sceirah ride, a
33m (100ft) long slide which has you
charging down to the pool at break-
neck speed. There are plenty of less
exhilarating rides for young children
and budding surfers can have a go on
the Wipeout Flowrider, one of only four
such rides in the world. The machine's
technology generates artificial waves,
which are perfect for body-boarding.

Eau Zone p145

The Marina & Around

The Marina is the heart of what is referred to, with tongue in cheek, as 'new Dubai' – Old Dubai being the bits around the Creek that sprung up in the '70s and '80s, and distinct from the Old Town development, due for completion around 2010, near the Burj Dubai. The Marina is past the **Mall of the Emirates** when driving towards Abu Dhabi, and despite ongoing construction work, is forging its own identity.

Skyscrapers abound, and with them come venues with breathtaking views of the **Palm** development. Bar 44 at the Grosvenor House hotel boasts a vista of almost 360 degrees around one of the biggest marinas in the world. The district is popular with residents, as websites aren't subject to the same strict censorship policy as elsewhere in Dubai. **Jumeirah Beach Residence**, a collection of around 40 buildings, is one of the buzzy pockets with a mixture of chain restaurants and boutique shops, and as the name suggests, you don't have to walk far to get to a strip of sand. The metro system will pass through the Marina from early 2010.

Eating & drinking

Bar 44

Grosvenor House, West Marina Beach (04 317 6871/www.grosvenorhouse-dubai.com). **Open** 6pm-2am Mon-Wed, Fri-Sun; 6pm-3am Thur. **$$**. **Bar**. **Map** p143 C2 ①
There's a plethora of classy venues in Dubai, but the vertiginous Bar 44,

The Marina & Around

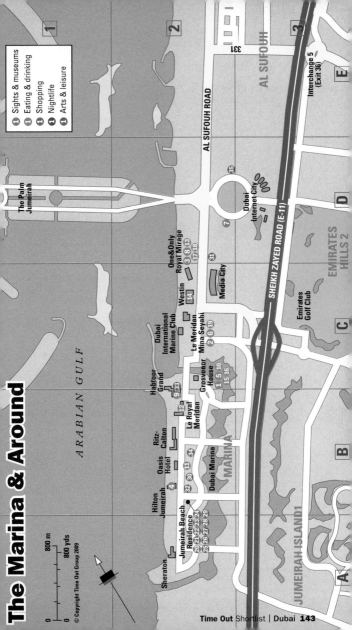

Legend:
- 🔴 Sights & museums
- 🔵 Eating & drinking
- 🟣 Shopping
- 🟠 Nightlife
- 🟢 Arts & leisure

ARABIAN GULF

The Palm Jumeirah

AL SUFOUH ROAD

AL SUFOUH

331

One&Only Royal Mirage
3 8 13
17 18

Westin
14

Dubai Internet City

35

7

Media City
31

Interchange 5
(Exit 36)

SHEIKH ZAYED ROAD (E-11)

EMIRATES HILLS 2

Emirates Golf Club

Dubai International Marine Club

Le Meridian Mina Seyahi
2 6 19

Grosvenor House
1 5 10
15 16

Habtoor Grand
9 33

12

Le Royal Meridian

Ritz-Carlton

Oasis Hotel
11 34
30

Hilton Jumeirah
32 4

Sheraton

Jumeirah Beach Residence
20 21 22 23 24
25 26 27 28 29

MARINA

Dubai Marina

JUMEIRAH ISLAND 1

800 m
0
800 yds
0

© Copyright Time Out Group 2009

Food chain

Go GM free at one of the few organic restaurants

Organic food is hard to come by in Dubai, which is why Az.u.r (pronounced 'as you are') is creating a stir among the city's foodies. The newly opened restaurant in the Harbour Hotel has a broad Mediterranean menu – take your pick from paella, tagine, mezze and plenty of vegetarian options. The concept behind the restaurant is 'farm to fork', a phrase that Chris Baker, executive chef at the hotel, explains as 'something that I got into a few years ago. It doesn't mean to say that the farmer drives it to you and then you cook it. It's about knowing the whole process of where it comes from, so if your beef comes from America, which farm in America? What is it fed, is it grass fed or grain fed. How does it get here, is it protected all the way along?'

The restaurant claims that about 75 per cent of the produce it uses is organic, and Baker is a fervent advocate of good, clean cooking. 'If I wouldn't serve a dish to my wife,' he says, 'why would I serve it to you? I love food and I don't like these chefs around the city who seem to prefer their Montblanc to their knife. You're not the star, your food is.' His attitude, and his food, make a healthy change.

Az.u.r
Harbour Hotel & Residence, Dubai Marina (04 319 4794/ www.emirateshotelsresorts.com)

so-called because it proudly stands on the 44th floor of the Grosvenor House – has plenty to elevate its standing. The views across new Dubai are incredible.

Barasti Bar
Le Méridien Mina Seyahi Beach Resort & Marina (04 318 1313/ www. starwoodhotels.com).
Open 11.30am-1.15am daily. **$$**.
Bar. Map p143 C2 ②
Permanently packed, this wood-decked, sun-drenched beach bar almost doubled in size during its recent refit, but you'll still struggle to find a table, particularly at the weekend. Alongside the usual alcoholic drinks, the bar does a nice sideline in shisha pipes, and offers the perfect setting for a puff overlooking the sea. Despite being in one of the more touristy locations, Barasti still generates a cheery local ambience.

The Beach Bar & Grill
One&Only Royal Mirage (04 399 9999/www.oneandonlyresorts.com).
Open 12.15-3.15pm, 7-11.30pm daily.
$$. Seafood. Map p143 D2 ③
This beachfront restaurant boasts low-lit lanterns, wooden walkways across the sand and a view of the Palm. Kick off with the black mussels in a marinara sauce and you won't be disappointed. Follow with a dish of pan-fried red snapper, its whole baked fennel and pretty scattering of clams offering a perfect foil to the smoke-infused fish.

Buddha Bar
Grosvenor House, West Marina Beach (04 399 8888/www.grosvenorhouse-dubai.com). **Open** 8pm-2am daily. **$$$**.
Asian. Map p143 C2 ⑤
A favoured haunt of Dubai's ostentatious in-crowd: candlelit tables buzz with chatter and well-trained staff mill about unobtrusively, serving up excellent food. The sushi appetisers are light and clean on the palate, and the lacquered Chinese duck is grease-free and covered with caramelised fruit compote, which tempers the gamey taste of the meat. The seafood bouillabaisse is not quite as successful, but the path to culinary enlightenment is never easy.

Barasti Bar

Bussola

*Le Méridien Mina Seyahi Beach
Resort & Marina (04 399 3333/
www.starwoodhotels.com).*
Open 7pm-midnight daily. **$$**.
Italian. Map p143 C2 ⑥

Customers are lured to Bussola by the promise of a gentle sea breeze. Yet despite the popularity, the starters fail to impress. Slightly more luck is to be had with the mains: the suckling pig comes in thick slices of pink meat and benefits from the bed of savoy cabbage mash. The chicken, soft and tender with a citrus kick in the middle, is a delight. Prices aren't too bad, considering the seaside setting.

Certo

*Radisson SAS Hotel, Dubai Media City
(04 366 9111/www.radisson.com).*
Open noon-3.30pm, 7pm-midnight
daily. **$$**. **Italian**. Map p143 D2 ⑦

It may be in a nondescript corner of a business hotel, but Certo serves Italian fare that's far too good to be hogged by the after-work crowd. When you're wrapped in the culinary embrace of an insalata di scoglio, a mix of seafood

treats given added lustre by the tang of capers and juicy olives, you'll be whisked away from the Gulf to the Mediterranean. From the main courses, try the perfectly crisped fillet of sea bass, sitting proudly atop a spinach and porcini mushroom salad with a balsamic dressing generous in its mellow acidity. A quality dining experience.

Eau Zone

*One&Only Royal Mirage (04 399
9999/www.oneandonlyresorts.com).*
Open noon-3.30pm, 7-11.30pm daily.
$$$. **European**. Map p143 D2 ⑧

A short stroll across a wooden footbridge amid quiet stretches of candlelit water transports you to this romantic dining spot. The shredded chicken in rice paper and the seared scallops make excellent starters, perfectly cooked, bursting with flavour and light enough to leave you hungry. For your main course, try the duck duo – tender slivers of meat on a perky pak choi base, served with a quail's egg. Such pleasures don't come cheap, but for a special occasion, this is a good bet.

DUBAI BY AREA

The Grand Grill

Habtoor Grand Resort & Spa (04 399 5000/www.grandjumeirah. habtoorhotels.com). **Open** 1pm-midnight daily. **$$$**. **Steakhouse**. **Map** p143 C2 ❾

This South African grill ticks every box for a fine steakhouse. The brawny 500g Aussie rump steak is magnificent for sheer size and flavour. It's a shame that the non-beef options, such as the seafood esperada, aren't as good, but it's still worth a whirl.

Indego

Grosvenor House, West Marina Beach (04 399 8888/www.grosvenorhouse-dubai.com). **Open** 7.30pm-midnight Mon-Wed, Sun; 7.30pm-1am Thur; 7.30pm-midnight Fri, Sat. **$$$**. **Indian**. **Map** p143 C2 ❿

This beautiful restaurant, which is full of bronze statues, exotic masks and antique Indian shoes, is tucked away in a hushed corner of the sweeping mezzanine lobby of Grosvenor House. Try the tandoori prawn starter, pricked with devilish spice and snappy fresh onion and a dollop of creamy-chunky potato. And the impossibly moist and yielding meat of the lamb shank rogan josh departs from the bone like a kicked-off slipper. It's one of the best Indian restaurants in town.

Johnny Rockets

Marina Walk, Dubai Marina (04 368 2339/www.johnnyrockets.com). **Open** noon-midnight Mon-Wed, Sat, Sun; noon-12.30am Thur, Fri. **$$**. **American**. **Map** p143 B2 ⓫

Inspired by Americana, Johnny Rockets delivers a feel-good '50s family diner experience with utter aplomb. This salubrious, kid-friendly joint proudly grills fresh beef right in front of your nose, and tosses it up into a sizzling hamburger with whopping slabs of tomato and onion. From the humble cheeseburger to the 'Number 12' hamburger – a dense puck of beef with slabs of lettuce, fresh onion and pickle, plus tillamook cheese and patented 'red, red sauce' – Johnny Rockets is one step short of patty heaven.

Maya

Le Royal Méridien Beach Resort & Spa (04 399 555/www.starwoodhotels.com). **Open** noon-2am daily. **$$$**. **Mexican**. **Map** p143 B2 ⓬

Maya has been challenging the restaurant-going public of Dubai with its contemporary take on Mexican cuisine for just over a year. The chefs have made lots of stabs at creating hybrid dishes, some of which are more successful than others. The braised lamb shanks are delicately cooked and full of flavour, but in a Mexican restaurant they feel slightly out of place. And the duck enchiladas are more like the pancakes that you would expect to find in a Chinese establishment.

Nina

One&Only Royal Mirage (04 399 9999/www.oneandonlyresorts.com). **Open** 7-11.30pm daily. **$$**. **Indian**. **Map** p143 D2 ⓭

Over the years, this large, inviting and usually bustling restaurant has delivered some of the most innovative food in the city. Worth booking ahead, it offers a taste of Indian fine dining. The savoury starters include a vibrant dosa, a South Indian rice-and-lentil-flour pancake with an unusual bean sprout, tomato and palm sugar relish; and tandoori-roasted chicken with papaya and coriander pesto. For a good main course, try the lamb dumplings, which are tender, warm and gorgeously spice, or the smooth tomato butter chicken. The decent wine list has plenty of fragrant Rieslings that could easily hold their own against the fieriest curry.

Oeno

The Westin Dubai Mina Seyahi Beach Resort and Marina (04 399 4141). **Open** 4pm-1am daily. **$$**. **Bar**. **Map** p143 C2 ⓮

For the best bottles in Dubai, Oeno is a safe bet. It has a fantastic selection of wines, from vintage champagnes to outstanding sweet Sauternes. There are two private rooms, one for wine tasting and one for sampling cheese, and the latter's menu is superb.

Ottomans

Grosvenor House, West Marina Beach (04 399 8888/www.grosvenorhouse-dubai.com). **Open** 8pm-12.30am Mon-Sat. **$$**. **Turkish**. **Map** p143 C2 ⑮

Beyond a candlelit marble water feature, there's a plush dining area with well-spaced tables, curtains and a slumber party of cushions. You'll be well rewarded with shrimp in pistachio, featuring a pair of huge prawns encased in spirited, crunchy batter shells on a bed of sweetened onion and bell pepper shavings. With the serene ambience and comfortable food, dining out here feels like a cosy night in.

Rhodes Mezzanine

Grosvenor House, West Marina Beach (04 399 8888/www.grosvenorhouse-dubai.com). **Open** 7.30pm-midnight Mon-Wed, Fri-Sun; 7.30pm-1am Thur. **$$$**. **European**. **Map** p143 C2 ⑯

From its high ceilings to its uncluttered floors, Mezzanine's airy and expansive dining room welcomes guests with a commodity that is sadly all too rare in Dubai's restaurants: space. Celebrity chef Gary Rhodes does his modern British bit here with all the flair you'd expect back home. The oxtail starter perches a creamy teardrop of mash on shortcrust pastry surrounding a treasure of moist shredded beef, and the expertly seared salmon main course is accompanied by delicate chunks of lobster and a splash of frothy bisque.

The Roof Top

Arabian Court, One&Only Royal Mirage, Al Sufouh Road (04 399 9999/www.oneandonlyresorts.com). **Open** 5pm-1am daily. **$$**. **Bar**. **Map** p143 D2 ⑰

A sedate sipping station, the Roof Top remains one of the most magnificent drinking venues in the city. The views, which take in the serene Gulf and the bizarre Jumeirah Palm, can't be beaten, and the soundtrack of commercial, chilled beats peppered with the odd classic is perfectly judged. Arrive early to be assured of a candlelit table around which you can enjoy a cocktail underneath the stars.

Tagine

One&Only Royal Mirage (04 399 9999/www.oneandonlyresorts.com). **Open** 7-11.30pm Tue-Sun. **$$**. **Moroccan**. **Map** p143 D2 ⑱

From the instant you enter the great wooden gates to this Moroccan paradise, you're in for a rare Dubai treat. The mezze, which include beetroot salad, a carrot concoction and a courgette mix, are exquisitely served in tiny blue and white ornamental plates. For mains, try the lamb tagine with ginger, parsley and a host of other flavours, a generous portion of juicy soft lamb and vegetables served with justifiable pomp. Perfect for a romantic evening out.

Tang

Le Méridien Mina Seyahi Beach Resort & Marina (04 399 3333/www.starwoodhotels.com). **Open** 7-11pm Mon-Fri, Sun. **$$$**. **European**. **Map** p143 C2 ⑲

The experiments in molecular gastronomy at Tang are a few steps behind the best efforts of Blumenthal and co, but make for a decent, alternative meal. The chocolate, cognac and tobacco dessert, for example, is an inventive, surprising and tasty dish. There may be nowhere in Dubai that offers food as challenging as Tang, but it hasn't hit the highest peaks yet, and can be a little over-reliant on foam.

Shopping

Baldinini

Jumeirah Beach Residence (04 424 3974/www.baldinini.it). **Open** 1-10pm daily. **Map** p143 B2 ⑳

If you want to look as though you've just left the catwalk, this is the shop for you. With shoe collections for men and women, you will be among the best heeled in town. Baldinini is an Italian company, so the footwear is well made and saucily designed.

Bendon

Jumeirah Beach Residence (04 424 3795/www.bendon.com). **Open** 2-10pm Mon-Thur, Sat, Sun; 3-10pm Fri. **Map** p143 B2 ㉑

DUBAI BY AREA

Solid bras for all busts are available, whether you're after sporty, romantic or everyday styles. There's also a bit of casual gear and underwear for expectant mums. As long as you're not after anything too fashionable or frilly, this is the place to head to.

Fabio Inghirami

Jumeirah Beach Residence (352 5551/www.inghirami.com). **Open** 10am-10pm daily. **Map** p143 B2 **22**

The Italian label for men who like to look sleek and chic, Fabio will have you ready for a polo event. You won't be surprised to learn this company was founded by a lawyer; it's all snappy suits and smart casual wear.

Fat Face

Jumeirah Beach Residence (04 427 0482/www.fatface.com). **Open** 10am-10pm daily. **Map** p143 B2 **23**

Great for beachwear and sloppy jeans: if you want to give the impression that you ride the waves or ski all day, then Fat Face delivers. Encouragingly, the company was set up by two men to fund their days on the slopes, so they know a thing or two about comfortable and practical sportswear.

Giordano

Jumeirah Beach Residence (04 423 3741/www.giordano-me.com). **Open** 10am-10pm Mon-Thur, Sat, Sun; 4-10pm Fri. **Map** p143 B2 **24**

Giordano offers excellent basics for a handful of dirhams. You can also purchase some pretty dresses, and accessories ranging from bags to earrings. This is definitely a place to come to if you've left a few things behind at home and need some cheap threads to see you through your trip.

The Men's Store

The Walk, Jumeirah Beach Residence (04 435 5681). **Open** 11am-11pm Mon-Thur, Sat, Sun; 3-11pm Fri. **Map** p143 B2 **25**

With so many shops for the fairer sex, it's good to see one which is dedicated to the male of the species. This one comes courtesy of Saks Fifth Avenue,

so expect labels of the expensive kind: Prada, D&G, Alexander McQueen, Christian Lacroix and Duchamp.

Pablosky

Jumeirah Beach Residence (04 424 3927/www.pablosky.com). **Open** 1-10pm Mon-Thur, Sat, Sun. **Map** p143 B2 **26**

Pablosky is the ideal place to buy fun and colourful footwear for sporty children who quickly outgrow their shoes. Whether you're looking for sensible, formal slip-ons, knockabout trainers, playful sandals or light cotton pumps, Pablosky has it covered.

Petit Bateau

Jumeirah Beach Residence (04 423 3854/www.petit-bateau.us). **Open** 10am-10pm Mon-Thur, Sat, Sun; 3-10pm Fri. **Map** p143 B2 **27**

Casual clothing for fresh-faced babies and children, all with a nautical flavour. There are lots of stripes, blues and the odd dash of red, and most designs are made of cotton or wool. Mums will be pleased to know there is a small range of daywear for them too.

Quiz

Jumeirah Beach Residence (04 424 3896/www.quizclothing.co.uk). **Open** 1-10pm Mon-Thur, Sat, Sun; 3-10pm Fri. **Map** p143 B2 **28**

Quiz offers a kaleidoscope of stylish party frocks for young women at very reasonable prices. Think satin, animal prints and bright colours. Buy a few bits here if you want to stand out from the rest of the Dubai crowd; this is one of the city's best kept secrets.

Zadig & Voltaire

Jumeirah Beach Residence (04 423 3768/www.zadig-et-voltaire.com). **Open** 1-9pm Mon-Thur, Sat, Sun. **Map** p143 B2 **29**

This is the place where you can pick up trendy watches that have a skull and crossbones, necklaces with a diamante gun and plenty of fashionably cut clothes for men, women and children. This is the first Zadig & Voltaire store to open in the Middle East.

Arts & leisure

Angsana Spa

Level 2, Marina Walk, Dubai Marina (04 368 4356/www.angsanaspa.com). **Open** 10am-10pm daily. **Map** p143 B2 ③⓪

The signature treatment is the Dhs500 Angsana massage, a two-hour pummelling with oils that mixes Asian and European techniques. Facials cost from Dhs320, and massages start at Dhs350. This is a lovely spacious spa with a small shop for visitors who would like to take some treats home.

Blue Banana

Office 1007, Business Central Towers, Dubai Media City (04 369 7378/www. bluebanana.ae). **Map** p143 D2 ③①

Blue Banana offers all sorts of Pepsi Max trips, ranging from desert adventures such as quad biking and rock climbing; to sailing and jet skiing; to skydiving and helicopter tours; and more sedate adventures such as hot air ballooning. The trips usually include pick up and drop off at your hotel.

Dubai Water Sport Academy

Dubai Marina, Marina Walk (050 303 9700). **Open** 6am-7pm daily. **Map** p143 B2 ③②

The Academy has qualified instructors for monoski, barefoot, wake and kneeboarding. These cost Dhs150 for 15 minutes. Sporty types should jog down to this adrenaline-pumping Dubaian institution; it's an excellent place to go to if you haven't tried out some of these water sports before.

Elixir Spa & Health Club

The Habtoor Grand Resort & Spa (04 399 5000/www. grandjumeirah. habtoorhotels.com). **Open** 9am-8.30pm daily. **Map** p143 C2 ③③

The Habtoor's spa has five treatment rooms, a dry float room and tanning booth. The spa menu offers something for men and women, with massages starting from Dhs320 and facials from Dhs450. The spa is next to one of the best beaches in town.

Franck Provost

Dubai Marina (04 362 9865/ www.franckprovost-dubai.com). **Open** 10am-10pm daily. **Map** p143 B2 ③④

It's hard to get a booking at this salon for a good reason: the stylists actually know what they are doing. Prices are surprisingly affordable (Dhs300 for a haircut). They also offer great packages of cut, colour and blow-dry, with prices starting at Dhs550.

Shapes Wellness & Spa

Dubai Knowledge Village (04 367 2137/www.shapeshealthclub.com). **Open** 6am-9pm Mon-Thur, Sat, Sun. **Admission** Dhs35. **Map** p143 D2 ③⑤

A great gym for men and women who are trying hard to lose the lard. The owner, Sam, doesn't believe in tedious treadmills, so there are lots of interesting classes to help you achieve your weight loss goals, such as salsa and belly dancing. There's also a separate

Dubai Water Sport Academy

View from Bidiya Mosque

Worth the Trip

Many of Dubai's best attractions lie beyond its city limits. Neighbouring emirates offer history, culture, Martian mountain ranges, towering sand dunes and beautiful beaches. Inter-emirate public transport is limited to infrequent (and often uncomfortable) buses, so a car is necessary. You can hire taxis for 12 hours for Dhs500 from Dubai Transport (04 208 0808), but hiring your own wheels, preferably a four-wheel drive, is a good idea. Otherwise, there's an army of firms keen to take you into the **Hajar mountains** sand boarding down dunes, or the typical 'desert safari' of dune-bashing, camel riding and dinner with shisha and belly dancing. Some are tacky, some are impressive, but they are the easiest way to see desert or mountain. Prices range from Dhs50 for 15 minutes of quad biking or Dhs180 for a desert safari, to Dhs350 for a dinner cruise or Dhs450 for a dune buggy safari. The main operators are Arabian Adventures (04 303 4888, www.arabian-adventures. com), Desert Rangers (04 422 0044, www.desertrangers.com), Arabian Desert Tours (04 268 2880, www.adt uae.com) and Desert Rose (04 335 0950, www.holidayindubai.com).

Sharjah

The emirate next door has become a de facto suburb of Dubai for workers driven north by high rents. It's overcrowded, traffic is a pain and it's conservative (alcohol is illegal, men and women should dress more modestly). But it also has the UAE's best collection of galleries and museums.

Sights & museums

Bait Al Naboodah

Al Shuwaiheyn, between the waterfront & Al Hosn Avenue 'Bank Street' (06 568 1738). **Open** 8am-8pm Mon-Thur, Sat, Sun; 4-8pm Fri. **Admission** Dhs5. Built in 1845, the Al Naboodah family home was inhabited until the '70s, but then fell into disrepair. In the early '90s, the Sharjah government declared the home a historical building, and began renovations. Today it's an excellent example of the simplicity of traditional life in the emirate, even for the wealthy. Next door is El Eslah School, which is worth a look. It's a small building and apparently the first school in the UAE.

Heritage area

Al Shuwaiheyn, between the waterfront & Al Hosn Avenue 'Bank Street' (no phone). **Open** 8am-8pm Mon-Thur, Sat, Sun; 4-8pm Fri. **Admission** varies. Around the courtyard of the former home of the Al Naboodah family, the buildings of the Heritage Museum are a fascinating example of traditional UAE architecture. Inside are displays of old clothing and heritage items. For the modern-day equivalent, visit the nearby Souk Al Arsah, an alley packed with antiques and jewellery.

Islamic Handicraft Museum

Heritage area (050 934 6429). **Open** 10am-7pm Mon-Thur, Sat, Sun. **Admission** free. This new centre, in a restored pearl trader's home, brings together local artisans. Their products are all for sale, so if you're after Persian rugs, Afghani tiles, Syrian wooden boxes and Turkish jewellery a trip here is essential. There's an atmospheric courtyard and majlis area where you can take tea, and the museum has a few guest rooms decorated in Arabian style.

Museum of Islamic Civilization

Corniche Street, Sharjah, nr Radisson SAS (06 565 5455). **Open** 8am-8pm Mon-Thur, Sat, Sun; 4-8pm Fri. **Admission** Dhs10; Dhs5 reductions.

Local talent

The Sharjah art scene is pushing to get Emirati artists recognised

Ebtisam Abdul Aziz was born and raised in Sharjah. She studied science and mathematics before moving into art in the early '90s. It's a grounding that is reflected in the precision and focus of her work. A 2005 video piece, 'Vision And Illusion', played with lightbox images of an eye-test screen and the conversations between an optician and his patient; another documented 2,000 hands to create an alternative archive of Sharjah's population. Now living in Dubai, Abdul Aziz has shown at the annual Creek Art Fair (p44) as part of Flying House Gallery's UAE Focus – an exhibition of well known and up-and-coming local artists, including Nuha Asad, Alia Al Shamsi and Hassan Sharif.

Much of Sharjah's art scene is based around the Arts Area by the waterfront and the Art Museum Al Shuwaiheyn (behind the bazaar and close to the waterfront, 06 568 8222). This area is also the centre of the Sharjah Biennial (06 568 5050/www.sharjahbiennial.org), a spring event that runs in odd-numbered years and offers local and foreign artists a chance to show off their talents.

It may be a while before the UAE scene is on a par with Paris's (or even Beirut's), but intrepid art buffs could do worse than to pay a visit to Dubai's little next-door neighbour.

DUBAI BY AREA

Sharjah Souk

This new museum displays art from the seventh to 20th centuries. Think glassware, ceramics, metalwork, woodwork, as well as ancient clothes and weapons. It also has an important collection of rare Arabic manuscripts, and a major Islamic mint exhibition featuring silver dinars and dirhams from the Abbasid and Umayyad periods (in the sixth century). There's a room dedicated to the Islamic faith, and another outlining the Arab world's contribution to science over the centuries. There's also a busy café and a shop.

East coast

Sights & museums

Al Bithnah

13km from Fujairah on the Fujairah-Masafi Road.
This village was once a stopover for trading caravans from the Far East, and its fort was used to control the main east-west pass through the mountain. What was used as a burial chamber from approximately 1350BC to 350BC

is now known as the T-shaped Tomb or the Chambered Tomb. It has had to be sealed off and covered to protect it from the elements, but the Fujairah Museum (see below) provides fascinating information about this archaeological site.

Bidiya Mosque

Bidiya, on coastal road between Dibba & Khor Fakkan.
Bidiya's claim to fame is that it is home to the oldest and smallest mosque in the UAE. The tiny structure dates back to 1446, predating the Portuguese invasion of the area by more than 50 years. It's a unique example of the building style of its time, with four small domes supported by a central pillar, stone carvings and special shelves for the holy Qur'an. The mosque can be visited outside prayer times if you're accompanied by a guide. It's also worth a short hike up the mountain to take in the view.

Fujairah Museum & Fort

Al Gurfa Street & Al Nakheel Road, Fujairah (09 222 9085). **Open** 8am-6.30pm Mon-Thur, Sat, Sun; 2.30-6.30pm Fri. **Admission** Dhs5.
There's a fairly decent collection of archaeological artefacts displayed in this rather grungy-looking museum, including local discoveries like ancient Islamic bronze coins excavated from a farm in Mirbah, rock art from Wadi Al Hail, old tools and Bedouin jewellery. A short distance away, the Fujairah Fort rises up on a rocky hilltop. Built in 1670, there are watchtowers and windows overlooking the sea. At the time of writing, the fort was undergoing restoration.

Hatta Heritage Village

Hatta (04 852 1374). **Open** 7.30am-8.30pm Mon-Thur, Sat, Sun; 2.30-8.30pm Fri. **Admission** free.
A great way to get an impression of how Hatta, the oldest town in the emirate once looked, is to pay a visit to the Heritage Village. The complex is dominated by two round towers built to protect the town from attacks during the rule of Sheikh Hasher bin Maktoum bin Butti in the late 1880s. As you stroll in, a group of UAE nationals enjoying

the quiet of village life will greet you at the entrance. Although the place is hardly a hive of activity, the traditionally built stone and mud houses and fort offer a fascinating insight into what life was like before electricity and modern construction took over. To drive to the Heritage Village, turn right at the Fort roundabout and follow the brown signposts.

Hatta rock pools

From the Dubai-Hatta highway, turn onto Mahdah 64 road, then left onto a gravel track at the Sumaini signpost.

The Hatta rock pools are the main draw to the area, and in the summer months attract masses of sweaty Dubaians trying to escape the heat of the city. The pools are situated 20 km (12 miles) south of Hatta in the rock crevices that have developed along the floor of the dried-out riverbeds known as wadis. The pools are safe to swim in, as are the two waterfalls; however, keep an eye on children, as in some parts the pools can change from shallow to deep quite quickly. The pools suffer from the same problem as other beauty spots in the UAE – litter louts and vandals. Although it isn't necessary to hire a 4x4

for the trip to the pools, you will need one if you are going to do a bit of wadi bashing (driving through the rocky dried-out river beds).

Khor Kalba mangroves

Head south along the east coast; the mangroves are about 10km (6 miles) past Fujairah town.

Part of the Sharjah enclave, the Kalba area is relatively untouched by development, with sweeping sandbanks right up to the delicate mangrove area known as Khor Kalba. With deserted sandy beaches and the remains of fishing boats pulled up on the shore, the area has a decidedly sleepy feel to it. It's this idyllic peace that makes the area special, in addition to being home to one of the world's oldest mangrove forests. The rare, white-collared kingfisher can be found here, and when the tide is high it's possible to canoe through the mangroves to seek one out. Visitors who would like to do so with a guide can turn to Dubai-based Desert Rangers (04 422 0044, www.desertrangers.com), which is the only company approved to take tourists through this delicate ecosystem. The water is shallow and clear (though there are a number of old plastic bags),

Fujairah Museum & Fort

A load of bull

Lock horns with bullfighting, Emirates style.

The origins of this unusual sport are shrouded in mystery, but if you happen to be in Fujairah on the east coast on a Friday afternoon, head to the bullfighting arena along Corniche Road, just after the coffee pot roundabout, next to Café Maria. Don't worry about blood and spears, though; this is a fight between two beasts, rather than bovine versus toreador. It draws car-loads of people from across the emirate every week.

Before the fight begins, the muscular, snorting bulls are led off trucks by their owners. The animals are tied to trees, allowing spectators to assess the competitors. Spectators and owners both throw handfuls of dirt onto the animals' backs and heads: 'It is for luck,' explains Mohammed Al Shaid, an owner who competes every Friday. 'The same way for a sick child; it is to help them be strong.'

The action kicks off when two bulls are led into the dirt arena. In a flurry of guttural grunting and dust, the animals butt each other, lock horns and push until one becomes submissive. Though the bulls run loose, a handler skirts around them brandishing a cane in case they become too wayward. A group of 20 men act as judges, sitting cross legged on the ground a few metres away, and a commentator describes the action over a megaphone.

It's quite thrilling to watch. The bulls charge and push with all their might. If the clinch ends in a stalemate, handlers leap up to pull the animals apart, their white *dishdashas* dragging in the mud.

There are inevitably some hairy moments, and as the bulls lurch too close, the crowd shriek and jump to their feet. But spectators are otherwise blasé about these vast beasts charging about a few feet away.

and it's lovely to paddle along in a canoe, eyes peeled for the elusive kingfisher. Herons, gulls and turtles are easier to see, along with the fish that leap playfully from the water and tiny crabs that scurry around the sand banks.

Al Gharbia

What's in a name? Well, apparently a lot in the case of Al Gharbia – previously known as the Western Region or, more colloquially, the 'massive sandy bit past Abu Dhabi'. The sparsely populated area to the west of the capital got its new name in an effort to promote its identity. This is meant to encourage tourists to a region with some dramatic natural gifts. Around 300km (186 miles) from Dubai and a further distance out to sea, Sir Bani Yas island is a wildlife reserve, and nearby Dalma Island will house an arts centre. The nearby island of Marsa will host restaurants, and there are claims that Discovery Islands will be an 'eco resort'. Inland, Qasr Al Sarab will boast a five-star desert resort next to a falconry school and a camel riding village. See www.desertislands.com for the latest information.

Sights & museums

Liwa

150km south-west of Abu Dhabi.

Liwa is a 180km-long crescent of oases on the edge of the vast Empty Quarter, a desert that stretches into Saudi Arabia, Oman and Yemen, and covers an area larger than the combined land mass of the Netherlands, Belgium and France. Liwa's main town, Madinat Zayed, is a functional but uninspiring starting point for exploring 300-metre-high dunes and a desolate natural beauty that simply cannot be found anywhere else in the country. The Liwa hotel (02 409 9999/ www.danathotelgroup.com) is the nearest place to stay.

Sir Bani Yas Island

Around 8km off the coast from Jebel Dhanna, 240km west of Abu Dhabi city (02 409 9999/ www.danathotelgroup.com).

The island of Sir Bani Yas is a recently re-opened nature reserve that houses an army of wildlife indigenous to the Gulf. The species found here include gazelles, oryx, desert hares and flamingos. Giraffes and ostriches have also made it on to this Arabian ark. Trips can be organised through the Danat Resort Jebel Dhanna.

DUBAI BY AREA

Khor Kalba

JW MARRIOTT®
DUBAI

Enchanting Hospitality in a Spellbinding City

Discover the best kept secrets of Dubai while you stay at the JW Marriott Dubai. Whether you enjoy the vigor of the bustling souks, the excitement of a desert safari, the buzz of shopping centres, the history of Arab civilisation or a leisurely cruise down the Creek, this city will impress you.

The JW Marriott Dubai remains your haven of elegance in this ever changing city. Strategically located in the business district of Deira and fifteen minutes from Dubai International Airport, our award-winning hotel offers the largest variety of suites and room choices along with 12 eclectic restaurants and lounges. Events by JW drives the superb convention facilities while the Griffins Health Club and the rooftop swimming pool give you time to relax and enjoy.

IT'S THE MARRIOTT WAY℠

To find out more on our room packages, visit **www.jwmarriottdubai.com**
You can also call the hotel on
+971 (4) 262 4444

JW Marriott Dubai
PO Box 16590,
Abu Baker Al Sidique Road,
Hamarain Centre, Dubai, UAE

Essentials

Radisson SAS Hotel p163

Hotels

Hotels in Dubai are more than somewhere to rest your head, they are the hub of the city's social scene. Hotels (and some social clubs) are the only places licensed to sell alcohol in their restaurants and bars. It's also quite common for visitors to spend more time relaxing in the grounds of Dubai's finest resorts than exploring the city itself. Some, such as the Burj Al Arab and Jumeirah Emirates Towers have become icons.

Prices are generally reasonable, but star ratings are generally nonsense. Some very tatty spots have chosen to stick four stars above their door, and the system is not policed to a proper standard. Currently, the most interesting development in the hotel sector is the arrival of more budget chains. The promised arrival of a number

of easyHotels, Holiday Inns and Rotana's new Centro chain in 2009 will add some lower rungs to Dubai's hotel ladder.

Geography often influences hotel type, with prices generally dropping the further you get from the shore. If it's the classic sun, surf and sand experience you're after, Jumeirah or the Marina are your best bet. Ritzy resorts dot Jumeirah Beach Road, but they're not cheap; the accommodation here is mainly five-star. It's worth bearing in mind, too, that when (or if) you tire of soaking up the sun, it's quite a trek to the heritage sights around the Creek.

The cloud-bothering Sheikh Zayed Road has most of the city's skyscrapers and the world's tallest building, the Burj Dubai. It is also home to the majority of the city's business hotels. Prices are as staggering as the architecture.

Stretching from the Creek to the coast, Bur Dubai offers a halfway house between Jumeirah's polish and Deira's urban delights. But although pockets such as Bastakia, Oud Metha, Satwa and Karama are some of the most charming in town, the central area is a heaving mass of high-rise towers. Good if you want to feel part of the action, but hardly conducive to a relaxing stay.

A colourful mix of souks, skyscrapers and shopping malls, Deira is one of the oldest areas of the city and a world away from the shiny new Dubai that is epitomised by the Marina. Hotels vary from high-class Creek-huggers to the cheap and less-than-cheerful establishments that can be found lining the rundown areas away from the water.

Money matters

The categories given in this guide indicate the average cost per night of a standard double room in high season (October to April), including the ten per cent municipal tax and ten per cent service charge. Unfortunately, rates at Dubai hotels vary wildly, and booking a room can be like playing the stock exchange, with huge fluctuations within the space of a few days not uncommon. Don't be scared off by the high prices; bookings through travel agents and websites can be a lot cheaper than the rates listed here. Discounts of up to 50 per cent can be had, particularly during Ramadan and Dubai's sizzling summer months (June-August).

The hotels are divided into four categories, according to the price for one night in a double room with shower/bath facilities: $ Dhs499 and below; $$ Dhs500-Dhs999; $$$ Dhs1,000-1,499; $$$$ Dhs1,500 and above.

SHORTLIST

For sleeping by the beach
- Atlantis (p171)
- Grosvenor House (p171)
- Le Méridien Mina Seyahi Beach Resort & Marina (p173)

For celebrity spotting
- Fairmont Dubai (p164)
- Shangri-La Hotel Dubai (p168)

For socialising
- Atlantis (p171)
- Fairmont Dubai (p164)
- Al Manzil (p167)
- Al Murooj Rotana (p168)

For guaranteed romance
- One&Only Royal Mirage (p173)
- Park Hyatt Dubai (p163)

For overwhelming opulence
- Burj Al Arab (p175)
- Raffles Dubai (p174)

For shoppers
- Kempinski Hotel Mall of the Emirates (p175)
- The Palace (p168)

For a taste of Arabia
- Mina A'Salam (p176)
- Al Qasr (p176)

For sealing the deal
- Hilton Dubai Creek (p163)
- Jumeirah Emirates Towers (p167)
- The Monarch Dubai (p167)

For bargain beds
- Dubai Youth Hostel (p161)
- Ibis (p167)

For something a bit different
- XVA (p161)
- Atlantis (p171)

For posh package deals
- Jumeirah Beach Hotel (176)

ESSENTIALS

Bur Dubai

Arabian Courtyard Hotel

Al Fahdi Street, opposite Dubai Museum (04 351 9111/www.arabian courtyard.com). $$

Set in the very heart of old Dubai, less than a stone's throw from the Creek and the Souk Al Kabir, the Arabian Courtyard is so heavily tilted on the heritage angle that you'll be surprised to discover it's one of the city's newer hotels. Spacious bedrooms, many of which have Creek views, make this a comfortable choice.

Ascot Hotel & Royal Ascot Hotel

Khalid Bin Waleed Road (04 352 0900/www.ascothoteldubai.com). $$

The Ascot was the first upmarket hotel to be built in Bur Dubai, and it's a homely, inviting place. Staff here are friendly and there are a number of restaurants and bars, including the ever-popular Irish-themed pub Waxy O'Connor's and the Thai Connection. A couple of hundred extra dirhams per night will bag you a posher room at the adjacent Royal Ascot Hotel.

Dhow Palace Hotel

Kuwait Street (04 359 9992/www.dhowpalacehoteldubai.com). $$

This relative newcomer is shaped like a ship, and all the staff wear sailing attire. Taste has bypassed the lobby area too, and reception staff are sometimes less than helpful. Rooms, however – there are 282 in total – are spacious and furnished in contemporary Arabic decor that doesn't overly assault the senses. The pool is surprisingly small and lacks sun loungers.

Four Points by Sheraton

Khalid bin Walid Street (04 397 7444/www.fourpoints.com/burdubai). $$

The Four Points is a small hotel in the centre of town that is geared towards the business traveller on a budget.

Dhow Palace Hotel

ESSENTIALS

With only 125 rooms and basic services, it doesn't draw large crowds, which is great if you're looking for somewhere quiet. The decor in the bedrooms is a tad old-fashioned, but rooms are clean and neat.

Golden Sands Hotel Apartments

Off Bank Street (04 355 5553/ www.goldensandsdubai.com). **$$**

Sizeable, fully serviced self-catering flats, ranging from one bedroom studios to three- and four-bedroom apartments, with additional services such as a gym, sauna and squash courts. Long-term visitors can extend their stay by the month. There are a dozen Golden Sands apartments in this area.

Majestic Hotel Tower

Mankhool Road (04 359 8888/ www.dubaimajestic.com). **$$**

This relatively new hotel is well positioned for exploring the historical Bastakia Quarter, and is only a short

taxi ride away from the five-star strips of Sheikh Zayed Road and Jumeirah. There's not much to complain about, but there's not much to get overly excited about either. The rooms are spacious enough and vaguely Arabian – think along the lines of varnished wooden floors and rich, opulent furnishings. Adding to the Majestic's appeal is a spacious pool area.

Rush Inn

Bank Street (04 352 2235). **$$**

At this well-priced hotel, the foyer is decorated with slightly dismal snapshots of karaoke stars working the plethora of themed in-house bars (one Pakistani, one Filipino and one African – the wonderful Club Africana), but the rooms are none too shabby. If you're looking for a tranquil getaway, this place is not for you.

XVA

Al Fahidi roundabout, Bastakia, behind Basta Art Café (04 353 5383). **$$**

This stunningly attractive, retro hotel is unique in Dubai. Built more than 70 years ago from coral and clay, it has been faithfully restored and re-opened as a triple treat: it's a gallery (don't be surprised if you see an artist working on a canvas), a café and a boutique guesthouse. Nestled in the pocket of old Dubai known as Bastakia, this is one of a handful of wind tower-topped buildings holding out against the lightning modernisation of the city.

Deira

Dubai Youth Hostel

Ousais Road, nr Al Mulla Plaza (04 298 8161/www.uaeyha.com). **$** No credit cards.

More of an upmarket boarding house than a hostel, this is deservedly popular. Dormitories are available alongside spruce, well-maintained family rooms, and the new wing has singles and doubles. Facilities are good for a hostel – a pool and gym are juxtaposed alongside a jacuzzi, spa, sauna and tennis court. Bear in mind that Dubai Youth Hostel

**DUBAI
GREEN COMMUNITY**
IT'S A NEW STAY℠

An oasis of serenity and harmony

Conveniently located in the Green Community, amidst a crystal blue lake and picturesque parkland, this hotel offers pure tranquility for business and leisure travellers.

Various dining options are available. The Pine Grill serves an array of international cuisines, juicy steaks and sizzling seafood. Italian trattoria cooki can be savored at Cucina and The Bar on the upper floor provides a great atmosphere for pre-dinner drinks and light snacks. Open 24 hours, the Rendezvous Lounge is a perfect setting to relax and unwind.

Courtyard by Marriott Dubai Green Community, Dubai Investment Park
P.O Box 63845, Dubai UAE
Tel: +971 (4) 8852222, Fax: +971 (4) 8852525
www.cydubaigreencommunity.com

is some distance away from the action, and any dirhams that are saved on accommodation could quite easily be spent on taxi fares.

Hilton Dubai Creek
Baniyas Road (04 227 1111/ www.hiltonworldresorts.com). **$$$**
One of Deira's classiest hotels, the Hilton was designed by Carlos Ott, the brains behind the Opéra Bastille in Paris. The hotel is also home to international über-chef Gordon Ramsay's award-winning restaurant Verre, sister restaurant the Glasshouse and some buzzy bars. Glide into the zen-like foyer, where peaceful water features lap against glass and gleaming chrome, and you will enter a world of designer purity. Chances are that you'll either love it or hate it.

Hyatt Regency Dubai & Galleria
Deira Corniche (04 209 1234/www. dubai.regency.hyatt.com). **$$$$**
Built in 1980, this vast 400-room stalwart sits close to the mouth of the Creek in central Deira. Deal makers, in particular those from East Asia, are drawn in their droves by the veteran hotel's reputation, professionalism and plush suites. The out-of-the-way location has created something of a siege mentality, and the hotel has a revolving restaurant, nightclub, cinema, ice skating rink, mini golf course and its very own (if paltry) shopping centre. The rooms are dominated by large glass windows offering fine views of Dubai, the Corniche and Sharjah, with fresh flowers and plants to offset the slightly dated furniture.

JW Marriott Hotel Dubai
Muraqqabat Street (04 262 4444/ www.jwmarriott.com). **$$$**
Huge sofas and lush cushions all but engulf guests in the lobby, and the enormous staircase is straight out of the fairytale of Cinderella. It's strange, then, that the classy ambience is undermined somewhat by an assemblage of plastic palm trees. Rooms here are

comfortable, offering an old-world formality that's rare in Dubai hotels, with signature Marriott beds ensuring you enjoy a deep slumber.

Al Mamzar Apartments
Sharjah border (04 297 2921). **$**
This complex boasts modest but fully furnished apartments with a swimming pool and gym, which can be used for a small extra charge. Although a short distance away from the town centre, its location is within easy reach of the delightfully peaceful Al Mamzar beach park; unlike the calm Jumeirah waters, it has waves that are perfectly suited to bodysurfing and boasts far fewer fellow tourists.

Park Hyatt Dubai
Dubai Creek Golf & Yacht Club (04 602 1234/www.dubai.park.hyatt.com). **$$$$**
Too good to leave only to golfers, this is also the destination hotel of choice for fashionistas; it's rumoured that Elle Macpherson, Tommy Hilfiger, Giorgio Armani and Diane von Furstenberg have stayed at this jaw-droppingly gorgeous hotel. The Park Hyatt oozes calm and luxury, from its white Moroccan low-rise architecture to the tasteful modern interior.

Radisson SAS Hotel, Deira Creek
Baniyas Road (04 222 7171/ www.radissonsas.com). **$$**
Almost as old as the United Arab Emirates itself, this '70s monolith was Dubai's first five-star hotel. Although impeccable service, brilliant restaurants and interesting decor still make the Radisson SAS (formerly known as the InterContinental) a fine place in which to stay you can't escape the feeling that time has taken its toll.

Sheraton Dubai Creek
Baniyas Road (04 228 1111/ www.sheraton.com/dubai). **$$$$**
Stunning from the outside, with its tower and thrusting waterfront extension, the Sheraton Dubai Creek is slick but businesslike within. A huge

escalator leads up to the dimly lit foyer, where there are several restaurants. Rooms are comfortable, and although they don't exactly ooze character, you can cheer yourself with the fact that they're excellent value for money. Some have amazing Creek views, for which you pay extra.

Al Sondos Suites by Le Méridien

Opposite Deira City Centre mall (04 294 9797/www.alsondos-lemeridien.com). $$$

These pleasant suites combine self-catering convenience with five-star service, making them popular with long-term guests. A short hop from the Creek, they are ideal for business stays. But getting a taxi here can be difficult, and you're some distance from the beach. There's an impressive, burnt-orange lobby, and the tiled rooms are clean, spacious and comfortable.

Sun & Sand Hotel

Nr Dubai Clock Tower, off Maktoum Road (04 223 9000). $$

One of the better options in the area, this small, reasonably well-equipped hotel includes a pool, gym and shuttle services to the shopping malls, airport and beach. Don't be fooled by the name though, because you're some way from the shore (although there is a rooftop swimming pool). The decor is dated (think in the vein of gilt-edged sofas and marble floors), but the amenities are fair and the staff are friendly.

Taj Palace Hotel

Between Al Maktoum Street & Al Rigga Road (04 223 2222/www.tajpalacedubai.ae). $$$$

A haven of extravagance in central Deira, the Taj Palace Hotel is a grand mass of glass and steel. Decked out with regal curtains, plush sofas and deep carpets, it is keen to uphold traditional Arabian ideals: no women work here past eleven at night, and it's one of only two top-end hotels in the city not to serve alcohol. These values have made the Taj hugely popular with visitors from Gulf countries.

Downtown & Sheikh Zayed Road

Crowne Plaza Hotel Dubai

Off Trade Centre roundabout, next to Fairmont (04 331 1111/www.ichotels.com). $$$

This Sheikh Zayed Road stalwart does a good tourist trade. Owing to its location at the Creek end of the road, guests are only a short drive from the beach, the malls or the Creek. The grand lobby area, which is reached via steep and narrow escalators, has aged well on the whole, although the once swish decor is looking a little tired. Standard rooms are on the small side, and the itsy-bitsy bathrooms are dated.

Dusit Dubai

Off Defence roundabout (04 343 3333/www.dusit.com). $$$

One of the most striking buildings on the street, the Dusit Dubai is a colossus of glass and steel. Its Thai-style decor is evident throughout, from the Asian-chic rooms to the smart sarong-wearing staff. Rooms are lovely, with rich browns and sweeping views. Guests can work out in the well-stocked gym with its bird's-eye city views, or laze in the 36th-floor open-air pool, before heading to the mini spa to beautify themselves for a night out. This used to be the closest you'd get to a high-class bargain on Sheikh Zayed Road, but prices have risen in recent times.

Fairmont Dubai

Sheikh Zayed Road, off Trade Centre roundabout next to Crowne Plaza (04 332 5555/www.fairmont.com). $$$$

An elegant beast, the Fairmont is set directly across from the Trade Centre. It has four illuminated turrets that change colour throughout the night and have acquired a unique place in Dubai's cityscape. At the centre is a massive foyer graced with groovy velvet sofas and a huge atrium, its walls splashed with every colour. Bedrooms are spacious, with large beds, huge windows and well-chosen furnishings.

Hilton Dubai Creek p163

InterContinental p169

Ibis World Trade Centre Dubai

Behind World Trade Centre (04 318 7000/www.ibishotel.com). $
The ever-popular Ibis is a fuss-free affair, there's no pool, and facilities are minimal, but the hotel has put its time and energy into the fundamentals, creating a sophisticated feel for a three-star address. The rooms are small and offer pretty drab glimpses of the Dubai World Trade Centre apartments.

Jumeirah Emirates Towers

Sheikh Zayed Road (04 330 0000/www. jumeirahemiratestowers.com). $$$$
Emirates Towers dominated the Sheikh Zayed Road skyline until the arrival of the Burj Dubai. Occupying the taller of the two towers (the other is a desirable office block), the hotel has a sophisticated lobby lounge – a top people-watching spot – and acres of atrium on the ground floor, while the glass lifts that shoot up the 52 storeys are a vertigo-inducing delight. Rooms are sizeable, with attractive dark wood tables, bright soft furnishings, and panoramas that should blow the socks off the most seasoned of travellers.

Al Manzil Hotel

Burj Dubai Boulevard (04 428 5888/ www.almanzilhotel.com). $$
Dubai has an outstanding new four-star hotel in Al Manzil. Although views are currently of a construction site, when the work is completed guests will be treated to vistas of the Burj Dubai. The decor is contemporary Arabic, and all rooms boast a unique open bath-room with a rainfall shower and a gigantic, oval-shaped bath in which you can wallow like a hippo and watch a film on the rotating plasma TV.

The Monarch Dubai

NEW *Trade Centre roundabout (04 501 8888/www.themonarchdubai.com). $$$$*
This hotel boasts the address One Sheikh Zayed Road. Standing next to a busy roundabout, it isn't for leisure travellers, but for business visitors who have meetings close by. Rooms are modern and masculine, with wood floors and neutral furnishings. Floor-to-ceiling windows offer excellent city views. Guests with wads of cash can reserve the Sky suite, which is literally suspended between two towers, and, of course, comes with butler service.

ESSENTIALS

Le Méridien Dubai

Al Murooj Rotana Hotel & Suites Dubai

Al Saffa Street, off Sheikh Zayed Road (04 321 1111/www.almuroojrotana hoteldubai.com). $$$$

Tucked behind Sheikh Zayed Road and surrounded by a moat-like, man-made lake, the Al Murooj Rotana offers the convenience of being close to Dubai's main thoroughfare without the traffic noise. The hotel lies in the shadow of the rapidly rising Burj Dubai, but with this privilege comes the ongoing drone of construction work, for the time being, at least. The rooms are comfortable and contemporary, the pool area pleasant, and there's a well-equipped gym and spa at which to purge your sins. One word of warning: avoid the second-floor rooms near to the busy and noisy Double Decker pub if you're a light sleeper.

The Palace

NEW *The old town, nr Burj Dubai (04 428 7888/www.sofitel.com).* $$$$
Built in old Arabian style, this new hotel is part of a development springing up around the imposing Burj Dubai, which is now the tallest building in the world. This hotel is going to be great when the surrounding construction has finished, but right now it's a noisy place to stay if you prefer to lie beside the swimming pool or sit and relax on the terraces or balconies. Already, the restaurants Asado, an Argentinean steakhouse, and Thiptara, a Thai eatery, are causing a stir with local residents. Rooms are tastefully decorated, with a modern twist on traditional Arabic design.

Shangri-La Hotel Dubai

Sheikh Zayed Road (04 343 8888/ www.shangri-la.com). $$$$
The Shangri-La towers above its more established competitors literally and figuratively. The serene foyer is immaculate, and the views over the structures of Sheikh Zayed Road are magnificent. The stylish, spacious standard rooms impress with their minimalist chic, and the Aigner-equipped bathrooms feature separate tub, shower and toilet spaces. Business facilities are state-of-the-art and suites dazzle with their luxurious fittings. The hotel boasts several top dining options, including the wonderful French-Vietnamese restaurant Hoi An and the seafood-heavy fine dining of Amwaj. You'll sleep happily here.

Festival City

Crowne Plaza

NEW *Dubai Festival City (04 701 2222/www.dubaihotels.crowne plaza.com).* **$$$**

This new hotel is well placed if you want to spend lots of time at the nearby golf courses. If you're a golf widow, good news: the hotel is adjacent to a new shopping centre. Rooms are warm and welcoming. The Crowne Plaza is slightly cheaper than its sister hotel next door – the InterContinental – but since it's so close, you can easily walk over to the spa and restaurants there.

InterContinental

NEW *Dubai Festival City (04 701 1111/www.ichotelsgroup.com).* **$$$$**

The InterContinental has an informal feel, and the rooms are modern and well designed. Reflets – Michelin-starred-chef Pierre Gagnaire's French restaurant – has just opened, making the hotel a real draw. There are two golf courses nearby, and DFC is close to the airport. The hotel overlooks the Creek, with views of the new marina and the old boatyard.

Garhoud

Le Méridien Dubai

Airport Road (04 282 4040/ www.lemeridien.com). **$$$**

A large, low-lying, two-storey hotel, the Méridien caters mainly for people in Dubai for a quick shop or an en-route layover. Rooms could be described as 'grandma chic', with dated decor and ageing white sofas. The grounds house Le Méridien Village, a throng of eateries set in their own gardens. The place comes alive at night, with people eating and drinking into the early hours.

Millennium Airport Hotel

Casablanca Road (04 282 3464/ www.millenniumhotels.com). **$$$**

As you'd expect from the name, this comfortable address is within spitting distance of Dubai's main airport terminal, so attracts business from European suits and airline crews. Muzak aside, the marble-heavy hotel foyer is elegant, and the large pool and banks of green grass make it a family favourite. Rooms are large (a twin share could easily sleep four adults), airy and have pleasant garden views.

Grosvenor House p171

REFRESHMENT THAT RISES ABOVE THE REST.

COPTHORNE
HOTEL
You are the Centre of Our World

Copthorne Hotel located in the heart of Dubai is just 5 minutes a
from the International airport and in close proximity to City Cer
Experience a refreshing stay at the Copthorne, with its luxuri
rooms overlooking the scenic Dubai creek accompanied by
world-class facilities.

Avail our attractive packages for hotel stay and Rest assured.

COPTHORN
HOTEL
DUBAI

You are the Centre of Our

For reservations call: 04 2094241 or
E-mail: reservations@cop-dubai.com
Port Saeed, P.O. Box: 119311, Dubai, U.A.E.

The Marina & Around

Atlantis

NEW *The Palm (04 426 1000/www. atlantisthepalm.com).* $$$$

This 1,500-room hotel is creating quite a buzz in Dubai. As the name suggests, the design is based on the mythical lost island of Atlantis, and facilities will include a 40-acre water park, an underwater gallery where you can view an interpretation of what Atlantis may have looked like, and a dolphin conservation area. The restaurants should be sensational, with a branch of Nobu and restaurants run by Michelin-starred chefs Giorgio Locatelli, Michel Rostang and Santi Santamaria.

Grosvenor House

West Marina Beach (04 399 8888/ www.starwoodhotels.com). $$$$

With 45 storeys, you're guaranteed an excellent view, either of the sea or the Dubai skyline. Rooms are spacious, furnished to a brown and cream colour scheme and complete with the essential plasma TV. There's a small spa, and after unwinding you can relax even more by heading up to Bar 44 for an aperitif and a view of the sunset across the Gulf. If you want to ensure full holiday bragging potential, the Grosvenor is a good choice, but not if you want to walk out of your room and straight on to the beach.

Habtoor Grand Resort & Spa

Al Sufouh Road, next to Jebel Ali Sailing Club (04 399 5000/www. grandjumeirah.habtoorhotels.com). $$$$

The luxurious Habtoor serves beach-bound holidaymakers, but at rather hefty prices. There are two floodlit tennis courts, a well-equipped gym and a stretch of beach. The rooms are conservative, but the bathrooms are ornate, decked out in green mosaics and those tiny glass sinks that were fashionable a few years ago. If you fancy some pampering, the Elixir Spa has a good range of treatments.

Coming soon

Atlantis won't be alone on the Palm for long.

Plenty of fancy pads are due to open up to visitors in 2009. The Al Fattan Resort (www.alfattan.com) will belong to Jumeirah, the company that owns Emirates Towers (p167), and will be suitably swanky. Kingdom of Sheba (www.kingdomofsheba.com) will be run by the people behind the Fairmont (p164), and will be decorated to Yemeni themes. The Trump Hotel (www.trumpdubai.com) is a 62-storey beast from the famous entrepreneur. It will include a restaurant by one of New York's best-known chefs, Jean Georges Vongerichten. The Royal Amwaj (www.seventides.com) will be located on the crescent of the Palm (rather than among the hoi-polloi on the trunk and fronds), and will have an Asian theme. Its spa will feature an 'ice grotto' and 'crystal steam room'. Only once it's open will we be able to discern what this actually means.

The Taj Exotica Resort and Spa (www.tajhotels.com) will be smaller than most Palm hotels, with only 200 or so rooms. It will be decorated in an Indian style and offer private jets and yachts to guests. And finally, there's the *QE2*, which is due to be moored off the coast of the Palm from early 2009 and turned into a fancy hotel. An on-board museum will be created to tell the colourful history of the ship.

ESSENTIALS

Le Royal Méridien

Le Méridien Mina Seyahi Beach Resort & Marina

Al Sufouh Road (04 399 3333/www. lemeridien-minaseyahi.com). $$$$
With a gem of a beach for sun worshippers, the Mina has a casual ambience that's at odds with its rather more formal big brother, Le Royal Méridien. Rooms are simple but comfortable, with beachside balconies overlooking the Palm Jumeirah (request a room with a view when you book). It is outside that the Mina really comes into its own. With more than 850m (2,800ft) of golden beach, the hotel boasts more sand than any other in Dubai.

One&Only Royal Mirage

Al Sufouh Road (04 399 9999/ www.oneandonlyresorts.com). $$$$
Modelled on an Arabian fort, the Royal Mirage is still Dubai's most romantic resort, despite some stiff competition from Madinat Jumeirah. It is composed of three hotels: the Palace, the Arabian Court and the Residence, each one plusher and more expensive than the last. Whereas many of Dubai's landmarks owe their success to a degree of shock and awe, the Royal Mirage presents an illusion of bygone days with welcome subtlety.

Le Royal Méridien

Al Sufouh Road (04 399 5555/www. leroyalmeridien-dubai.com). $$$$
Roses are a grand affair at Le Royal Méridien. In the rooms are finger bowls of petals floating in water; rose residue adorns the bed; and the bathroom has more blooms than a florist on February 13th. Such in-your-face opulence is typical of this hotel and the pools, gardens and great stretch of sand have been laid out in a timelessly classic style.

Westin Dubai Mina Seyahi Beach Resort & Marina

NEW *Al Sufouh Road (04 399 4141/ www.westin.com/dubaiminaseyahi).* $$$$
The Westin is a tasteful property that overlooks the sea and has a small private beach and a few swimming pools.

The lobby, with a fancy stained-glass atrium and trendy Murano light fittings, hints at the style in the bedrooms; ask for one with a balcony and sea view. All the facilities that you would expect from a five-star hotel are present and correct; a couple of restaurants, bars, spa and gym.

Oud Metha

Arabian Park Hotel

Nr Wafi City, opposite Grand Hyatt Dubai (04 324 5999/www. arabianparkhoteldubai.com). $$
Think not of beautiful views – construction sites surround the hotel – but rather of convenience: the Arabian Park Hotel is close to the airport, the World Trade Centre and Wafi City Mall. Rooms here tend to be on the small side, but are comfortable and simply but tastefully decorated.

Grand Hyatt

Qataiyat Road (04 317 1234/www. dubai.grand.hyatt.com). $$$$
With 674 rooms, the Grand Hyatt is an impressive exercise in hotel-based bombast. It houses a running track, three outdoor pools, four tennis courts, a spa, 14 busy restaurants and bars and (gulp) its own indoor rainforest with four-tonne dhows hung overhead. Rooms are decorated with contemporary Arabic touches, and bathrooms are smallish – although the massaging shower and colossal tub, which could house three people plus the family pet, quickly subdue any spatial quibbles.

Mövenpick Hotel Bur Dubai

19th Street, Oud Metha (04 336 6000/ www.moevenpick-burdubai.com). $$
Comfortable without being stuffy, the Mövenpick has an inviting atmosphere. The view from the medium-sized rooms is all inner-city Dubai, but the beds are comfy and the fittings are adequate. The suites and executive rooms are a leap up, with jacuzzis in the bathrooms. Meanwhile, the rooftop boasts a lovely pool deck area and a jogging track.

ESSENTIALS

Grand Hyatt p173

Raffles Dubai

NEW *Oud Metha (04 324 8888/ www.dubai.raffles.com).* $$$$

In line with Raffles in Singapore, this is a luxury hotel. Raffles Dubai is a lot younger, but what it does have in common with its Singapore sister is that it's tastefully decked out. The high-ceilinged lobby has real wow factor, and the opulent but not ostentatious decor follows through to the suite-only rooms. If you have time to go for a dip, the tiled floor surrounding the pool has an underwater cooling system so your feet don't get burnt.

Satwa & Jumeirah

Capitol Hotel

Mankhool Road, Satwa (04 346 0111/www.capitol-hotel.com). $$

A good alternative to Dubai's garish glitz, the Capitol is a pleasantly basic affair, with reasonably sized standard rooms boasting huge beds but banal views of built-up Satwa. Sadly, the

Capitol is let down by its facilities: the rooftop is home to an underwhelming swimming pool and a lonely Lebanese restaurant, the Chinese eatery is dismal, and the gym is pokey.

Dubai Marine Beach Resort & Spa

Jumeirah Beach Road, Jumeirah (04 346 1111/www.dxbmarine.com). $$$$

The Dubai Marine Beach Resort & Spa is the beachfront hotel closest to the city's heart. Accommodation is scattered in 33 low-rise, villa-style buildings spread throughout the resort, with each containing just six suites. The quiet, green gardens and a sun-drenched stretch of sand make Dubai Marine a great chill-out spot.

Jumeirah Rotana Dubai

Al Dhiyafah Road, Satwa (04 345 5888/www.rotana.com). $$

The Jumeirah Rotana is misleadingly named: it is actually set in the shore-free area of Satwa. That said, this busy hotel has a casual atmosphere and an even mix of business and leisure guests. The spacious and light bedrooms have generously sized beds, plenty of wardrobe space and entertaining views over the back streets.

Rydges Plaza

Satwa roundabout, Satwa (04 398 2222/www.rydges.com/dubai). **$$$$**
This old fashioned, nine-storey Aussie hotel delivers far more in terms of comfort, style and facilities than its mundane exterior promises. The good position, attentive staff and faux-classical swimming pool area attract business travellers and elderly tourists. Bedrooms are spacious and comfortable, but the furnishings, although in good condition, match the somewhat dated style of the hotel.

Umm Suqeim

Burj Al Arab

Off Jumeirah Beach Road (04 301 7777/ www.burj-al-arab.com). **$$$$**
Dubai's most famous hotel is every bit as extravagant and outrageous as you have been led to believe. The landmark building has a sail-like structure that recalls dhow-trading vessels and is a tribute to the region's seafaring tradition. The Burj Al Arab stands proudly on its own man-made island that lies 280m (920ft) offshore and is connected to the mainland by a slender, gently curving causeway. Taller than the Eiffel Tower in Paris, the hotel has its own helicopter pad on the 28th floor to receive guests who prefer to fly the 25km (16 mile) from Dubai's airport. A triumphant waterfall cascades into the lobby, and is flanked by floor-to-ceiling aquariums so vast that the staff have to don scuba gear just to clean them. It's just about worth the extravagance.

Hilton Dubai Jumeirah

Al Sufouh Road (04 399 1111/ www.hiltonworldresorts.com). **$$$$**
A classic resort hotel, this is more a package deal holiday rather than an out-and-out luxury destination. The decent-sized rooms are comfortable and functional, rather than decadent, with cute little balconies that offer views across the Gulf. Pleasant terraced gardens lead down to the white sandy beach, where you can try a number of different water sports.

Hilton Dubai Jumeirah

Jumeirah Beach Hotel

*Jumeirah Beach Road (04 348 0000/
www.jumeirahbeachhotel.com). $$$$*
A Dubai landmark, the wave-shaped
Jumeirah Beach Hotel is the city's best-
known hotel after the neighbouring
Burj Al Arab. For all its outer grandeur,
however, it's a down-to-earth spot
patronised by young European families in search of a spot of winter sun.
In the shadow of its arching, blue glass
walls is a decent children's club and
a family adventure playground; just
across the road lies the Wild Wadi
water park, venue for aquatic tomfool-
ery on an epic scale.

Kempinski Hotel Mall of the Emirates

*Mall of the Emirates, Al Barsha
Interchange (04 341 0000/
www.kempinski.com). $$$$*
The Kempinski is attached to the
biggest shopping mall outside North
America, which is home to the only
indoor ski slope in the UAE. So if your
idea of a holiday centres on bagging as
many designer labels as you can, and
fitting in a spot of skiing, the Kempinski
is very much the place for you.

Mina A'Salam

*Al Sufouh Road (04 366 8888/
www.madinatjumeirah.com). $$$$*
This was the first hotel completed as
part of the Madinat Jumeirah resort.
Built around a network of Venetian-
style waterways filled with abras that
ferry guests around the resort, it has a
more laid-back look than its neighbour,
the iconic Burj, and marries Dubai's
modern-day opulence with its old-world
architecture. The sand-coloured buildings are topped with legions of wind
towers, and the interior is palatial.

Al Qasr

*Al Sufouh Road (04 366 8888/
www.madinatjumeirah.com). $$$$*
More stately than its sister hotel Mina
A'Salam, Al Qasr was designed as the
'jewel in the crown' of the Madinat
resort. It's certainly grandiose: the huge
lobby with Arabian lanterns and plump
cushions leads to an opulent cigar
lounge. What makes Al Qasr stand out,
however, is its 24-hour butler service,
its long private beach and the Talise
Spa, one of the best in the Gulf.
Transportation through the vast resort
is by water taxis and golf buggies.

Mina A'Salam

Getting Around

Airports

Dubai International Airport

04 224 5555/flight information
04 216 6666/www.dubaiairport.com.
One of the most highly acclaimed airports in the world, DXB is currently undergoing an elaborate and extravagant expansion programme. This includes a new terminal (the airport's third terminal) exclusively for Emirates airline flights.

Almost all major airlines arrive at Terminal 1. Here the Dubai Duty Free (04 224 5004) is the last port of call for the purchase of alcohol before entering Dubai's 'hotel only' licensing restrictions (p182 Customs). Airport facilities include internet and banking services, shops, restaurants, business services, a bar, a hotel and a regular raffle that gives you the chance to win a luxury car. Tickets cost Dhs500, but odds are favourable as there is a draw every time 1,000 are sold. The smaller Terminal 2 caters largely for charter flights, cargo and commercial airlines from Iran and the CIS countries. There is also a VIP terminal, which is known as Al Majlis.

A card-operated system enables residents who carry the relevant smart card to check in and travel unhindered, using nothing more than their fingerprints for identification; for more information see the airport website. For a fee of US$20, the Marhaba welcome service will usher you from plane to taxi and ease you though immigration. For more information, see www.marhabaservices.com.

To and from the airport

DXB is in Garhoud, about five kilometres (three miles) south-east of the city centre. If you're staying at one of the big international hotels, you'll get a complimentary shuttle **bus** or **limousine** transfer to and from the airport.

Otherwise, **taxis** are the most convenient and practical form of transport. There is a Dhs20 surcharge on pick-up from the terminal (instead of the usual Dhs3). This means that the journey from the airport to the city centre costs around Dhs45, while the return journey is Dhs25 or so. It takes about ten minutes to travel to Bur Dubai, and Jumeirah and the hotel beach resorts are about half an hour away.

There are bus links to and from both terminals every 20 or 30 minutes for around Dhs3, although frequency is somewhat erratic and routes can be lengthy. Route 401 goes from the airport to Al Sabkha bus station, and the 402 goes to Al Ghubaiba, running through the centre of the city. From Deira station, located opposite the Al Ghurair Centre on Al Rigga Road, the numbers 4, 11, 15, 33 and 44 will take you straight to Terminal 1, as will the 33 and 44 from Bur Dubai. Fortunately, all buses are air conditioned. Call 04 227 3840/800 9090 or see www.rta.ae for more details.

Airport parking

There are short- and long-term car parking facilities at the airport. Tariffs range from Dhs10 per hour in the short-stay car park to Dhs120 per day for up to ten days in the long-stay area.

Airlines

All airlines operating regular flights into DXB are listed on the airport website; some of the most popular are listed below. Note that some airlines ask you to reconfirm your flight 72 hours before departure, and that cheaper tickets will often incur a penalty fee for alteration or cancellation.

Air France *Information*
04 602 5400/www.airfrance.ae.
British Airways *Reservations*
& ticket sales 04 307 5777/8000
441 3322/www.britishairways.com.
Emirates *04 214*
4444/www.emirates.com.
Etihad Airways *02 505*
8000/www.etihadairways.com.
Gulf Air *04 271*
3111/3222/www.gulfairco.com.
KLM *04 319*
3777/www.klm.com.
Lufthansa *04 343*
2121/www.lufthansa.com.
Qatar Airways *04 229 2229/221*
4210/www.qatarairways.com.
Royal Brunei *04 351*
4111/www.bruneiair.com.
(No alcohol served on board).

By road

The UAE is bordered to the north and east by Oman, and to the south and west by Saudi Arabia. Road access to Dubai is via the Abu Dhabi emirate to the south, Sharjah to the north, and Oman to the east.

There is no charge for driving between emirates, but travel to or from Oman or Saudi Arabia requires your passport, driving licence, insurance and visa. Crossing the Oman border costs Dhs30 per person for those who have UAE residency and Dhs60 for those on a visit visa. Check www.omanaccess.com for the latest visa requirements before you leave. Your car will be searched: carrying alcohol is prohibited. All the highways linking Dubai to other

emirates and Oman are in good condition. Ensure that your vehicle and the air-conditioning are in working order, as it is inevitably hot and the drive through the Hajar Mountains to Muscat, the capital of Oman, takes around five hours. Check with Immigration (04 398 0000) before you leave for any changes in travel policy.

RTA (traffic enquiries)
800 9090/www.dubaipolice.gov.ae.

By sea

There are boats to Dubai from Iraq and Iran; journey time is more than two days, and costs around Dhs580 return. For schedules and details contact the **Dubai Ports Authority** (04 881 5555/www.dpa.co.ae).

Navigation

Thanks to its modern highway system, most of Dubai is fairly easy to get around. However, in some places the existing infrastructure has struggled to cope with the growth of the city, most notably Maktoum bridge spanning the Creek and the Shindagha tunnel underneath it. During rush hours (7-9am, 1-2pm, 5-7pm Mon-Thur, Sun), serious tailbacks can develop.

The new Business Bay bridge opened in 2007, and the floating bridge, which is open during the day, is helping to ease congestion. A new toll system and the wider Garhoud Bridge have helped. **Hire cars** will come with a Salik tag on the windscreen and costs will be added to your fee.

Despite the relatively good road system, Dubai can be a dangerous place to drive around. There are high numbers of road accidents and deaths, caused largely by speeding and poor lane discipline. Many drivers tailgate, chat away

ESSENTIALS

on their mobiles, and do not use their indicators or mirrors.

The easiest way to get around is by **taxi**. Water taxis or **abras** are also available on the Creek. Dubai's public **buses** are not tourist-friendly, and are primarily used by people who are unable to afford cars or taxis.

The biggest problem with getting around Dubai, though, is the lack of an accurate system of street names. Some of the larger roads and streets are known by their name, but most are just numbered. This means your destination is usually identified by a nearby landmark, usually a hotel or building.

Public transport

Buses

The relative convenience of taxis (and their low cost) means the public bus system is rarely used by tourists. The service is extremely cheap, but routes can be convoluted and frequency erratic.

Timetables, prices and route maps are available from the main bus stations of Al Ghubaiba in Bur Dubai and by the Gold Souk in Deira (04 227 3840). You can also call the main bus line (800 9090) or visit www.rta.ae.

Should you fancy a bus trip, try to have the correct money, since change for larger notes is rarely available. All bus stops are request stops. Eating, drinking and smoking are not allowed on board; the front three rows of seats are reserved for women. Passengers without tickets are liable to prosecution.

Monthly bus passes can be purchased for Dhs95 (only valid on certain city routes), or you can buy a rechargeable pre-pay card. These are available from the depots at Al Ramoul and Al Qusais.

Metro

In September 2009, Dubai's metro system is due to open. The Red Line will run from Rashidiya and the airport down to Deira, and then along Sheikh Zayed Road. The Green Line will loop around in an inverted U shape from Al Qusais on the Sharjah border, under Deira, Bur Dubai and the mouth of the Creek, then back up to Business Bay. Prices and timetable information will be announced on www.rta.ae.

Taxis

Official taxis are well-maintained, air-conditioned and metered. A taxi will be beige with a red, green, blue or yellow roof, depending on the firm that runs it. The fare is Dhs1.6 per kilometre (0.3 miles) with a Dhs3-Dhs3.50 cover charge depending on the time of day.

Nice as they are, getting one can be a problem. The two biggest firms are Dubai Transport Company (04 208 0808) and National Taxis (04 339 0002). Dubai Transport is the only company with a telephone booking system, but at popular times it can be impossible to get through. When you do, the promised car often fails to arrive, so hailing one from the street can be your only option. There are usually taxis waiting outside big hotels and shopping centres, but queues can be monstrous. If faced with an hour-long taxi queue, head to the street outside and try to flag one down there. It is illegal for drivers to refuse a fare, but they often do, particularly if you're heading into heavy traffic. They have been known to refuse to take Asian passengers.

Unofficial taxis may pull up if they see you waving. These tend to be older cars with poor air-con, and

ESSENTIALS

may try to rip you off, so be sure to agree on a price before entering the car. Taxi drivers usually have a reasonable grasp of English, so you shouldn't find it too difficult to explain where you want to go.

Fares for longer journeys outside Dubai should be agreed in advance. There is also a 12-hour service available, with petrol and driver included: call 04 208 0808.

Official drivers have a reputation for returning lost items, so if you leave something in a taxi, your driver may find a way to return it to you. Failing this, call the firm you used and they will help.

Water taxis

Abras are water taxis that ferry Dubai workers and tourists across the Creek for Dhs1. The boats run between 5am and midnight, carry about 20 people and take just a few minutes to make the crossing from Bur Dubai on the south bank of the Creek (near the textile souk) to Deira on the north side, or vice versa. See also p67 Abracadabra.

Driving

People drive on the right in Dubai. Seatbelts are compulsory in the front and highly recommended in the back. In residential areas, the speed limit is usually between 40kph (25mph) and 80kph (50mph). On the city highways it is 100kph (60mph); outside the city limits it's 120kph (75mph). Most western licences entitle the owner to drive in a hire car for up to three months.

There are, in theory, fines and bans for a variety of offences, but the enforcement of these is erratic. Although you may have to pay up to Dhs1,500 if you're caught going through an amber or red light, don't expect much in the way of road rules if you venture out by car.

Traffic fines & offences

A comprehensive traffic police website (www.dubaipolice.gov.ae) lists details of licence requirements, contact numbers and fines for offences. They are listed under 'Kiosk Locations and Violations'.

There is a zero tolerance policy in regard to drinking and driving. If you are caught driving or parking illegally by the police, you'll be issued with a *mukhalifaa* (fine). If clocked by a speed camera you'll normally be fined Dhs200. When hiring a car, it's routine to sign an agreement of responsibility for any fines you may incur. To check whether you've racked up any traffic offences call 800 7777, or see www.dubaipolice.gov.ae. Fines can be paid online, or at the Muroor (Traffic Police Headquarters), near Galadari roundabout on the Dubai-Sharjah road.

Traffic accidents

If you are involved in a serious accident, call 999; if it's a minor collision, call the police on 04 398 1111. If you do not report scratches or bumps to the traffic police, insurers will almost certainly reject your claim. Third-party vehicle insurance is compulsory.

If the accident was a minor one and no one was hurt, move the car to the side of the road and wait for the police to arrive. If there is any doubt as to who is at fault, or if there is any injury, do not move the car, even if you are blocking traffic. If you help or move anyone injured, the police may hold you responsible if anything happens to that person.

Breakdown services

There are two 24-hour breakdown services, the **AAA** (Arabian Automobile Association; 800 4900/www.aaauae.com) and

IATC Recovery (International Automobile Touring Club; 800 5200/www.iatcuae.com). If you are driving when the car breaks down, pull over to the hard shoulder. The police are likely to stop and give assistance. If you're in the middle of high-speed traffic, it will be unsafe to get out of the car. Instead, use a mobile to call the police from the safety of your vehicle. Other services (not 24-hour) include:

Ahmed Mohammed Garage
050 650 4739.
Dubai Auto Towing Service
04 359 4424.

Vehicle hire

Most major hire companies have offices at the airport (15 companies operate, some of which are open 24 hours a day) and hotels. Before renting a car, check the small print, especially clauses relating to insurance cover in the event of an accident, as this can vary considerably from company to company.

Drivers must be over 21 to hire a small car, or 25 for a medium (two-litre) or larger 4x4 vehicle. You'll need your national driving licence (an International Driving Permit is best, although it isn't legally required). You'll also need your passport and a major credit card. Prices range from Dhs160 per day for a small manual car to Dhs1,400 for something like a Lexus LS460. Motorbikes are not available for hire in Dubai.

Autolease *04 224 4900.*
Avis *04 224 5219.*
Budget *04 224 5192.*
Cars *04 224 5524.*
Diamond Lease *04 220 0325.*
Europe *04 224 5240.*
Fast rent a car *04 224 5040.*
Hertz *04 224 5222.*
Patriot *04 224 4244.*
Thrifty *04 224 5404.*
United Car Rentals *04 224 4666.*

Fuel stations

At the time of writing, the cost of petrol was Dhs6.25 a gallon, so you should expect to pay about Dhs70 to fill up. There are 24-hour petrol stations on all major highways. Most petrol stations also have convenience stores selling snacks.

Parking

Many areas in the city centre have introduced paid parking to reduce congestion. Prices are reasonable (Dhs1 or Dhs2 for a one-hour stay, depending on location), but this hasn't made it easier to secure a space. Paid parking areas operate at peak times (usually from 8am to noon and 4pm to 9pm). It's free to park outside these hours, on Fridays and public holidays. If you exceed your time limit or park illegally the penalty charge is Dhs100-Dhs150.

Road signs

Road signs are in English and Arabic, which makes matters easier for Western visitors, but the sheer scale of the American-style highway system (up to five lanes on either side at some points) means you have to stay alert, especially at the junctions on Sheikh Zayed Road that have multiple exits.

Walking

Due to the intense heat and humidity, an outdoor stroll is unpleasant between May and September. The city is simply not designed with pedestrians in mind; certain areas lack pavements and the size of some highways can mean waiting up to 20 minutes just to cross. In pleasant weather, the best places for a walk include the Creek-side areas of Bur Dubai and Deira, and the stretches of beach in Jumeirah and Umm Suqeim.

ESSENTIALS

Resources A-Z

Accident & emergency

For **police** call 999, for **ambulance** call 998 or 999, and for the **fire brigade** call 997. The **coastguard** can be contacted on 04 345 0260, and there is also a **helicopter service**. If you dial 999 in an emergency, Dubai Police can sometimes send a helicopter.

Dubai has well-equipped public and private hospitals. Emergency care for all UAE nationals, visitors and expatriates is free from the Al Wasl, New Dubai and Rashid hospitals. All other treatments are charged to tourists, so it's advisable to have medical insurance as well as travel insurance.

Al Wasl Hospital
Oud Metha Road, south of Al Qataiyat Road, Za'abeel (04 324 1111).

American Hospital Dubai
Off Oud Metha Road between Lamcy Plaza & Wafi Centre, Al Nasr, Bur Dubai (04 336 7777).

Emirates Hospital
Opposite Jumeirah Beach Park, next to Chili's restaurant, Beach Road, Jumeirah (04 349 6666).

Iranian Hospital
Corner of Al Hudeiba Road & Al Wasl Road, Satwa (04 344 0250).

New Dubai Hospital
Opposite Hamria Vegetable Market, after Hyatt Regency Hotel, Deira (04 271 4444).

Rashid Hospital
Oud Metha Road, nr Al Maktoum Bridge, Bur Dubai (04 337 4000).

Welcare Hospital
Next to Lifco supermarket in Garhoud, Deira (04 282 7788).

Credit card loss

American Express *04 408 2222.*
Diners Club *04 349 5800.*

MasterCard *+1 636 722 7111 (reverse charges).*
Visa *+1 410 581 9994 (reverse charges).*

Customs

There is a duty-free shop in the airport arrivals hall. Each person is permitted to bring into the UAE four litres of spirits or two cartons of beer, 400 cigarettes, 50 cigars and 500g of tobacco.

No customs duty is levied on personal effects which are brought into Dubai. For more extensive explanations on duty levied on particular products, see the Dubai Airport website at www.dubaiairport.com, or call 04 224 5555.

The following goods are prohibited in the UAE, and importing these items will incur a heavy penalty: controlled substances (drugs), firearms and ammunition, pornography (including sex toys), unstrung pearls, pork, raw seafood and fruit and vegetables that come from cholera-infected areas. Some recent high-profile cases (including arrests for prescription painkillers and fractions of a gram of hashish) have highlighted just how seriously smuggling is taken here. For further information, see the website www.dxbcustoms.gov.ae.

Dental emergency

Good dentists are readily available, but prices can be hefty. Dubai Smile Dental Centre offers 24-hour emergency care.

Dr Michael's Dental Clinic
04 349 5900.

Dubai Smile Dental Centre
04 398 6662.
Scandinavian Dental Clinic
04 349 3202.

Disabilities

Although things are beginning to improve, many places are still not equipped to facilitate wheelchair access. Most hotels have made token efforts at improving their facilities, but functionality still plays second fiddle to design. Those hotels that do have specially adapted rooms include the Burj Al Arab, City Centre Hotel, Crowne Plaza, Jumeirah Emirates Towers, Hilton Dubai Creek, Hilton Dubai Jumeirah, Hyatt Regency, Jumeirah Beach Hotel, JW Marriott, Oasis Beach Hotel, Madinat Jumeirah, the Ritz-Carlton Dubai, Renaissance, One&Only Royal Mirage and Sheraton Jumeirah.

The airport and major shopping centres such as the Mall of the Emirates have good wheelchair access. Some **Dubai Transport** taxis are fitted to accommodate wheelchairs. For more details, call 04 208 0808.

Electricity

The domestic electricity supply is 220/240 volts AC, 50Hz. Sockets are suitable for three-pin 13 amp plugs of British standard design; however, it is a good idea to bring an adaptor with you to Dubai, because some buildings also have two-pin sockets. Adaptors can be purchased cheaply in local supermarkets. Appliances that are bought in the UAE will generally have two-pin plugs attached. For more information on local networks, call the Ministry of Electricity on 04 262 6262.

Embassies & consulates

For information about passport, visa, commercial and consular services, press and public affairs, contact your country's embassy or consulate. In Dubai, they're usually open 8.45am-1.30pm, Sunday to Thursday. If you need to contact an official urgently, don't despair: there is often a number on the embassy's answer service, which you can call for help outside working hours.

Australia *1st floor, Emirates Atrium Building, Sheikh Zayed Road, between Interchange 1 & 2 (04 508 7100/www. austrade.gov.au).* Open 8am-3.30pm Mon-Wed, Sun; 8am-2.45pm Thur.
Canada *7th floor, Juma Al Bhaji Building, Bank Street, Bur Dubai (04 314 5555/www.dfait-maeci.gc.ca).* Open 8am-4pm Mon-Thur, Sun.
France *18th floor, API World Tower, Sheikh Zayed Road (04 332 9040/ www.consulfrance-dubai.org.ae).* Open 8.30am-1pm, Mon-Thur, Sun.
India *Al Hamria Diplomatic Enclave, Consulate area, nr BurJuman Centre (04 397 1333/www.cgidubai.com).* Open 8am-4.30pm Mon-Thur, Sun.
Ireland *1301 Crown Plaza Commercial Tower Sheikh Zayed Road (04 331 4215/www.embassyofireland.org.sa).* Open 9am-1pm Mon-Thur, Sun.
New Zealand *15th floor, API Tower, Sheikh Zayed Road (04 331 7500/www.nzte.govt.nz).* Open 8.30am-5pm Mon-Thur, Sun.
Pakistan *Khalid binWaleed Road, nr BurJuman Centre (04 397 3600).* Open 7.30am-noon Mon-Thur, Sun.
South Africa *3rd floor, Dubai Islamic Bank Building, Bank Street, Bur Dubai (04 397 5222/www.southafrica.ae).* Open 8am-4pm Mon-Thur, Sun.
United Kingdom *British Embassy Building, Al Seef Road, Bur Dubai (04 309 4444/www.britain-uae.org).* Open 7.30am-2.30pm Mon-Thur, Sun.
USA *21st floor, Dubai World Trade Centre, Sheikh Zayed Road (04 311 6000/www.dubai.usconsulate.gov).* Open 8.30am-5pm Sun-Thur.

ESSENTIALS

Internet

Most hotels have good access, but many sites are blocked by the government censor. This means any that are 'inconsistent with the religious, cultural, political and moral values of the United Arab Emirates'. So no online poker, dating or overt criticism of the government. Or cheap international phone calls. Internet cafés are clustered in Khaled bin Waled (Computer) Street, Bur Dubai, and in parts of Deira, Karama and Satwa. Otherwise, try one of these:

Coffee Bean Café *Aviation Club, Garhoud (04 282 4122).* Dhs15/hr.
Giga Planet Network Café *Garhoud, nr International School (04 283 0303).* Dhs5/hr.
Al Jalssa Internet Café *Al Ain Centre/Computer Plaza Bur Dubai (04 351 4617).* Dhs10/hr.

Opening hours

The working week runs from Sunday to Thursday. Working hours are typically 9am to 6pm, but a few firms still operate a split-shift system (normally 8am-noon and 4-8pm). Malls tend to open from 10am to 10pm.

Police

In the case of an emergency, call 999. If you just want information, www.dubaipolice.gov.ae is a good resource. If you want to report something confidentially or think you have witnessed something illegal, call Al Ameen Service on 800 4888, or go to www.alameen.ae.

Post

The UAE's post is run solely by Empost, and works on a PO Box system, although a postal delivery service is planned for the future.

Hotels will handle mail for guests, and you can buy stamps at post offices, Emarat petrol stations and card shops. Shopping malls such as Mercato have postal facilities. Delivery takes between two and three days within the UAE, but up to ten days (or more) for deliveries to Europe and the USA. The service can be erratic, so don't be surprised if sending something to your home country takes longer than planned. All postal enquiries can be directed to the Empost call centre on 600 599 999 (7am-10pm Mon-Thur, Sat, Sun). Alternatively, call the Emirates Post Head Office on 04 262 2222 (7am-10pm daily).

Central Post Office *Za'abeel Road, Karama (04 337 1500/ www.empostuae.com).* **Open** 8am-10pm Mon-Thur, Sat, Sun.

Smoking

A smoking ban came into force in January 2008, which has made all Dubai restaurants non-smoking indoors. However, smoking is still permitted in bars and outdoors on terraces. Indoor smoking is permitted if the restaurant has a designated room, but most venues do not.

Telephones

The international dialling code for the UAE is 971, followed by the individual emirate's code. For Dubai, this is 04. Other area codes are as follows: Abu Dhabi 02, Ajman 06, Al Ain 03, Fujairah 09, Ras Al Khaimah 07 and Sharjah 06. For mobile telephones, the code is 050 or 055. Drop the initial '0' of these codes if dialling from abroad.

Operator services can be contacted on 100; directory enquiries are available on 181, or 151 for international numbers.

Alternatively, consult the Yellow Pages directory online at www.yellowpages.ae, which in many cases can be quicker and less frustrating.

Making a call

Until recently, the corporation Etisalat (www.etisalat.com) had a monopoly on all telecommunications in the UAE, but 2006 saw the launch of rival company Du (www.du.ae), which offers some competition, especially in the mobile phone market. Local calls are very inexpensive, and direct dialling is available to more than 100 countries.

Pay phones, which are both card- and coin-operated, are located throughout the UAE. To make a telephone call within Dubai, dial the seven-digit phone number; for calls to other regions within the UAE, dial the area code followed by the seven-digit phone number.

To make an international phone call, dial 00, then the appropriate country code (UK 44; Australia 61; Canada 1; the Republic of Ireland 353; New Zealand 64; South Africa 27; USA 1; France 33; India 91; Pakistan 92; Russia 7). Next, dial the area code, omitting the initial 0, followed by the telephone number.

Public telephones

There are plenty of public telephones, which accept either cash or phone cards. Cards for local and international use are available in various denominations (including Dhs25 and Dhs40) from most Etisalat offices, garages, pharmacies and supermarkets. Coin-operated phones accept Dhs1 and 50 fils coins.

Mobile telephones

Dubai has one of the world's highest rates of mobile phone usage, and practically everyone has at least one cellular phone. A reciprocal agreement exists with over 60 countries allowing GSM international roaming service for other networks in the UAE. There is also a service (Wasel) that enables temporary Etisalat SIM cards and numbers lasting 60 days – or until your Dhs300 credit runs out. Calls are charged at local rates, with good network coverage.

Tickets

Tickets can often be bought from the venue or on the door, but it's wise to book ahead for any major gigs. The Time Out ticket line (800 4669/www.timeoutdubai.com) sells tickets to most big events.

Time

The time in UAE is GMT plus four hours, and has no seasonal change. So, for instance, if it is noon in London (winter time), it is 4pm in Dubai; after British clocks move forwards for BST, noon in the UK is 3pm in Dubai.

Tipping

Hotels and restaurants usually include a 15 per cent service charge in their bills; if not, adding ten per cent is normal, if not obligatory. Unfortunately this inclusive charge usually goes straight to the restaurant, and rarely reaches the pockets of the people who served you; so if you are particularly impressed with the service, you will need to tip in addition to the inclusive total. It is common to pay taxi drivers a small tip: rounding up

ESSENTIALS

the taxi fare to the nearest Dhs5 is the norm. For other services, including those of supermarket baggers, bag carriers, petrol pump attendants and hotel valets, it is usual to give at least a couple of dirhams.

Tourist information

The Department of Tourism & Commerce Marketing (DTCM) is the government's sole regulating, planning and licensing body for the tourism industry in Dubai. It has information centres dotted around the city, the most useful being located in the airport arrivals lounge (04 224 5252). These one-stop information centres aim to answer any visitor queries, provide maps, tour guides and hotel information, as well as business and conference advice. Most of the larger shopping malls have their own centres providing visitor information.

Department of Tourism & Commerce Marketing
10th-12th floor, National Bank of Dubai Building, Baniyas Road, Deira (04 223 0000/www.dubaitourism.ae).
Open 7.30am-2.30pm Mon-Thur, Sun.

Visas

Visa regulations are always liable to change, so it is worth checking them with your travel agent or the UAE embassy in your home country before leaving. Overstaying on your visa can result in detention and fines (a penalty charge of around Dhs100 per day over). Nationals of Israel may not enter the UAE. Your passport must have at least two months (in some cases six) left before expiry for you to be granted admission into the UAE, so make sure that you check before booking your flight.

UK
Citizens of the UK will be granted a free visit visa on arrival in the UAE: passports will be stamped with the visa as you pass through immigration at any airport in the UAE. Although the visa is usually stamped for 30 days, it entitles the holder to stay in the country for 60 days, and may be renewed once for an additional period of 30 days, for a fee of Dhs500.

Multiple-entry visas
Multiple-entry visas are available to business visitors who have a relationship with either a multinational company or other reputable local business, and who visit the UAE regularly. This type of visa is valid for six months from the date of issue and the maximum duration of each stay is 30 days. It is not renewable. The cost of such a visa is Dhs1,000. The visitor must enter the UAE on a visit visa and obtain the multiple entry visa while in the country. The visa is stamped in the passport.

96-hour visa for transit passengers
As a way of promoting Dubai's city tours, passengers from Europe, US, Asia and Africa who stop at Dubai International Airport for a minimum of five hours are eligible for a 96-hour transit visa which enables them to go into the city for that period of time. This visa is available only to those travelling onwards from Dubai, who have a ticket for their forthcoming journey.

What's on

Time Out Dubai is available from all good newsagents and comes out every Wednesday. The magazine contains listings and reviews on entertainment-related places in the city.

ESSENTIALS

Vocabulary

Arabic is the official language of Dubai, and Urdu and Hindi are widely spoken, but English is likely to be all you'll need to get by. That said, using a few Arabic phrases is always appreciated. Some basic words and phrases are given below, written phonetically. Capitals are not used in Arabic, but are used below to indicate hard sounds.

Useful phrases

hello *marhaba*; how are you? *kaif il haal?* good morning *sabaaH il khayr*; good evening *masaa' il khayr*; greetings *'as-salamu 'alaykum*; goodbye *ma' 'is-salaama*; excuse me *afwan*; sorry *'aasif*; God willing *insha'allah*; please (to a man) *min fadlak*, (to a woman) *min fadlik*; thank you (very much) *shukran (jazeelan)*; yes/no *na'am/laa*; I don't know *lasto adree* or *laa 'a-arif*; who?/what? *man?/matha?* where?/why? *ayina?/lematha?* how much? (cost) *bekam?* how many? *kam?* the bill, please *alfatourah min faDlak*

Pleasantries

do you speak English? *titkallam inglizi*; I don't speak Arabic *ma-atkallam arabi*; nice to meet you *yusadni moqapalatak*; what's your name? *ma esmok?* my name is... *esmei...* how old are you? *kam amrk?* what's your job?/where do you work? *ma heya wazefatuk? /ayna tam'al?* where do you live? *ayna taskun?* I live/I work in Dubai *askun/a'amal fi Dubai*; how is the family? *kayfa halou l'a ila?* congratulations *mabrook*; with pleasure *bikul siroor*; have a good trip *atmna lak rehla muafaqa*; thanks for

coming *shukran limajee, ak*; best wishes *atyab al-tamniyat*; when will I see you? *mata sa'araak?*; wait a little *intazarni kaliln*; calm down *hadia nafsak*; can I help you? *hl astateea'i musaa'adatuk?*

Numbers & time

0 *sifr*; 1 *waahid*; 2 *itnain*; 3 *talata*; 4 *arba'a*; 5 *khamsa*; 6 *sitta*; 7 *sab'a*; 8 *tamanya*; 9 *tis'a*; 10 *'ashra*; 100 *me'ah*; Sunday *al-ahad*; Monday *al-itnayn*; Tuesday *al-talata*; Wednesday *al-arba'a*; Thursday *al-khamees*; Friday *al-jum'a*; Saturday *al-Sabt*; day *yom*; month *shahr*; year *sanah*; hour *sa'aa*; minute *daqiqa*; today *al yom*; yesterday *ams/imbarah*; tomorrow *bukra*

People

I/me *ana*; you (to a man) *anta*, (to a woman) *anti*, (to a group) *antom*, (to several women) *antonna*; he/she *houwa/hiya*; we *nahnou*; they (men and women), *hom* (women only) *honna*; father *ab*; mother *umm*; son *ibn*; daughter *ibnah*; husband *zauj*; wife *zaujah*; brother *akh*; sister *ukht*; child *tifl*

Getting around

airport *matar*; post office *maktab al barid*; bank *bank*; passport *jawaz safar*; luggage *'aghraad*; ticket *tath karah*; taxi *taxi*; car *say-yarra*; city *madina*; street *share'h*; road *tareeq*; bridge *jisr*; mosque *jame'h* or *messjed*; bazaar *souk*; boat *markab*; beach *il-shat'i*; customs *jumrok*; library *maktabeh*; shop *mahall*; museum *mathaf*

Menu Glossary

Arayess: Deep-fried lamb sandwich.

Baba ghanoush: Chargrilled eggplant, tahini, olive oil, lemon juice and garlic served as a dip

Baharat: Arabic mixed spices

Baklava: Dessert of layered pastry filled with nuts and steeped in honey-lemon syrup – usually cut into triangular or diamond shapes

Burghul: Parboiled and dried wheat kernels processed into grain, used in tabouleh and mixed with lamb in kibbeh

Ejje: Arabic omelette

Falafel: Small deep-fried patties made of highly-spiced ground chickpeas

Fatayer: Pastry pockets filled with spinach, meat or cheese

Fattoush: Salad of croutons, cucumber, tomato and mint

Haleeb: Milk

Hammour: Red sea fish of the grouper family

Kabsa: Classic Arabian dish of meat mixed with rice

Kibbeh: Oval-shaped nuggets of ground lamb and burghul

Koshary: Cooked dish of pasta, rice and lentils to which, onions, chillis and tomato paste are added

Kufta: Fingers, balls or a flat cake of minced meat and spices that may be baked or charcoal-grilled on skewers

Laban: Tangy-tasting sour milk drink widely used in cooking as a substitute for milk

Labenah: Thick creamy cheese, often spiced and used as a dip

Lahma bi ajeen: Arabic pizza

Ma'amul: Date cookies shaped in a wooden mould called a *tabi*

Makloubeh: Meat or fish with rice, broad beans and cauliflower

Mantou: Dumplings stuffed with minced lamb

Mouhammara: Mixture of ground nuts, olive oil, cumin and chillis, eaten with Arabic bread

Moutabel: Aubergine dip made with tahini, olive oil and lemon juice

Rocca: Aromatic salad green with a peppery mustard flavour, used in salads or mixed with hot yoghurt

Sambusek: Triangular pies filled with meat, cheese or spinach

Sayyadiya: Delicately-spiced fish dish served on a bed of rice

Shaour: Red sea fish from the emperor family

Shawarma: A cone of pressed lamb, chicken or beef roasted on a vertical spit. Meat is shaved off from the outside while the spit is turning. Also Arabic bread filled with shawarma meat, salad, hot sauce and tahini

Shisha: Pipe for smoking tobacco leaves or dried fruit through a water filter

Shish taouk: Skewered chicken pieces cooked over charcoal

Shourba: Soup

Snober: Pine nuts

Sumac: Ground powder from the cashew family, used as a seasoning

Tabouleh: Salad of burghul, tomato, mint and parsley

Tahini: An oily paste made from ground sesame seeds, used in hommus, moutabel and baba ghanoush

Taratour: A thick mayonnaise of puréed pine nuts, garlic and lemon, used as a sauce or dip

Umm ali: 'Ali's mother' is a pastry pudding with raisins and coconut steeped in milk

Warak enab: Stuffed vine leaves

Zatoon: Olives

Zattar: Blend of spices including thyme, sumac and marjoram

ESSENTIALS

Index

ESSENTIALS

ESSENTIALS

Traditional
Dinner Cruise
by the Creek

al mansour dhow

The Radisson SAS Hotel, Dubai Deira Creek's legendary Al Mansour Dhow welcomes you aboard to experience an unforgettable dinner cruise featuring a sumptuous buffet with a spread of Arabian cuisine and live performances by our Oud player while you enjoy Dubai Creek's beautiful sights for only Dhs. 185 per person.

* Boarding daily at 8 pm

Radisson SAS Hotel, Dubai Deira Creek
Baniyas Road, P.O. Box 476, Dubai, UAE
For Bookings, please call 04-205 7033
infocenter.dxbza@radissonsas.com
deiracreek.dubai.radissonsas.com

Radisson SAS
HOTEL, DUBAI DEIRA CREEK